Guide to Business Information
on
Central and Eastern Europe

Tania Konn

FITZROY DEARBORN PUBLISHERS
CHICAGO • LONDON

© Tania Konn 2000

Published in the UK by
Aslib/IMI
Staple Hall
Stone House Court
London EC3A 7PB

Published in the USA by
Fitzroy Dearborn Publishers
919 North Michigan Avenue
Chicago, Illinois 60611

Printed and bound in Great Britain by
Hobbs the Printers
Brunel Road
Totton
Hampshire SO40 3WX

A Cataloging-in-Publication record for this book is available from the Library of Congress.

ISBN 1-57958-263-X Fitzroy Dearborn

Contents

Introduction 1

Background 1
Coverage 2
Aims 2
Arrangement and Content 3

Central and Eastern Europe 7

Overview 7
Current Developments 15
Companies and Contacts 25
Industries and Services 27
Legislation 54
Organisations 56

Albania 59

Overview 59
Current Developments 62
Companies and Contacts 64
Industries and Services 64
Legislation 64
Organisations 65

Bosnia and Herzegovina 68

Overview 68
Current Developments 70
Companies and Contacts 71
Industries and Services 71
Legislation 72
Organisations 73

Bulgaria 75

Overview 75
Current Developments 80
Companies and Contacts 82
Industries and Services 84
Legislation 86
Organisations 87

Croatia **90**

Overview 90
Current Developments 93
Companies and Contacts 95
Industries and Services 96
Legislation 97
Organisations 97

Czech Republic **100**

Overview 100
Current Developments 104
Companies and Contacts 107
Industries and Services 110
Legislation 114
Organisations 117

Hungary **120**

Overview 120
Current Developments 125
Companies and Contacts 129
Industries and Services 130
Legislation 132
Organisations 133

FYR Macedonia **136**

Overview 136
Current Developments 138
Companies and Contacts 140
Industries and Services 140
Legislation 140
Organisations 141

Poland **144**

Overview 144
Current Developments 149
Companies and Contacts 153
Industries and Services 155
Legislation 160
Organisations 161

Romania **164**

Overview 164
Current Developments 168
Companies and Contacts 171
Industries and Services 172
Legislation 174
Organisations 175

Serbia and Montenegro **178**

Overview 178
Current Developments 180
Companies and Contacts 181
Industries and Services 181
Legislation 182
Organisations 182

Slovakia **185**

Overview 185
Current Developments 189
Companies and Contacts 191
Industries and Services 192
Legislation 194
Organisations 195

Slovenia **198**

Overview 198
Current Developments 202
Companies and Contacts 203
Industries and Services 204
Legislation 206
Organisations 206

Index **209**

Introduction

Background

Opening the economies of central and eastern Europe (CEE) to market forces transformed their business information sectors. In conditions of dramatic economic and market changes demands for new types of data and information, generated externally and internally, became the engine propelling CEE business information sectors into a new era. The same forces also indicated new market possibilities for western information entrepreneurs. This recognition rejuvenated what had been a lethargic information sector.

The lead in meeting the explosion of information demands was taken by a variety of western publishers. Operating from well-established bases, they were in the best position to take advantage of unparalleled information opportunities. This they did with enthusiasm. In a relatively short time, however, indigenous business information sectors responded with their own services and products.

For the CEE countries, providing information and data to meet the demands generated by external forces was an expansive factor. Indigenous information producers quickly learned how to meet western business information demands, and in a language other than their own – English. Their adaptability, in this case, was encouraged by a driving need to attract foreign investors and capital – essentials for economic progress based on market forces. It required little analysis to understand that more foreign investors were reached through English than any other language. This latter factor contributed markedly to the character of the developing English language information sectors, especially on the information activities of government and government related agencies.

As a result of these factors, CEE countries were placed in the unusual situation of developing their own local language business information sectors while, at the same time, developing externally orientated English language sectors. This guide describes some of the information products and services resulting from this process, as well as highlighting the contributions of western publishers.

At this point a word of caution is needed. The English and local language sectors are not identical, either in content or aims. Beyond a certain stage of investigation it is always sensible to exploit local language sources, if necessary through translation services.

Coverage

The countries included in this guide are Albania, Bosnia-Herzegovina, Bulgaria, Croatia, Czech Republic, Hungary, FYR (Former Yugoslav Republic) Macedonia, Poland, Romania, Serbia and Montenegro (Yugoslavia), Slovak Republic, Slovenia. The mere listing of these countries indicates that they do not constitute a homogeneous group in economic, business, political, geographic or demographic terms. The differences condition the nature of national business information systems. As might be expected the more advanced economies have progressed further in information terms. For example, Poland, Hungary and the Czech Republic, regarded as (relatively) economically progressive, are leaders in the use of the Internet for business purposes, and also have the most developed sectors of conventional business information sources. Economic success is the sustenance for maintaining and expanding business information sectors in CEE countries and in the west.

Aims

The aim of this guide is to serve as an introduction to English language sources, in electronic and conventional print forms, dealing with CEE business issues. Attention has been concentrated upon recent sources, i.e. those published during and since 1997, with an occasional earlier exception. However, even with this limitation the constraints of space inevitably impose a severe, perhaps distorting, selectivity both on the range and number of sources discussed. It is worth noting that, even as recently as six years ago, this would not have been the position for compilers of a guide such as this. Then, many categories of business information were scantily provided with English-language sources. The developments since have been remarkable.

Naming sources is often the easiest part of an information trail. Getting to see and use them, especially those in print formats, often present difficulties. The hunt for business information sources is best started at the East European Trade Council and at the Department of Trade and Industry (see details under Central Europe – Organisations). There are general business information services in the larger public libraries such as Birmingham and Manchester, and in national institutions such as the Science Library of the National Library of Scotland. There is a limit to the amount of assistance that can be expected from such organisations, however. Once that limit has been reached then the next step is to search out services that specialise in central and east European business information sources. There are not many of these, and the free use of their sources is not to be expected. An example of a fee-based business information retrieval service is the Business Information Centre of the European Bank for Reconstruction and Development (see details under Central Europe – Organisations).

Not all business people are willing to pay for information. Many show a disinclination to enter a public, or any other type of library, in search of business information. Many prefer to serve themselves rather than be served. For such reluctants and independents there is another option – the Internet. By some the Internet is seen as the future of business information provision on a self-service basis whether provided freely or at a price. There is no doubt that the use of the Internet can assist in information searching and provision. However, there are problems – largely of quality control, confusing duplication of services, dead links, lack of authoritativeness. There is also the frustrating fugitiveness of web sites to cope with. *On average*, it has been claimed, a web site address changes once every 44 days. Initially finding a useful web site is one problem, monitoring that site to check its continued existence another, relocating a lost site still another. As matters now stand the reality of Internet use for serious purposes is well short of the hype horizon; but the situation is changing, especially with the increasing Internet presence of paid-for business services such as, for example, *ISI Emerging Markets.*

For those needing to monitor information developments in a systematic manner it is worth noting that the most complete collection of sources is to be found in *The EBRD Directory of Business Information Sources on Central and Eastern Europe and the CIS* (Effective Technology Marketing, 1999. 4th edition). There is also the monthly *European Business Intelligence Briefing* (Headland Business Information) which carries a regular *East European Update* column.

Arrangement and Content

Under each country information sources are grouped in broad categories. These are: Overview, Current Developments, Companies and Contacts, Industries and Services, Legislation, Organisations. These headings need some explanation.

Overview includes the types of sources designed to answer general, exploratory, country and regional questions such as, for example, population and its characteristics, form and structure of government, main historical events, political issues, the economy, business customs, business climate, how to do business. In short, background information.

Current Developments overlaps somewhat with Overview but the emphasis here is upon sources that appear more frequently than annually – daily, weekly, monthly, etc. The range of subjects appearing in such sources is extensive – recent changes in tax and other laws affecting foreign investors, assessments of the impact of political events upon business expectations, foreign investment, trends in foreign direct investment, economic indicators, latest project tenders, privatisation developments, latest news regarding EU applications, for example.

Companies and Contacts concentrates upon general directory-type sources providing locational and other contact and descriptive data about firms.

Industries and Services presents a selection of specific industrial and service sectors with illustrative sources. In most cases the variety of sectoral sources in local languages is greater than in English. Sectoral company directories appear here.

Legislation needs little explanation beyond pointing out that attention is focused upon aspects of law and regulations impinging directly upon business people, companies and their operations.

Organisations is a listing of agencies and bodies able to provide assistance, information and data to business people. All CEE countries have acknowledged their need for foreign direct investment. All have set up agencies to encourage and assist foreign investors in a variety of ways. Inevitably, perhaps, for a bureaucracy, the importance of this task has led the OECD to conclude that attracting foreign direct investment needs a 'highly developed profession which requires appropriate national institutions and structures, a supportive business environment, with skills and knowledge to attract foreign direct investment within a highly competitive international market'. Since 1996 steps have been taken to establish a Network of European Investment Promotion Agencies. From the documents available it does not seem the majority of small country investment promotion agencies have reached the standards implied by the OECD's statement of higher bureaucratic aims. However, they remain sources of business information and assistance that should not be ignored.

Chambers of Commerce and Industry in CEE countries retain some of the authority of the 'old' days. It is still the case, for example, that in some countries membership of a Chamber is compulsory; unregistered enterprises cannot engage in business. Most Chambers have promotional, informational and assistance programmes. They are always willing to help potential investors, so they can be used as information sources. However, staff, though willing, may not be too certain of western attitudes to business information, or accustomed to the idea of strict deadlines.

National statistical offices and their products and services have been placed under this heading. Statistical compilations produced by other sources are grouped at appropriate points, but mainly in the Overview sections.

The foregoing categories are applied to all the separate country sections. They also apply to the largest single section – Central and Eastern Europe. The need for such a comprehensive category is explained by publishing practices. A marked response to the re-shaping of the CEE business information world, especially by western publishers, has been to seek enlarged markets for their products and services. One way of achieving this aim is by producing sources covering a number of countries, i.e. multi-country sources. By this procedure a number of countries, usually the better economic performers, are grouped for presentation; or, a regional approach may be adopted. In an increasing number of instances individual CEE countries, even the region as a whole, find places in compilations with worldwide coverage. This trend towards broader coverage has been applied to many sectors of the information business – company directories, analytical reports, financial analyses, country information, Internet services, legislation, alerting services, for example. The scale of the response has been such as to warrant acknowledgement in a separate, lengthy, section. One practical consequence of this movement is the need, always, to be aware of what multi-country sources, compiled on different coverage criteria, have to offer in specific information circumstances. In some instances a multi-country source may be preferred to a specific national source. In others the choice may be to rely on a national source, or, in some circumstances to use both types in complementary fashion.

The broadly classified arrangement adopted highlights the degree to which a handful of western and CEE based information providers dominate the English language business information sector. A number of these have adopted a standardised approach to providing country specific information. In such cases titles in the same series, although appearing under different country headings, have been described in identical terms.

The stress is upon business information sources that are publicly disseminated, either freely or for a price, in hard copy or in the various electronic formats. However, there is one important type of CEE business information source that has been excluded. This is the business conference and its associated documentation. The value of conferences varies, of course; but the best attract knowledgeable speakers bringing with them the latest and most authoritiative version of business events and developments. In many instances, for those who cannot attend, documentation is made available at a price. In circumstances of change and uncertainty such sources can prove extremely valuable.

Finally, numerous Internet sites are noted in the text. Many such sites, as experience teaches us, come and go at will, and change their addresses and names with disconcerting rapidity. So, it should be noted that the sites were last searched during the period June/July 1999.

Chapter 1

Central and Eastern Europe

Information suppliers, like other entrepreneurs, try to expand markets for their products. One way of doing so in this field is to produce business information sources and services that take in all, or a number of, CEE countries; or, on an even grander scale, include CEE countries in compilations with worldwide coverage. The popularity of extended geographical coverage with information suppliers means that the different kinds of multi-country English language sources considerably outnumber those found in individual national business information sectors. From the many sources available only a small selection can be described here.

Overview

An obvious initial business requirement is to get to know something about the country of intended operations. Questions on the following topics, for example, are typical: population size and characteristics; main cities, their size and characteristics; assessments of the transport infrastructure; general history fundamentals; cultural briefings; differences in business customs; how to do business; the state of the economy; attitudes towards foreign business interests, the political climate.

Satisfying such requirements is one of the more straightforward tasks of information work. There are numerous multi-country sources to choose from. The problem becomes one of evaluation, of knowing which sources can best satisfy a particular information need, bearing in mind that 'sources' come in different shapes and sizes – as Internet sites, in CD-ROM format, as hefty reference books, as diskettes, as journals and magazines, as email, as reports and newspapers. There is no special formula to assist in what is, in essence, a process of sifting. Hard-won experience is the only reliable guide, especially in discovering and monitoring rapidly shifting developments on the Internet. The selection that follows is intended to demonstrate the range and types of multi-country sources providing individual and regional overviews currently in the public domain.

Business Executive Resources Worldwide
This Internet site covers almost all East European countries. For each country it provides *Business Briefing* – 'a variety of reports on business

protocol, negotiating, social etiquette'. Another service is *Pre-Departure Country Reports* – these are intended to provide the business traveller with enough information to avoid inadvertent social and business gaffes, as well as touching upon 'other important issues you may not find in travel guides'. Rather lightweight compared to available printed sources, but nothing wrong with the advice proferred.

Contact details: Worldwide Business Executive Resources, PO Box 514, Deerfield, IL 60015, USA. Tel. +1 847 945 9516 Fax +1 847 945 9614. URL: http://www.worldbiz.com/index.html

Cost: On application

Business International
This Internet site is maintained by Deion Associates & Strategies, Inc. It identifies other Internet sites which provide information about CEE countries, and which have been highly rated by their own staff. This application of critical judgment is a valuable time-saver; often, on the Internet, so much rubbish has to be sifted through to find usable information. The links provided take in most CEE countries.

Contact details: URL: http://www.deionassociates.com/hplist/index.htm

Business Strategies for Eastern Europe
A report (1997) presenting information and advice for 'companies new to the region'. Topics include the nagging problems of corruption and security and securing payment, issues of personnel management and local business customs. There are case studies to push home the lessons. The report is available in print, and through online databases, direct network feeds and the Internet.

Contact details: Economist Intelligence Unit, PO Box 200, Harold Hill, Romford, RM3 8UX, UK. Tel. +44 (0)20 7830 1007. Fax +44 (0)1708 371 850. Email: london@eiu.com URL: http://www.eiu.com

Cost: £295

CEEBIC net
This Internet site is maintained by the Central and Eastern Europe Business Information Center of the U.S. Department of Commerce. One of the best single sources for regional and country coverage of business related issues and data. Available on the site are trade and investment leads, market research, sources of finance, U.S. Embassy reports, conferences and trade fairs, taxes and tariffs, key contacts. All the CEE countries are covered.

Contact details: URL: http://www.iep.doc.gov/eebic/ceebic.html

CEESource: Central and East European Legal, Political, Business and Economics WWW Resources
This Internet site, maintained by Gonzaga Law Library, in the USA, provides links to other sites relevant to CEE countries and issues. Directional sites of this type require frequent updating of links if they are to be of use as effective guides.

Contact details: URL: http://law.gonzaga.edu/library/ceeurope.htm

Central and East European Business Directory (CEEBD)
This is a new-ish Internet service which has had rather a rocky start. Against a background of country, sector, company and product information, investment and partnership opportunities are highlighted.

Contact details: CEEBD. Fax +44 (0)20 7209 2364.
Email: admin@ceebd.co.uk URL: http://www.ceebd.co.uk/

Cost: On application

CIA Factbook
The initials CIA, these days, are not a guarantee of high-quality for certain types of information on this region. However, for those searching for basic country data – population, climate, economic indicators, holidays, political parties, trade figures, brief descriptions of an economy, for example – this Internet site, with material from the *CIA Factbook,* can prove useful and conveniently packaged.

Contact details: URL: http://www.odci.gov/cia/publications/factbook/

Corporate Security in Eastern Europe
This report (1998) reviews the different scale and nature of security problems in 17 east European countries, and offers coping advice. It is an example of a specific business issue treated on a regional basis. The report is available as hard copy, and 'through online databases, direct network feeds and the Internet'.

Contact details: Economist Intelligence Unit, PO Box 200, Harold Hill, Romford, RM3 8UX, UK. Tel. +44 (0)20 7830 1007. Fax +44 (0)1708 371 850. Email: london@eiu.com URL: http://www.eiu.com. In the US: Economist Intelligence Unit, The Economist Building, 111 West 57th Street, NY, NY 10019, USA . Tel. +1 212 554 060/1 800 938 4685 (USA and Canada only). Fax +1 212 586 0248. Email: newyork@eiu.com URL: http://www.eiu.com

Cost: £365/$595

Eastern Europe: A Directory and Sourcebook
Among the countries covered in this reference source are Bulgaria, Czech Republic, Hungary, Poland, Romania and Slovakia. A useful mix of general and business information (company data, marketing statistics, etc.) is provided.

Contact details: Euromonitor, 60-61 Britton Street, London EC1M 5NA, UK. Tel. +44 (0)20 7251 1105. Fax +44 (0)20 7251 0985. Email:info@euromonitor.com URL: http://Euro.imrmall.com/

Cost: £295/$590

Eastern Europe and the Commonwealth of Independent States
This is a convenient starting point for background data for all the countries included in this volume. Each country has succinct sections on the economy, history, important events, selected statistics, geographical details and much more. This is the substantial type of work found in public and academic reference libraries. The last edition, the 4th, was published in 1998.

Contact details: Europa Publications, 18 Bedford Square, London WC1B 3JN, UK. Tel. +44 (0)20 7580 8236. Fax +44 (0)20 7636 1664. Email:sales@europapublications.co.uk
URL:http://www.europapublications.co.uk
In the US: Europa Publications, P.O. BOX 97974, Pittsburgh, Pennsylvania 15227, USA. Tel. 1-800-821-1447. Fax 1-786-549-6228. Email:europasales@europapublications.com
URL: http://www.europapublications.com/

Cost: £255/$510

Eastern Europe at a Glance
A compact reference source (1997) for frequently asked for data and information. There are concise descriptions of all the CEE countries aimed at business people. Coverage in these sections includes, for example, the economy, social and political background, demography, the business environment, main economic indicators.

Contact details: Economist Intelligence Unit, PO Box 200, Harold Hill, Romford RM3 8UX, UK. Tel. +44 (0)20 7830 1007. Fax +44 (0)1708 371 850. Email: london@eiu.com URL: http://www.eiu.com
In the US: Economist Intelligence Unit, The Economist Building, 111 West 57th Street, NY, NY 10019, USA . Tel. +1 212 554 060/1 800 938 4685 (USA and Canada only). Fax +1 212 586 0248. Email: newyork@eiu.com URL: http://www.eiu.com

Cost: £265/$395

Eastern Europe's Emerging Cities: Operating Beyond the Region's Capitals
This report (1999) concentrates critical attention on the expected economic and business development of areas away from the capital regions. The business potential of the various candidate cities are reviewed and compared.

Contact detail: Economist Intelligence Unit, PO Box 200, Harold Hill, Romford, RM3 8UX, UK. Tel. +44 (0)20 7830 1007. Fax +44 (0)1708 371 850. Email: london@eiu.com URL: http://www.eiu.com
In the US: Economist Intelligence Unit, The Economist Building, 111 West 57th Street, NY, NY 10019, USA. Tel. +1 212 554 060/1 800 938 4685 (USA and Canada only). Fax +1 212 586 0248. Email: newyork@eiu.com URL: http://www.eiu.com

Cost: £395/$625

EBRD Country Profiles
Twenty-six CEE countries are profiled **annually** in economic and financial terms. The main headings for each country are – economic survey, investment climate, financial sector, multilateral funding, EBRD activities, contact list. The *Profiles* are prepared for the Annual Meeting of the European Bank for Reconstruction and Development. The set is available in CD-ROM format. Individual printed country profiles are available also. These are listed under appropriate country headings.

Contact details. Effective Technology Marketing, PO Box 171, Grimsby DN35 0TP, UK. Tel/Fax +44 (0)1472 816660.Email:sales@etmltd.demon.co.uk URL: http://www.etmltd.demon.co.uk

Cost: £175/$290 (CD-ROM)

EBRD Transition Report
The *Report* is produced **annually** as a review of the Bank's support activities in CEE countries. The reform progress of individual countries is assessed, with supporting statistics. The latter are updated in *Transition Report Update*, again on an **annual** basis.

Contact details: Publications Desk, European Bank for Reconstruction and Development, One Exchange Square, London EC2A 2JN, UK. Tel. +44 (0)20 7338 6102. Fax +44 (0)20 7338 6102. Email:pubsdesk@ebrd.com URL: http://www.ebrd.com/english/region/tranrep/main.htm
US orders: Bernan Associates, 4611-F Assembly Drive, Lanham, MD 20706-4391, USA. Tel. 1 800 274 4888. Fax 301 459 0056

Cost: £30 (Report); £15 (Update). US price available on application.

EIU Country Forecasts
The CD-ROM service assesses likely future developments on a **five-year** basis in Bulgaria, Czech Republic, Hungary, Poland, Romania and Slovakia. Factors weighed include political stability, demographic trends, operating climate, economic performance. Each individual country report is available in hard copy and entered in this fashion under the appropriate country heading.

Contact details: Economist Intelligence Unit, PO Box 200, Harold Hill, Romford RM3 8UX, UK. Tel. +44 (0)20 7830 1007. Fax +44 (0)1708 371 850. Email: london@eiu.com URL: http://www.eiu.com In the US: Economist Intelligence Unit, The Economist Building, 111 West 57th Street, NY, NY 10019, USA . Tel. (212) 554 060/1 800 938 4685 (USA and Canada only). Fax: (1.212) 586 0248. E-mail: newyork@eiu.com URL: http://www.eiu.com

Cost: £3800/$7100 pa (CD-ROM)

EIU Country Risk Service
Risks attend CEE business dealings. Perhaps not as much as the stories highlighted in our newspapers might suggest, but bad enough to be taken seriously. The *Risk Service*, in the CD-ROM version, analyses the elements of risk facing businesses in each of the countries under review with the exception of Albania and Bosnia-Herzegovina. The individual titles, in hard copy, are to be found under their country headings.

Contact details: Economist Intelligence Unit, PO Box 200, Harold Hill, Romford RM3 8UX, UK. Tel. +44 (0)20 7830 1007. Fax +44 (0)1708 371 850. Email: london@eiu.com URL: http://www.eiu.com In the US: Economist Intelligence Unit, The Economist Building, 111 West 57th Street, NY, NY 10019, USA . Tel. (212) 554 060/1 800 938 4685 (USA and Canada only). Fax (1.212) 586 0248. Email: newyork@eiu.com URL: http://www.eiu.com

Cost: £7300/$11,800 pa (CD-ROM)

Investor's Guide to Eastern Europe
This is a survey (1998) of all CEE countries, presenting likely future economic and political scenarios shaping forecasts of developments in individual countries. The main sectors highlighted for analytical treatment are energy, automotive, telecommunications, banking and consumer goods.

Contact details: Economist Intelligence Unit, PO Box 200, Harold Hill, Romford RM3 8UX, UK. Tel. +44 (0)20 7830 1007. Fax +44 (0)1708 371 850. Email: london@eiu.com URL: http://www.eiu.com In the US: Economist Intelligence Unit, The Economist Building, 111 West 57th Street, NY, NY 10019, USA. Tel. +1 212 554 060/1 800 938

4685 (USA and Canada only). Fax +1 1 212 586 0248. Email:
newyork@eiu.com URL: http://www.eiu.com

Cost: £295/$475

Managing Human Resources in Eastern Europe
Recruiting, salaries, benefits, mass redundancies, expatriate issues, hard-
ship postings – these are some of the topics in this report (1999) which
examines a critical aspect of business and management. In so doing it
provides informative insights into business attitudes and expectations in
all the CEE countries.

Contact details: Economist Intelligence Unit, PO Box 200, Harold
Hill, Romford, RM3 8UX, UK. Tel. +44 (0)20 7830 1007. Fax +44
(0)1708 371 850. Email: london@eiu.com URL: http://www.eiu.com
In the US: Economist Intelligence Unit, The Economist Building, 111
West 57th Street, NY, NY 10019, USA . Tel. +1 212 554 060/1 800
938 4685 (USA and Canada only). Fax +1 212 586 0248. Email:
newyork@eiu.com URL: http://www.eiu.com

Cost: £395/$625

Opening and Operating Offices in Eastern Europe and the CIS
This report (1997) offers information and advice on establishing business
offices in most CEE countries. Among the topics covered are property
issues, legal constraints on foreign business people, communication problems, staffing matters. A fund of good sense based on experience.

Contact details: Economist Intelligence Unit, PO Box 200, Harold
Hill, Romford RM3 8UX, UK. Tel. +44 (0)20 7830 1007. Fax +44
(0)1708 371 850. Email: london@eiu.com URL: http://www.eiu.com
In the US: Economist Intelligence Unit, The Economist Building, 111
West 57th Street, NY, NY 10019, USA . Tel. +1 212 554 060/1 800
938 4685 (USA and Canada only). Fax +1 212 586 0248. Email:
newyork@eiu.com URL: http://www.eiu.com

Cost: £395/$625

PlanEcon Trade and Finance Review
This is an **annual** review and analysis of Bulgaria, Czech Republic, Hungary, Poland, Romania, Slovakia and Slovenia in terms of foreign trade,
balance of payments, level of debts, etc. Short term projections are presented based on the analysis. The level of statistical support is impressive.

Contact details: PlanEcon, 111 14th Street NW, Suite 801, Washington,
DC 20005-5603, USA. Tel. +1 202 898 0471. Fax +1 202 898 0445. URL:
http://www.planecon.com

Cost: $8000 (for all countries); $1000 (individual country reports).

Reconnaissance
This Internet site covers all the countries discussed in this volume in terms of 'history, politics, government, economies, business, culture, transport, agriculture, environment, etc.'. There are 'files on all main industries'. This is not a free service, but contacted users speak favourably of it.

Contact details: City Mutual, PO Box 13614, London W4 1GS, UK. Tel. +44 (0)1935 817800. Fax +44 (0)1935 812999.
Email: nicholai@citymutual.com
URL: http://www.citymutual.com/recon.htm

Cost: On application (free trial period).

REESWeb
This Internet site provides a most comprehensive coverage of web sites relating to central and eastern Europe. Directions to country specific sites lead to all types of information and data. There is a search facility. For the Internet literate this is an excellent site to begin any process of familiarisation.

Contact details: URL: http://www.ucis.pitt.edu/reesweb/

Requests for country information often reduce to questions of statistical data – population figures, economic indicators, mortality rates, gross domestic product, trends in consumer spending, educational statistics, energy consumption, and so on. All the sources listed above include selected economic, business, social and other forms of statistics. Most are derived from the work of national statistical agencies with the responsibility for gathering and presenting such data. The latter agencies in CEE countries now aim to produce data sets roughly comparable to those available in the west and, in many cases, offering convenient data access through the Internet. Details of these will be found in the country sections under the Organisations heading.

However, there are specialist sources that flourish on the re-packaging of officially compiled statistics, or by ensuring quicker publication than is afforded by official hard copy timetables; or, in some instances, going out to collect their own statistics. Examples of these multi-country statistical compilations are:

Countries in Transition
The national statistics of a number of CEE countries, including Bulgaria, Croatia, Czech Republic, Hungary, Poland, Romania, Slovakia and Slovenia, are gathered to form a useful regional reference source. Among the selected economic indicators are – employment, consumption, investment, standard of living. The elements of selection and summarisation

have to be remembered. The **annual** compilation is available as hard copy and as a CD-ROM.

Contact details: Vienna Institute for International Economic Studies, Oppolzergasse 6, Vienna A-1010, Austria. Tel. +43 1 533 6610. Fax +43 1 533 6610 50. URL: http://www.wiiw.ac.at/

Cost: On application

Consumer Eastern Europe
This well-established **annual** compilation with its emphasis upon consumer goods and spending vividly reflects the change in economic and business attitudes in CEE countries – Bulgaria, Czech Republic, Hungary, Poland, Slovakia, among other east European countries. The coverage of product sectors is wide and related to such measures as, for example, market shares, sales volumes. There are data for household characteristics, consumer expenditure, retail distribution, and much else having a bearing on consumers and consuming. As part of *World Consumer Markets* the volume is available in CD-ROM format.

Contact details: Euromonitor, 60-61 Britton Street, London EC1M 5NA,UK. Tel. +44 (0)20 7251 1105. Fax +44 (0)20 7251 0985. Email: info@euromonitor.com URL: http://Euro.imrmall.com/

Cost: £425/$1050

Consumer Lifestyles in Eastern Europe
A collection of statistics (1997) designed to reflect the social changes taking place especially in relation to consuming and leisure habits. The data offer intriguing insights into ordinary lives in Bulgaria, Czech Republic, Hungary, Poland, Romania, Slovakia among others.

Contact details: Euromonitor, 60-61 Britton Street, London EC1M 5NA, UK. Tel. +44 (0)20 7251 1105. Fax +44 (0)20 7251 0985. Email: info@euromonitor.com URL: http://Euro.imrmall.com/chapters/ 0011/index.shtml

Cost: £895. Country chapters can be purchased separately.

Current Developments

Enquiries about country information, in the sense discussed above, are often a prelude to more specific questions. For example, information about current and immediate future economic conditions, the anticipated risk factors for business, evaluations of the implications of specific political events for business expectations, the latest news about the progress of privatisation programmes. In short, current news and information about almost everything to do with business operations in rapidly changing times.

The demand for the latest business information, especially from western investors accustomed to high standards of information provision, has had to be satisfied. One of the languages for this purpose had to be English although, for some countries, German was a close runner-up. With such a strong demand it is not surprising that the sector devoted to monitoring and reporting on current business and related developments has become crowded and highly competitive. It is not surprising, either, that the sector supports numerous information-at-a-price services. Paradoxically, however, the same demand has resulted in far more 'free' business information being made available on the Internet. As a consequence the market has become one in which potential customers are spoiled for choice, and one in which all the formats for rapid, and not-so-rapid, dissemination of information are deployed – email, the Internet, online, fax, daily print services, weeklies, monthlies, etc. Some examples are:

BBC Summary of World Broadcasts
Weekly economic reports which offer news monitored from foreign media. Part 2 covers Central Europe, the Balkans. Can be supplied in full or in sections in machine-readable form. Also available through a closed user group on the Internet via a File Transfer Protocol.

Contact details: BBC Monitoring, Caversham Park, Reading RG4 8TZ, UK. Tel. +44 (0)118 9469 254/247/245

Cost: On application

BNA's Eastern Europe Reporter
This substantial **fortnightly** has authority and staying power. In 1999 it took over and extinguished the new (1998) title – *Emerging European Markets* – put out by FT Finance. The news coverage of current business events and developments is extensive, with helpful national grouping of news items.

Contact details: BNA International, Heron House, 10 Dean Farrar Street, London SW1H 0DX, UK. Tel. +44 (0)20 7222 8831. Fax +44 (0)20 7222 5550. Email: bnai@bna.com

Cost: $995 pa (USA); £660 pa (elsewhere).

Business Central Europe
This is a lively, glossy, analytical, **monthly.** A typical issue has features and brief items about business, finance, politics, supported by a statistical section. An excellent monitoring source. With subscription comes *Business Central Europe: The Annual* – 'an analysis of the main political and business developments in the region's 27 countries', plus forecasts for the coming year. A handy quick reference source.

Contact details: Business Central Europe, Economist Newspaper Limited, PO Box 14, Harold Hill, Romford, Essex RM3 8EQ, UK. Tel. +44 (0)1708 381 555. Fax +44 (0)1708 381 211.

Cost: £35 pa

Business Eastern Europe
This is a **weekly** newsletter providing brief, alerting, items of news – significant legislative changes, economic developments, financial and banking issues, etc. A key resource.

Contact details: Economist Intelligence Unit, PO Box 200, Harold Hill, Romford, RM3 8UX, UK. Tel. +44 (0)20 7830 1007. Fax +44 (0)1708 371 850. Email: london@eiu.com URL: http://www.eiu.com In the US: Economist Intelligence Unit, The Economist Building, 111 West 57th Street, NY, NY 10019, USA . Tel. +1 212 554 060/1 800 938 4685 (USA and Canada only). Fax +1 212 586 0248. Email: newyork@eiu.com URL: http://www.eiu.com

Cost: £765/$1395 pa.

Business Europa: Central European Business Magazine
This is a **bi-monthly** publication aimed squarely at executives. Sharp, glossy, features with reports on business developments in the region; 'who's bought whom, for how much. Who's invested in whom. Who's started, who's stopped'. There is a diary of selected coming events, very selective statistical presentations. Not boring. The company's web site provides links to other sites.

Contact details: Business Europa, 2 Market Street, Saffron Walden, Essex CB10 1 HZ, UK. Tel. +44 (0)1403 782644. Fax +44 (0)1799 524805.Email: waldenpub@easynet.co.uk URL: http://www.business-europa.co.uk/

Cost: £30/$60 pa (Europe); £45/$90 pa (USA and Canada); £48/$95 (elsewhere).

Central and South-East Europe Monitor
This **monthly** newsletter reports on business events and conditions in all the CEE countries. The news items are brief, but coverage is wide – for example, privatisation, sectoral performances, political and legal changes impacting on business operations, selected economic indicators, the business climate.

Contact details: Business Monitor International, 179 Queen Victoria Street, London EC4V 4DU, UK. Tel. +44 (0)20 7248 0468. Fax +44 (0)20 7248 0467. URL: http://www.businessmonitor.com

Cost: £265/$630 pa

Central Europe Business Journal

This is an Internet service maintained by an established news gathering agency. Its newspapers and alerting services are available in electronic format and updated **daily**. The news coverage is wide, but with a strong emphasis upon economic and business issues. A convenient way of keeping in touch with local developments within the CEE.

Contact details: URL: http://www.ceebiz.com/

Cost: Services are individually priced ranging from $190 to $2490.

Central Europe Daily Bulletin

The *Bulletin* is distributed by fax and email. The brief news items highlight market and general business issues. For a price each original news item can be received as a fuller report.

Contact details: Newsbase, 22 Forth Street, Edinburgh EH1 3LH, UK. Tel. +44 (0)131 478 7000. Fax +44 (0)131 478 7001. URL: http://www.newsbase.co.uk/

Cost: £275 pa

Central Europe Online

This Internet site provides a wide range of CEE business and business-related news items on a **daily** basis, including selected stock market and currency data. An interesting site to explore.

Contact details: URL: http://www.centraleurope.com

Central Europe Review

This **quarterly** reports mainly on Croatia, the Czech Republic, Hungary, Poland, Slovakia and Slovenia. It carries news of sectoral and market surveys and of companies, but its main value is in the review and analysis of economic developments.

Contact details: Dresdner Kleinwort Benson, Central Europe Research, 20 Fenchurch Street, London EC3P 3DP, UK. Tel. +44 (0)171 475 1473. Fax +44 (0)171 475 1488.

Cost: On application

Central European

The *Central European* appears **10 times a year.** It covers events and developments in the business world, and is especially strong on money and financial matters. The system and depth of the reporting makes an interesting contrast with the unrefined presentations characteristic of many freely accessed Internet sites.

Contact details: Euromoney Publications, Nestor House, Playhouse Yard, London EC4V 5EX, UK. Tel. +44 (0)20 7779 8999. Fax +44 (0)20 7779 8300. URL: http://www.euromoney.com/

Cost: £240/$435 pa.

Central European Business and Finance
A **monthly** newsletter providing the usual brief, alerting, news items about business, industrial, legal, banking and financial developments in the Czech Republic, Hungary, Poland, Slovakia.

Contact details: East European News Group, PO Box 579, Tower Hill House, Le Bordage, St. Peter Port, Guernsey GY1 6LQ, Channel Isles. Tel. +44 (0)1481 727730. Fax +44 (0)1481 727731.

Cost: £295 pa.

Central European Business Daily
This Internet site carries business and economic news about a number of east European countries including the Czech Republic, Hungary, Poland, Slovenia and Slovakia. The news reports are drawn from local sources. The site is better organised than many others. A useful monitoring service.

Contact details: Central European Business Daily, 10 Carteret Street, Queen Anne's Gate, London SW1H 9DR, UK. Tel. +44 (0)20 7222 3450. Fax +44 (0)20 7222 3460. URL: http://www.nsl.co.uk/cebd/

Cost: $230 pa (Europe); $300 (elsewhere).

Central European Business Weekly
This **weekly** newspaper provides broad business coverage of CEE countries focusing on financial information, property news and reports of foreign investor developments.

Contact details: VP International, Red Hill House, Hope Street, Chester CH4 8BU, UK. Tel +44 (0)1244 681619. Email: helen@vpinternational.com URL: http://www.vpinternational.com/

Cost: £185/$280 pa.

Central European Economic Review
The *Review* is published **10 times a year**. It is received as a supplement to *The Wall Street Journal* Europe, but can be purchased separately. Coverage includes banking and finance, company news, country surveys, sectoral analyses and reviews, stock markets, politics, as well as significant items of general news and cultural notices. It is also available on the Internet as part of the *The Wall Street Journal Interactive Edition*.

Contact details: Dow Jones Publishing Company (Europe), PO Box 2845, DH Heerlen, NL 6401, Belgium. Tel. +32 45 576 1222. Fax +32 45 571 4722. Email: subs.ceer@cor.dowjones.com URL: http://www.wsj.com/ceer/

Cost: £45 pa (separate subscription); $29 pa (Internet, for those with a print subscription; $59 pa otherwise).

East European Business Intelligence on Disc
The numerous EIU reports and journals – *Business Eastern Europe, Country Reports, Country Profiles, Country Forecasts*, etc. – are repackaged into a single, searchable, business information system covering all the CEE countries. There are monthly updates.

Contact details: Economist Intelligence Unit, PO Box 200, Harold Hill, Romford RM3 8UX, UK. Tel. +44 (0)20 7830 1007. Fax +44 (0)1708 371 850. Email: london@eiu.com URL: http://www.eiu.com In the US: Economist Intelligence Unit, The Economist Building, 111 West 57th Street, NY, NY 10019, USA . Tel. +1 212 554 060/1 800 938 4685 (USA and Canada only). Fax +1 212 586 0248. Email: newyork@eiu.com URL: http://www.eiu.com

Cost: £3200/$5000

East European Emerging Markets
This is a **fortnightly** newsletter aimed at foreign investors eyeing business prospects in CEE countries. It provides standard business fare – news of company activities, developments in privatisation, investment decisions, etc.

Contact details: East European Emerging Markets, Glebe House, 12 Glebe Road, London, N8 7DB, UK. Tel. +44 (0)20 8372 8932. Fax +44 (0)20 8374 1153. Email: 100766.2735@compuserve.com

Cost: £695 pa

Eastern Europe Consensus Forecasts: A Digest of Economic Forecasts
This new (1999) **bi-monthly** service provides the averaged predictions of a large panel of experts regarding future financial and economic developments in individual CEE countries. Unlike many other forecasting agencies it regularly assesses its own predictive success.

Contact details: Consensus Economics, 53 Upper Brook Street, London W1Y 2LT, UK. Tel. +44 (0)20 7491 3211. Fax +44 (0)20 7409 2331.

Cost: £315/$490 pa.

Eastern Europe Monitor
This is a **monthly** reporting on business related developments in Poland, Hungary, Bulgaria, Romania, Czech Republic, Slovakia, Slovenia and Albania. Issues reported include political risk, the business environment, economic prospects, major industrial developments.

Contact details: Business Monitor International, 179 Queen Victoria Street, London EC4V 4DD, UK. Tel. +44 (0)20 7248 0468. Fax +44 (0)20 7248 0467. Email: busmon@dial.pipex.com URL: http://www.businessmonitor.com/home.htm

Cost: £265/$435 pa

Economic Trends in Eastern Europe
This periodical appears **three times a year.** It reports and analyses events and developments in CEE countries, focusing attention on economic changes and illustrating discussions with statistics. The articles have an academic flavour, but the features are interesting and informative because of their Hungarian standpoint.

Contact details: Kopint-Datorg, Szende Pál u. 5, H-1051 Budapest, Hungary. Tel. +36 1 266 5060. Fax +36 1 266 5782. URL: http://www.kopint-datorg.hu/

Cost: $157 pa

EIU Country Reports
This series, presented on CD-ROM, covers 27 CEE countries, including those under review in this volume. The *Reports* appear **quarterly,** covering such topics as the outlook for the coming year, the political scene, economic policy, the performance of the economy, trade, business news, statistics. The individual titles that make up the series are given separate treatment under appropriate country headings.

Contact details: Economist Intelligence Unit, PO Box 200, Harold Hill, Romford RM3 8UX, UK. Tel. +44 (0)20 7830 1007. Fax +44 (0)1708 371 850. Email: london@eiu.com URL: http://www.eiu.com In the US: Economist Intelligence Unit, The Economist Building, 111 West 57th Street, NY, NY 10019, USA . Tel. +1 212 554 060/1 800 938 4685 (USA and Canada only). Fax +1 212 586 0248. Email: newyork@eiu.com URL: http://www.eiu.com

Cost: £3800/$7100 pa (CD-ROM)

EIU ViewsWire Eastern Europe
This **daily** Internet service provides, for all the CEE countries, '10 - 15 articles ... of reasoned analysis of critical developments in the region'. The stress is upon the analytical and interpretative, not simply news report-

ing. Other features include briefings on developments in '6 key areas – corporate strategy, economy, finance, politics, regulations and industry'. Country forecasts and background data are also part of the service. Marketed as a 'pioneer' service.

Contact details: EIU Electronic, Economist Intelligence Unit, 15 Regent Street, London SW1Y 4LR, UK. Tel. +44 (0)20 7830 1183. Fax +44 (0)20 7830 1023. Email: london@eiu.com URL: http:// www.eiu.com (general). URL: http://www.ee.viewswire.com (specific).
In the US: Economist Intelligence Unit, The Economist Building, 111 West 57th Street, NY, NY 10019, USA . Tel. +1 212 554 060/1 800 938 4685 (USA and Canada only). Fax +1 212 586 0248. Email: newyork@eiu.com URL: http://www.eiu.com

Cost: £2200/$3600 pa (for single user; special rates for multiple users)

EMIC's Guide to Export Sites
The Department of Trade and Industry has produced a guide to web sites, throughout the world, which provide free information and data relating to exports. Countries covered include Croatia, Czech Republic, Hungary, Poland, Romania, Slovakia, Slovenia and Yugoslavia. The guide is in hard copy format, and is also available on the Internet.

Contact details: DTI Export Publications Orderline, Admail 528, London SW1W 8YT, UK. Tel. +44 (0)870 1502 500. Fax +44 (0)870 1502 333. URL: http://www.dti.gov.uk/ots/publications/ export_publications_home.html

Cost: £10 (print)

Euro-east
A **monthly** news bulletin focusing on the increasingly important process for CEE countries of European Union enlargement. Topics discussed include progress reports on individual applications to join the EU, the current state of official relations, project tendering, aid projects.

Contact details: European Information Service, avenue Adolphe Lacomblé 66, B-1130, Brussels, Belgium. Tel. +32 2 737 7709. Fax +32 2 732 6757. Email: eis@eis.be URL: http://www.eis.be

Cost: BEF 23,200 pa.

Image on Central + Eastern Europe
This newsletter appears irregularly. It is well produced and written, and informative. A typical issue will contain a country profile, an editorial feature, an investment update monitoring, country by country, changes

in tax legislation and labour law, and also reports of developments in the fields of finance and privatisation.

Contact details: KPMG Regional Headquarters Central and Eastern Europe, Váci út. 99, H-1139 Budapest, Hungary. Fax +36 1 270 72 78. Email: kathrins@kpmg.hu URL: http://www.eu.kpmg.net

Cost: Free on application

International Country Risk Guide (ICRG)

Risk analysis is an integral part of business operations. There are specialist services to help in assessing levels of risk attending operations in various countries. The exercise is usually based on a formula that takes in political, economic and financial factors. ICRG's world wide **monthly** coverage of risk factors includes the major east European economies. There are hard copy and CD-ROM versions.

Contact details: The PRS Group, 6320 Fly Road, Suite 102, PO Box 248, East Syracuse, NY 13057-0248, USA. Tel. +1 315 431 0511. Fax +1 315 431 0200. Email: custserv@polrisk.com URL: http://www.polrisk.com/

Cost: $3300 pa (hard copy); $6800 (monthly CD-ROMs).

ISI Emerging Markets

This much lauded Internet service, acquired by Euromoney Publication plc in January 1999, provides 'searchable current news and archives, public and private company financials, macroeconomic statistics, analysis and economic forecasts, equity and debt market daily quotes, industry and company reports and privatisation updates, legal and regulatory information'. Among the countries covered by this fee-based service are Bulgaria, the Czech Republic, Hungary, Poland, Romania. The range and detail of data on offer, as well as the local perspectives reported, make it a convenient and effective tool of research. An established market leader.

Contact details: Internet Securities, 7 Helen's Place, London EC3A 6AU, UK. Tel. +44 (0)20 7570 0057. Fax +44 (0)20 7570 0058. URL: http://www.securities.com In the US: Internet Securities, Inc., 695 Atlantic Avenue, Boston, Massachusetts 02111. Tel +1 617 204 3100. Fax +1 617 204 3101

Cost: On application.

New Europe

This is a **weekly** newspaper providing general coverage of events and developments in central and east European countries. It has a strong business, economic and financial orientation.

Contact details: New Europe Group, 3D Stefanias Avenue, Pale Penteli Attikis, 15236 Athens, Greece. Tel. +30 1 601 6700. Fax +30 1 600 6999. Email: ne@new-europe.com URL: http://www.new-europe.gr/

Cost: $350 pa

New Markets Monthly
This is a bright and breezy business magazine reporting business and sectoral news from all CEE countries. A legal briefing section is a regular feature. A good general monitoring source.

Contact details: New Markets Monthly, STE Publishing Ltd., 45 Beech Street, London EC2Y 8AD, UK.

Cost: £60/$160 pa

PlanEcon Report
This is a stalwart of the CEE information business concentrating upon macroeconomic indicators. The *Report* appears **fortnightly**, generally concentrating upon one of the countries kept under review – Bulgaria, Croatia, Czech Republic, Hungary, Poland, Romania, Slovakia, Slovenia. It is an excellent source of independently interpreted statistical material. Also available via email.

Contact details: PlanEcon, 1111 14th Street NW, Suite 801, Washington, DC 20005-5603, USA. Tel. +1 202 898 0471. Fax +1 202 898 0445. URL: http://www.planecon.com

Cost: $1800 pa

PlanEcon Review and Outlook
Published **twice a year** this is a well-established, authoritative, source of current and likely future developments in the economies of CEE countries. There are four volumes, each devoted to a particular region, but the country chapters can be purchased individually. Each economy is surveyed and a five-year projection of the major economic indicators presented, together with an assessment of the possible risk factors.

Contact details: PlanEcon, 111 14th Street NW, Suite 801, Washington, DC 20005-5603, USA. Tel. +1 202 898 0471. Fax +1 202 898 0445. URL: http://www.planecon.com

Cost: $7000 (for all countries); $850 (individual country reports)..

Transition
This **bimonthly** differs from the usual newsletters in that it considers broad reforming issues in a reflective, essay style – banking developments, privatisation, social welfare changes, foreign investment, etc.

Contact details: World Bank, PO Box 7247-7956, Philadelphia PA 19170-7956, USA. Tel. +1 703 661 1580. Fax +1 703 661 1501. Email: books@worldbank.org URL: http://www.worldbank.org

Cost: $30 pa

Uniting Europe
This is a **weekly** newsletter which, as the title suggests, reports on issues associated with the process of European Union enlargement.

Contact details: Agence Europe, Rue de la Gare 36, Brussels B-1040, Belgium. Tel. +32 2 737 9494. Fax +32 2 736 3700.

Cost: BEF 10,000 pa

Companies and Contacts

Contact at company level is essential for business transactions. In the CEE countries the provision of sources to facilitate such contacts went through an initially hectic development phase which gradually steadied into a severely weeded set of sources providing relatively standardised forms of company information. In the main the elements of the latter are – names and addresses, telephone, fax, email numbers, date of establishment, names of senior management, numbers of employees, product and service descriptions. In some cases bank details and turnover figures are given, in fewer still balance sheet details may be provided. More detailed profiles are rarely found in multi-country sources. As a rule of thumb it may be assumed that the greater the geographical spread of the standard, printed, company information services the more selective will be the coverage, only the main companies and basic details finding their way into the record.

Faced with the increasing pace of change, and the short life of many new enterprises in turbulent circumstances, the usefulness of less frequently updated sources is quickly diminished. The Internet, with its rapid updating facility, has the potential to provide a solution to the problems of coverage and updating. Currently, however, the CD-ROM format, less flexible than online services, but both more flexible and versatile than the hard copy forms, is a solution much favoured by compilers of company directories. Many publishers satisfy market appeal by providing print and CD-ROM versions of their sources and, in some cases, Internet versions as well. The examples chosen all provide general sectoral coverage. Company directories concentrating upon specific sectors are listed under their sectoral headings below.

Central and Eastern European Directory
This directory (1999) lists the major companies of the Czech Republic, Slovakia, Croatia, Hungary, Poland and Slovenia. The company profiles consist of locational and contact data, names of top personnel, descriptions of activities and products, number of employees, turnover.

Contact details: Dun & Bradstreet, Holmers Farm Way, High Wycombe, Bucks HP12 4UL, UK. Tel. +44 (0)1494 422000. Fax +44 (0)1494 422929.

Cost: £495

Directory of Consumer Brands and their Owners 1998: Eastern Europe
This source provides a classified list of brand names with the usual locational company details as well as brand market shares and financial data.

Contact details: Euromonitor, 60-61 Britton Street, London EC1M 5NA, UK. Tel. +44 (0)20 7251 1105. Fax +44 (0)20 7251 0985. Email: infor@euromonitor.com URL: http://Euro.imrmall.com/

Cost: £495/$990

East European Business Database
This CD-ROM (1998) lists over 50,000 enterprises in CEE countries. There is a handy search facility but the company information provided does not go beyond basic locational, contact and product descriptions. Differential pricing is common in the business information sector, but rarely as great as in this instance.

Contact details: National Technical Information Service, 5285 Port Royal Road, Springfield VA 2216, USA. Tel. +1 703 605 6060. Fax +1 703 605 6900. URL: http://www.ntis.gov

Cost: $395 (USA/Canada); $790 (elsewhere).

Kompass Eastern Europe
Over 160,000 companies, in 15 CEE countries, are listed in this **annually** produced CD-ROM source. Apart from the usual contact data company profiles include sales figures, number of employees, descriptions of activities and products. In addition to an extensive range of search options the CD-ROM can be used to produce labels and specialist listings. Subscribers receive one update a year.

Contact details: Kompass UK, Reed Information Services, Windsor Court, East Grinstead House, East Grinstead, West Sussex RH 19 1XA, UK. Tel. +44 (0)1342 326 972. Fax +44 (0)1342 335612.

Cost: £2890

Major Companies of Central and Eastern Europe and the
Commonwealth of Independent States
This standard directory (1998) provides the usual basic company data. Each year it increases its coverage of firms. Now the total stands at around 10,000 with, as a new service, country summaries and comparative tables. Available in hard copy and as a CD-ROM.

Contact details: Graham & Whiteside, Tuition House, 5-6 Francis Grove, London SW19 4DT, UK. Tel. +44 (0)20 8947 1011. Fax +44 (0)20 8947 1163. Email: sales@major-co-data.com URL: http://www.major-co-data.com

Cost: £545/$980 (hard copy); £880/$1585 (CD-ROM)

Industries and Services

As various industrial and commercial sectors of CEE countries slowly and hesitantly adapted to the new demands being made upon them sectoral information sources were produced which monitored their development and scanned the future economic horizon. There was, for example, a lively interest in the destinations of foreign investments, assessments of likely future possibilities were necessary for internal planning and for outside investors, production performance and market shares were significant issues, as were the incursions of foreign firms into previously protected CEE markets. Inevitably, it was the most economically promising sectors that received the most attention from information providers.

The financial sector, not surprisingly, is the best served by information sources of all types. Banks, insurance companies, stock exchanges, shares, government borrowing policies, taxation issues, project finance – all are reflected in specialised multi-country information sources. Information activity in this sector, however, was soon matched by that associated with the energy industries which soon supported a western style information structure. Not far behind came the media and telecommunications sections now flourishing under more liberal regimes. Others sectors have followed more slowly, but the change over a period of ten years or so has been remarkable. The repertoire of sectoral sources takes in reports, journals of various descriptions, directories of companies, products and personnel, market research surveys, statistical services. Even more than in other areas sectoral sources reveal the extent to which providers have emerged to cater for narrower activity markets. The following examples, for a limited selection of sectors, illustrate these points.

Agriculture

The Agrarian Economies of Central and Eastern Europe and the Commonwealth of Independent States: Situation and Perspectives.
This report (1998) 'presents an overview of the agricultural situation and the status of the reforms in the agrarian sectors' of CEE countries. The transformation to market economies has been 'a far more complicated and complex process than imagined'.

Contact details: OECD Paris Centre, 2 rue André-Pascal, Paris 75775 Cedex 16, France. Tel. +33 (0)1 49 104235. Fax +33 (0)1 49 104276. Email: sales@oecd.org. Also – The Stationery Office, PO Box 276, London SW8 5DT, UK. Tel. +44 (0)870 600 5522. Fax +44 (0)20 7873 8247. URL: http://www.tso-online.co.uk

Cost: $22

Agricultural Policies in Emerging and Transition Economies
This **annual** is a major reference source for the agricultural and agro-food sectors. Among the countries selected for review and analysis of agricultural policies are Albania, Bulgaria, Croatia, Romania, the Slovak Republic, Slovenia. In addition to an examination of such themes as productivity and competitiveness there are numerous statistical tables.

Contact details: OECD Paris Centre, 2 rue André Pascal, Paris 75775 Cedex 16, France. Tel. +33 (0)1 49 104235. Fax +33 (0)1 49 104276. Email: sales@oecd.org. Also – The Stationery Office, PO Box 276, London SW8 5DT, UK. Tel. +44 (0)870 600 5522. Fax +44 (0)20 7873 8247. URL: http://www.tso-online.co.uk

Cost: £29/$48

Central and East European Agriculture and the European Union
This report (1997) 'examines the development and current state of agricultural policy and trade in each of the countries of Central and Eastern Europe' in the light of possible effects of EU enlargement upon an industry struggling to come to terms with levels of modernisation required by market forces.

Contact details: Agra Europe, 80 Calverley Road, Tunbridge Wells, Kent TN1 2UN, UK. Tel. +44 (0)1892 533813. Fax +44 (0)1892 544895. Email: marketing@agra-europe.com URL: http://www.agra-food-news.com

Cost: £275

Dairy Industry in Eastern Europe
This report (1997) concentrates on the causes of falling milk production, and suggests courses of action to remedy the situation.

Contact details: Agra Europe, 80 Calverley Road, Tunbridge Wells, Kent TN1 2UN, UK. Tel. +44 (0)1892 533813. Fax +44 (0)1892 544895. Email: marketing@agra-europe.com URL: http://www.agra-food-news.com

Cost: £175

East Europe Agriculture and Food
This **monthly** is one of the major sources for keeping abreast of developments in this sector. It includes excellent statistical surveys, market reports, price movements, assessments of national policies, the activities of major companies.

Contact details: Agra Europe, 80 Calverley Road, Tunbridge Wells, Kent TN1 2UN, UK. Tel. +44 (0)1892 533813. Fax +44 (0)1892 544895. Email: marketing@agra-europe.com URL: http://www.agra-food-news.com

Cost: £440 pa (UK); £485 pa (Europe); £530 pa (elsewhere).

Automotive

Automotive Emerging Markets
This is a **monthly** newsletter monitoring developments in the sector in central and eastern Europe, and in other emerging economies. Production data, forecasts, company statements, trading figures, and other sector relevant data and information are to be found here.

Contact details: FT Automotive, Maple House, 149 Tottenham Court Road, London W1P 9LL, UK. Tel. +44 (0)20 7896 2241. Fax +44 (0)20 7896 2275. URL: http://www.ftauto.com

Cost: £495/$782 pa.

The Automotive Sectors of Central and Eastern Europe
This report (1997) examines national production and demand trends, reviews developments in the components sector, and presents medium-term forecasts. Major enterprises are profiled.

Contact details: Economist Intelligence Unit, PO Box 200, Harold Hill, Romford, RM3 8UX, UK. Tel. +44 (0)20 7830 1007. Fax +44 (0)1708 371 850. Email: london@eiu.com URL: http://www.eiu.com In the US: Economist Intelligence Unit, The Economist Building, 111 West 57th Street, NY, NY 10019, USA . Tel. +1 212 554 060/1 800 938 4685 (USA and Canada only). Fax +1 212 586 0248. Email: newyork@eiu.com URL: http://www.eiu.com

Cost: £645/$995

Central Europe Automotive Report (CEAR)
If there has to be a standard example of aggressive selling of an information product through the Internet this service would be a prime candidate.

A number of information services, all relating to the automotive industry, are on offer, with loads of hype and explanation. The sources produced include 'interviews with local automotive executives, market information, news, investment, legal, accounting and tax analysis, partnership opportunities and supplier directories'. There is a standard **monthly** print edition of the *Report*, a **monthly** email version which has extra data, a **monthly** specialist analyst edition subscription which has further added data and faster delivery of information and data. To add icing to the cake there is also the bait of an *AutoNewsFast* subscription – a **weekly** email sectoral news service. This really is an Internet site with attitude.

Contact details: CEAR, 4800 Baseline Road, Suite E104-340 Boulder, CO 80303, USA. Tel. +1 440 843 9658. Fax +1 206 374 5282.
Email: cetmlic@ibm.net URL: http://www.cear.com/
UK subscribers should contact: VP International, Red Hill House, Hope Street, Hope House, Chester CH4 8BU, UK.
Tel. +44 (0)1244 681619. Email: helen@vpinternational.com
URL: http://www.vpinternational.com/

Cost: $500 pa (Standard print edition and email version); $900 pa (special analyst edition); $1850 pa (AutoNewsfast, plus special analyst edition).

East European Automotive Industry Forecast Report
This report is published **twice a year**. Close analysis of national industries, their performance, and influencing factors such as foreign investment, government and tax policies, is followed by sectoral projections and forecasts.

Contact details: Standard & Poor's DRI, Wimbledon Bridge House, 1 Hartfield Road, London SW19 3RU, UK. Tel. +44 (0)20 8545 6216. Fax +44 (0)20 8545 6255.

Cost: $9500 pa

New Vehicle Distribution in Central and Eastern Europe
This two volume **annual,** covering all the CEE countries, analyses national markets in terms of sales of new vehicles, together with supporting background material – economic, sectoral, distributor networks, etc.

Contact details: Central Europe Automotive Report, 4800 Baseline, Suite E104-340, Boulder, Colorado 80303, USA. Tel. +1 440 843 9658. Fax +1 206 374 5282. Email: info@cear.com URL: http://www.cear.com

Cost: $800 (for 2 volumes)

Chemicals

Chemical Producers in Central and Eastern Europe

This **annual** provides profiles of over 3000 companies in Bulgaria, the Czech Republic, Croatia, Hungary, Poland, Romania, Slovenia, Slovakia and Yugoslavia. The profiles are basic – locational, contact, activities and products. Available in hard copy and in CD-ROM format.

Contact details: EXIN, Šeřikova 32, 63700 Czech Republic. Tel. +420 5 4323 6040. Fax +420 5 4122 0005. Email: exin@brn.pvtnet.cz URL: http://www.pvtnet.cz/www/EXIN/

Cost: 200 EUR (hard copy); 400 EUR (CD-ROM)

Directory of Chemical Producers and Products

An **annual,** basic, listing of companies in CEE countries – locational and contact data, number of employees, product descriptions.

Contact details: UN Economic Commission for Europe, Palais de Nations, CH-1211 Geneva 10, Switzerland. Tel. +41 22 917 3254. Fax +41 22 917-178.

Cost: On application

East Europe and CIS Chemicals Briefing

This **monthly** newsletter monitors, on a regional basis, current developments in sectors of the chemical and petrochemical industries. The main product focus is olefins and aromatics and their derivatives. There is a **monthly** email version – *East Europe and CIS ChemNet*.

Contact details: CIREC, 36 St. Christopher's Mews, Wallington, Surrey SM6 8AP, UK. Tel. +44 (0)20 8 669 5126. Fax +44 (0)20 8 669 5126. Email: andrew@andspar.demon.co.uk URL: http://www.andspar.demon.co.uk/

Cost: On application

Plastic and Rubber Processing Firms in Central and Eastern Europe

This **annual** directory is another from the bare bones output of EXIN. It 'profiles more than 3600 plastics and rubber processing firms'. The company data is sufficient for contact purposes, and includes activity/product descriptions. The countries covered are Bulgaria, Czech Republic, Croatia, Hungary, Poland, Romania, Slovenia, Slovakia, Yugoslavia among others. For many business enquiries this is all that is needed.

Contact details: EXIN, Šeřikova 32, 63700 Czech Republic. Tel. +420 5 4323 6040. Fax +420 5 4122 0005. Email: exin@brn.pvtnet.cz URL: http://www.pvtnet.cz/www/EXIN/

Cost: 200 EUR (hard copy); 400 EUR (CD-ROM)

Construction

Central European Construction Journal

The country coverage of this **monthly** sectoral source takes in the Czech Republic, Hungary, Poland and Slovakia. Content includes, for example, company news, building projects and tenders, changes in legal requirements, price trends, statistical data.

Contact details: Roberts Publishing, Husenická 33, 130 00 Prague 3, Czech Republic. Tel. +420 2 628 4348. Fax +420 2 627 8643.

Cost: £72/$120 pa.

Eastern Europe's Largest Construction Companies

This directory (1997) profiles the construction companies of the Czech Republic, Poland, Slovakia and Hungary. Profiles include assessments of the current business standing of companies, past performances and forecasts of future developments. Data include, for example, net capital, pre-tax profit, turnover. In other words, more financial details than in general directories.

Contact details: European Construction Research, Bredgade 35B, DK-1260 Copenhagen, Denmark. Tel. +45 33 162 100. Fax +45 33 162 900. Email: ecr@cybernet.dk URL: http://www.epi.no/ecr/index.htm

Cost: £295/$495

International Construction Week: Eastern Europe

This **weekly** newsletter monitors the progress and technical details of major construction projects in CEE countries. Provides important operational information.

Contact details: ICW Publications, The Chapter House, Hinderton Hall Estate, Neston, South Wirral L64 7TS, UK. Tel. +44 (0)151 353 1234. Fax +44 (0)151 353 1011.

Cost: £767 pa

Cosmetics

Cosmetics and Toiletries in Eastern Europe

A market research report (1998) in the standard Euromonitor style – trends and developments review, profiles of major companies in the sector, a five-year forecast of market performance, useful statistics. Countries covered include Bulgaria, Czech Republic, Hungary, Poland, Romania and Slovakia.

Contact details: Euromonitor plc, 60-61 Britton Street, London EC1M 5NA, UK. Tel. +44 (0)20 7251 1105. Fax +44 (0)20 7251 0985. URL: http://Euro.imrmall.com/chapters/0188/index.shtml

Cost: £1905/$3900. Country chapters can be purchased separately.

Electronics

East European Report
This **monthly** newsletter analyses 'microelectronics and electronic markets, industry and technology as the change occurs. Topics covered include forecasts, production, end-use consumption, business activity, government and economic issues, and company operations'. In addition to news items there is a monthly research editorial. Email and print versions.

Contact details: Future Horizons, Blakes Green Cottage, Stone Street, Near Seal, Sevenoaks, Kent TN15 0LQ, UK. Tel. +44 (0)1732 762896. Fax +44 (0)1732 763914. Email: mail@future-horizons.net URL: http://www.future-horizons.net

Cost: £550 pa

Energy

Central European Downstream Service
This analytical report on the oil industry appears **annually,** covering the Czech Republic, Hungary, Poland and the Slovak Republic. The industry is reviewed, trends analysed and a future scenario advanced. Subscription to the **annual** review allows access to the analysts and the receipt of what are, in effect, updating reports. An illustrated 'electronic book' (i.e.. CD-ROM) version, with search, copy and paste facilities, is available.

Contact details: Wood Mackenzie Consultants, Kintore House, 74-77 Queen Street, Edinburgh EH2 4NS, UK. Tel. +44 (0)131 243 4530. Fax +44 (0)131 243 4495. Email: energy@woodmac.com URL: http://www.woodmac.com/

Cost: £6000 pa

CIS and East European Energy Databook
This **annual** provides a detailed and comprehensive statistical survey of energy production and consumption in 26 CEE countries.

Contact details: Eastern Bloc Research, Newton Kyme, Tadcaster, North Yorkshire LS24 9LS, UK. Tel. +44 (0)1937 835691. Fax +44 (0)1937 835756.

Cost: £350

East European Energy Report
An authoritative **monthly** which reviews and analyses developments within the sector. A typical issue will carry news about companies, statistical data, exploration, production, prices, projects, etc. An essential for the reference shelf.

Contact details: FT Finance, Maple House, 149 Tottenham Court Road, London W1P 9LL, UK. Tel. +44 (0)20 7896 2297. Fax +44 (0)20 7896 2274. URL: http://www.ft.com/

Cost: £600/$948 pa

Eastern Bloc Energy
This **monthly** provides a readable survey of developments throughout the CEE countries. All energy sectors are covered; factual reportage is accompanied by analysis, forecasts and useful statistical data.

Contact details: Eastern Bloc Research, Newton Kyme, Tadcaster, North Yorkshire LS24 9LS, UK. Tel. +44 (0)1937 835691. Fax +44 (0)1937 835756.

Cost: £320 pa.

Energy Markets Service: Europe
This comprehensive service covers all CEE countries. The main country sections are – energy and energy policy, energy industry organisation, energy infrastructure, energy demand by sector, electricity, energy flow by fuel. There is a CD-ROM version.

Contact details: Wood Mackenzie Consultants, Kintore House, 74-77 Queen Street, Edinburgh EH2 4NS, UK. Tel. +44 (0)131 243 4530. Fax +44 (0)131 243 4495. Email: energy@woodmac.com URL: http://www.woodmac.com/

Cost: On application

LPG in Eastern Europe
A research report (1997) focused on liquid petroleum gasoline markets. Demand and supply conditions of the various product forms are detailed. Major companies and their market shares are described. Likely future developments are forecast, with supporting statistics throughout.

Contact details: MarketLine International, 16 Connaught Street, London W2 2AF, UK. Tel. +44 (0)20 7624 2200. Fax +44 (0)20 7372 1030. URL:http://www.mktline.demon.co.uk/
MarketLine US, Datamonitor Group, 1 Park Avenue, 14th Floor, New York, NY 10016-5896. Tel. +1 212 686 7400. Fax +1 212 686 2626.

Cost: $1250

Opportunities in the Energy Markets of Central and Eastern Europe
A market research report (1997) highlighting prospects for Western companies in all the CEE countries. Each national energy set-up is described, analysed, and recent developments reported. Major companies are profiled in terms of, for example, structure, financial performance, operations, future plans.

Contact details: MarketLine International, 16 Connaught Street, London W2 2AF, UK. Tel. +44 (0)20 7624 2200. Fax +44 (0)20 7372 1030. URL:http://www.mktline.demon.co.uk/
MarketLine US, Datamonitor Group, 1 Park Avenue, 14th Floor, New York, NY 10016-5896, Tel. 1 212 686 7400. Fax +1 212 686 2626.

Cost: £995/$1950

Overview of Nuclear Legislation in Central and Eastern Europe and the NIS
This compilation and review (1998), from the OECD, is intended as a basis for regular updating. For each country the regulations and laws controlling the use of nuclear energy are set out in a standard fashion emphasising the intended comparative usefulness of the work.

Contact details: OECD, 2 rue André-Pascal, Paris 75775 Cedex 16, France. Tel. +33 1 45 249689. Fax +33 1 45 241843.
URL: http://www.oecd.org/

Cost: £15/$25

PlanEcon Energy Outlook
The *Outlook* consists of an **annual** package of a main report and two updates. Current developments are reviewed and analysed, and 20-year projections of future trends set out.

Contact details: PlanEcon, 1111 14th Street NW, Suite 801, Washington, DC 20005-5603, USA. Tel. +1 202 898 0471. Fax +1 202 898 0445. URL: http://www.planecon.com

Cost: $8000 pa

Power Generation in Central and Eastern Europe
A market research report (1997) reviewing the current situation and likely future developments in power generation. National political and economic backgrounds are described as context for the discussion of specialist issues. Major operators are profiled.

Contact details: Espicom Business Intelligence, Lincoln House, City Fields Business Park, City Fields Way, Chichester, West Sussex PO20

6FS, UK. URL:http://www.energybase.com/
In the US: Espicom Inc., 116 Village Boulevard, Suite 200, Princeton
Forrestal Village, Princeton, New Jersey 08540 5799, USA. Tel. 1 609 951
2227. Fax 1 609 734 7428.

Cost: £395/$695

Finance and Banking

Central and East European Tax Directory
This **annual** describes the corporate income tax, personal income tax,
value added tax and social security contributions systems of all the CEE
countries.

Contact details: IBFD Publications Bv, PO Box 20237, 1000 Amsterdam,
Netherlands.Tel +31 20 626 7726. Fax +31 20 622 8658.

Cost: NLG285

Central Europe Portfolio: The Central European Securities Newsletter
Central Europe Portfolio appears **fortnightly.** It reports on activities and
trends in all the securities markets of the region. A typical issue will provide brief news items, fund movements, company news, bond notes, market
summaries, economic endnotes, corporate earnings and actions.

Contact details: Global Investor Publishing, 50 Follen Street, Suite 14,
Cambridge, MA 02138, USA. Tel. +1 617 864 4999. Fax +1 617 864 4942.
Email: subscribe@gipinc.com URL: http://www.gipinc.com

Cost: $1075 pa (US/Canada); $1175 (elsewhere)

East European Banking Review
This **monthly** review reports on recent banking developments in all eastern Europe countries.

Contact details: East European Banking Review, PO Box 579, 9-11
Mansell Street, St. Peter Port, Guernsey, Channel Islands, UK. Tel. +44
(0)1481 727 730. Fax +44 (0)1481 7277 31.

Cost: £250 pa

East European Insurance Report
This **monthly** newsletter reviews and analyses sectoral developments –
legislative changes, company results, internal corporate changes, merg-
ers, etc.

Contact details: FT Finance, Maple House, 149 Tottenham Court Road,
London W1P 9LL, UK. Tel. +44 (0)20 7896 2297. Fax +44 (0)20 7896
2274. URL: http://www.ft.com/

Cost: £535 pa (UK); £555 pa (elsewhere)

East European Privatisation News
This **fortnightly** newsletter could do with a more descriptive title. It certainly covers privatisation issues in CEE countries, but it also covers banking and corporate finance. The latter sections are gaining in importance.

Contact details: East European Privatisation News Group, PO Box 579, Tower Hill House, Le Bordage, St. Peter Port, Guernsey GY1 6LQ, Channel Islands. Tel. +44 (0)1481 727730. Fax +44 (0)1481 727731.

Cost: £295 pa

Equity Central Europe 1998-1999
This **annual** service concentrates on providing information on publicly traded companies in the Czech Republic, Hungary, Poland, Romania and Slovakia. Company profiles include future prospects, main shareholders, share price performance, evaluation and comparative statistics.

Contact details: New World Publishing, Szent István Krt. 11, IIIem, Budapest, Hungary. Tel. +36 1 374 3344. Fax +36 1 374 3345. Email: jdol@pronet.hu

Cost: $19.95

Emerging Markets Database
This is a major source of 'information and statistics on stock markets in developing countries' including those of CEE countries. The performances of stock markets are tracked and compared employing standardised indexation. Subscribers can receive data via email, FTP, or online delivery through an EMBD distributor.

Contact details: EMDB, International Finance Corporation, 2121 Pennsylvania Avenue, Rm. F-6K-124, Washington DC 20433, USA. Tel. +1 202 473 9520. Fax +1 202 974 4805. Email: emdb@ifc.org URL: http:// www.ifc.org/emdb/pubs.htm

Cost: On application

Emerging Markets Monitor
This **weekly** has global coverage. CEE countries, because of developments within the region, feature every week. The *Monitor* is described as a 'brief on debt, bonds, equities and money', providing analyses of market developments. The reports are grouped by region and cover such topics as, for example, financial instruments, fund management, market views, market leaders, statistical data.

Contact details: Business Monitor International, 179 Queen Victoria Street, London EC4V 4DD, UK. Tel, +44 (0)20 7248 0468. Fax +44 (0)20 7248 0467. Email: busmon@dial.pipex.com

Cost: £895/$1470 pa

Emerging Markets Securities Handbook: Europe and Central Asia 1998/ 1999
This substantial reference source devotes separate chapters to all the east European countries; profiling them in terms of background data, economic and demographic data, economy assessments, history and current descriptions of stock exchanges, listing of member firms. There are country, sub-regional and sectoral overview sections as well.

Contact details: Garlickhill Ltd., 44B St Martin's House North, King Edward Street, Perth, PH1 5UT, UK. Tel. +44 (0)1738 636633. Fax +44 (0)1738 639933. Email: mail@garlickhill.com

Cost: £140

Emerging Stock Markets Factbook
This **annual's** worldwide coverage includes CEE countries. Contents include a listing of stock exchanges 'showing principal officers, addresses, hours of operation, and telephone/fax numbers'; statistical description and analysis of the various markets, commentaries, methodological consideration of the process of comparative indexation. The comparative time series cover a period of 10 years.

Contact details: EMDB, International Finance Corporation, 2121 Pennsylvania Avenue, Rm. F-6K-124, Washington DC 20433, USA. Tel. +1 202 473 9520. Fax +1 202 974 4805. Email: emdb@ifc.org URL: http://www.ifc.org/emdb/pubs.htm

Cost: On application

Emerging Stock Markets Review
This, the sister publication of the *Factbook*, provides **monthly** coverage of, for example, indexation issues, analyses of the 'largest stocks', the best and worst performing stocks, comparative tables.

Contact details: EMDB, International Finance Corporation, 2121 Pennsylvania Avenue, Rm. F-6K-124, Washington DC 20433, USA. Tel. +1 202 473 9520. Fax +1 202 974 4805. Email: emdb@ifc.org URL: http://www.ifc.org/emdb/pubs.htm

Cost: $3000 pa (Includes copy of *IFC Indexes* and *Emerging Stock Markets Factbook*)

Euromoney Bank Register
The *Register*, an **annual,** is another example of a source providing worldwide coverage, including CEE countries. All major banks are listed with

basic locational and descriptive details. There are CD-ROM and Internet versions.

Contact details: Euromoney Publications, Nestor House, Playhouse Yard, London EC4V 5EX, UK. URL http://www.bankregister.com

Cost: £180/$315 (hard copy); £750/$1250 (CD-ROM Read Only version); £1750/$3000 (CD-ROM full version)

European Banker
This **bi-weekly** report reviews and analyses developments in Europe's banking systems and financial services.

Contact details: Lafferty Publications, IDA Tower, Pearse Street, Dublin 2, Ireland. Tel: +353 1 671 8022. Fax +353 1 671 8520. Email: cuserv@lafferty.ie URL:http://www.lafferty.co.uk Lafferty Publications, Suite 2531, The Graybar Building, 420 Lexington Avenue, New York, NY 10170, USA. Tel. 1 212 557 6726. Fax 1 212 557 7266. Email:tom.stenson@lafferty.com

Cost: £699/$1159 pa

Finance East Europe
This **bi-monthly** newsletter monitors developments and changes in the financial and banking sectors. The range is wide, taking in, for example, legal issues associated with foreign investments, changes in government policies impinging upon the sectors, privatisation progress, movements in the capital markets, national budgets and their implications.

Contact details: FT Finance, Maple House, 149 Tottenham Court Road, London W1P 9LL, UK. Tel: +44 (0)20 7896 2279. Fax +44 (0)20 7896 2274. URL: http://www.ft.com/

Cost: £470/$800 pa

Financial Markets of Eastern Europe and the Former Soviet Union
One of the more down-to-earth assessments of CEE financial markets (1998).With the exception of Poland all other financial markets are severely criticised for their shortcomings. Not a read for the nervous investor.

Contact details: Gresham Books, Abington Hall, Abington, Cambridge CB1 6AH, UK. Tel. +44 (0)1223 891 358. Fax +44 (0)1223 893 694. Email: woodhead@dial.pipex.com

Cost: £150

Foreign Direct Investment in Central and Eastern Europe
The benefits and problems associated with foreign direct investment are much debated. This book (1997) provides a useful review of the arguments, illustrated through case studies.

Contact details: Royal Institute of International Affairs, Chatham House, 10 St. James's Square, London SW1Y 4LE, UK. Tel. +44 (0)20 7957 5700. Fax +44 (0)20 7957 5710. URL: http://www.riia.org

Cost: £45

Fundline: Investment Funds and Equity Resources for Eastern Europe and the Former Soviet Union
This is an Internet site maintained by the World Bank's Private Sector Development Department 'to facilitate communciation between potential equity investors and enterprises in the region. [The service] includes portfolio investment funds, private equity funds and companies, venture capital funds, and other private equity vehicles'. Funds are searchable by country of investment, form of investment, fund name, industry, major investors, management company, management company headquarters, and by type of firm.

Contact details: URL: http://wbln0018.worldbank.org/PSD/ invfund.NSF/

Global Treasury News
This is an example of an Internet site maintained by a newspaper – the Central European Business Daily. The service has an alerting function – with brief financial news items and short features characteristic of newsletters. It also has available a series of *Cash Management Guides*. These provide data describing the financial environment and cash management techniques in many CEE countries; for example, electronic banking, tax environment, account types, payment and collection methods, FX Risk Management Techniques, funding and investment options.

Contact details: GTNews. Tel. +44 (0)20 7222 3440. Fax +44 (0)20 7233 3440.Email: news@gtnews.com URL: http://www.gtnews.com/ ce_europe/

Insurance in East and Central Europe
This report (1997) describes the insurance sectors and their workings in all the CEE countries. The regulatory system is described, as are the various sub-sectors of the insurance business, methods of marketing, the current state of markets in various countries, etc. The largest companies are profiled, and future forecasts made.

Contact details: FT Finance, Maple House, 149 Tottenham Court Road, London W1P 9ALL, UK. Tel. +44 (0)20 7896 2279. Fax +44 (0)20 7896 2274. URL: http://www.ft.com

Cost: £470/$800

Insurance Market in Central and Eastern Europe
A report (1997) on the insurance business from established market re-search specialists. The sector is surveyed in regional and country terms. The country chapters include a review of the regulatory context and su-pervisory bodies, a description of insurance developments, and profiles of the main operators.

Contact details: Datamonitor Europe, 106 Baker Street, London W1M 1LA, UK. Tel. +44 (0)20 7316 0001. Fax +44 (0)20 7316 0002. URL: http://www.datamonitor.com/

Cost: £1995

Investment Guide to Central and Eastern Europe
This Internet site has the backing of the Chartered Institute of Banking. The result is a sound, authoritative, source with the bonus of being free. There are profiles of all countries other than Bosnia and Serbia. There is a section 'designed to provide indepth analysis of financial services'. The details of the latter include corporate finance, leasing, capital markets, fund management, equities, repos, international cash management, for-eign exchange. Other sections cover manufacturing, food and agriculture, telecomms and technology, news round-up.

Contact details: Kensington Publications, 111 Southwark Street, London SE1 0JF, UK. Tel. +44 (0)20 7717 0077. Fax +44 (0)20 7717 1000. Email: postmaster@kenpubs.co.uk URL: http://www.kenpubs.co.uk/ investguide/

Lafferty Cards Databank: Central and Eastern Europe
This report (1998) profiles the cards markets 'including the latest statis-tics on credit, debit and ATM cards usage; profiles of the major issuers; analysis of Europe's private-label cards, which outnumber bank-issued credit cards in the region; and smart cards initiatives ...'.

Contact details: Lafferty Publications, IDA Tower, Pearse Street, Dublin 2, Republic of Ireland. Tel. +353 1 671 8022. Fax +353 1 671 8520. URL: http://www.lafferty.co.uk/manreports/crse.html
In the US: Lafferty Publications, Suite 2531, The Graybar Building, 420 Lexington Avenue, New York, NY 10170, USA. Tel. 1 212 557 6726. Fax 1 212 557 7266. Email:tom.stenson@lafferty.com

Cost: £1849/$3051

Opportunities in Life, Health and Pensions in Central and Eastern Europe
A market research report (1998) focusing on recent regional developments in the insurance sectors covering life, health and pensions. Potential op-portunities are assessed critically.

Contact details: Datamonitor Europe, 106 Baker Street, London W1M 1LA, UK. Tel. +44 (0)20 7316 0001. Fax +44 (0)20 7316 0002. URL: http://www.datamonitor.com/

Cost: £1995

Privatisation and Emerging Equity Markets
A report (1998) reviewing the effect of privatisation on the emergence and workings of the new stock markets, and of the investment opportunities arising.

Contact details: World Bank, PO Box 7247-7956, Philadelphia PA 19170-7956, USA. Tel. +1 703 661 1580. Fax +1 703 661 1501. Email: books@worldbank.org URL: http://www.worldbank.org

Cost: $125

Retail Banking in Central and Eastern Europe
A critical account (1997) of the development of banking and financial institutions and services in response to more liberal market conditions.

Contact details: Datamonitor Europe, 106 Baker Street, London W1M 1LA, UK. Tel. +44 (0)20 7316 0001. Fax +44 (0)20 7316 0002. URL: http://www.datamonitor.com/

Cost: £1995

Taking Stock Central Europe: The Investor's Guide to Central Europe's Stock Markets
Describes the details of share acceptances and operations of the stock markets of Poland, Hungary, Czech Republic and Romania. A useful starter source (1997) for those considering investing in local companies. Company information, even of the basic kind, rarely comes as cheap.

Contact details: Budapest Business Journal, Ferenciek tere. 7-8, Iem. 4, 1053 Budapest, Hungary. Tel. +361 266 6088. Fax +361 118 0215.

Cost: £9.95/$14.95

Taxation in Central Europe: International Tax and Business Guide
A useful, concise, introduction (1998) to the tax regimes of CEE countries for potential foreign investors. The countries covered include Bulgaria, Czech Republic, Hungary, Poland, Romania, Slovak Republic and Slovenia. Informative and readable.

Contact details: Deloitte Touche Tohmatsu International, Stonecutter Court, 1 Stonecutter Street, London EC4A 4TR, UK. Tel. +44 (0)20 7936 3000. Fax +44 (0)20 7353 8648.

Cost: £6

Thomson Bankwatch
This service provides reports on the performance and ratings of banks in Bulgaria, Croatia, Czech Republic, Hungary, Poland, Romania, Slovakia, Slovenia. A highly specialised and, in times of uncertainty, when banking systems are under stress, a crucial source.

Contact details: Thomson Bankwatch UK, Aldgate House, 33 Aldgate High Street, London EC3N 1DL, UK. Tel. +44 (0)20 7369 7865. Fax +44 (0)20 7247 8019.

Cost: $16,500. Individual country reports are available – at a price.

Value Added Taxes in Central and Eastern European Countries: A Corporate Survey and Evaluation
An official comparative report (1998) of national VAT systems. A convenient one-stop source for data that can be time-consuming to establish.

Contact details: OECD, 2 rue André-Pascal, 75775 Paris Cedex 16, France. Tel. +33 1 45 24 9689. Fax +33 1 45 24 1843. URL: http://www.oecd.org/

Cost: £19/$32

Food, Drink, Tobacco

Alcoholic Drinks in Eastern Europe
A market research report (1997) reviewing recent developments in the sector, with a five-year forward look. The major operators are profiled. Included in the country coverage are Bulgaria, Czech Republic, Hungary, Poland, Romania, Slovak Republic.

Contact details: Euromonitor plc, 60-61 Britton Street, London EC1M 5NA, UK. Tel. +44 (0)20 7251 1105. Fax +44 (0)20 7251 0985. URL: http://Euro.imrmall.com/chapters/0125/index.shtml

Cost: £1905/$3900. Country chapters can be purchased separately.

Baby Food in Central and Eastern Europe
This research report (1998) covers the Czech Republic, Hungary, Poland, Slovakia, among others. Analyses market trends for the various sectors, consumption levels, segmentation trends, for example, and, against the background of past performance, assesses likely future developments.

Contact details: ERC Statistics International, 5-11 Shorts Gardens, London WC2H 9AT, UK. Tel. +44 (0)20 7497 2312. Fax +44 (0)20 7497 2313. URL: http://www.erc-world.com

Cost: £7500

Biscuits Market in Eastern Europe

Eastern Europe in this instance includes the following countries – the Czech Republic, Hungary, Poland, the Slovak Republic. The research report (1998) analyses developments in various biscuit sectors, assesses market trends, measures brand shares and market segmentation, describes and analyses retail aspects and discusses future market prospects. This type of report carries a heavy load of added value based on experience and market knowledge.

Contact details: ERC Statistics International, 5-11 Shorts Gardens, London WC2H 9AT, UK. Tel. +44 (0)20 7497 2312. Fax +44 (0)20 7497 2313. URL: http://www.erc-world.com

Cost: £7500

Cigarettes – Central and Eastern Europe

This report (1999) presents a review and analysis of markets, distribution and retail issues, with data on market leaders. The future in this sector is assessed for the Czech Republic, Hungary, Poland and the Slovak Republic. Excellent statistics.

Contact details: ERC Statistics International, 5-11 Shorts Gardens, London WC2H 9AT, UK. Tel. +44 (0)20 7497 2312. Fax +44 (0)20 7497 2313. URL: http://www.erc-world.com

Cost: £6950

Confectionery in Central and Eastern Europe

This market survey (1998) covers a number of countries including the Czech Republic, Hungary, Poland and Slovakia. The country reports contain individual market surveys, analyses of the various sub-sectors of the industry with supporting statistics. The retail and distribution sectors are reviewed. Future prospects are assessed.

Contact details: ERC Statistics International, 5-11 Shorts Gardens, London WC2H 9AT, UK. Tel. +44 (0)20 7497 2312. Fax +44 (0)20 7497 2313. URL: http://www.erc-world.com

Cost: £7500

Eastern Europe Snacks

This research report (1998) describes and analyses opportunities available in the markets for biscuits, confectionery, ice-cream, snacks, etc. The major companies in the various sectors are profiled.

Contact details: Datamonitor Europe, 106 Baker Street, London W1M 1LA, UK. Tel. +44 (0)20 7316 0001. Fax +44 (0)20 7316 0002. URL: http://www.datamonitor.com/

Cost: £1995

Food and Drink in Central/Eastern Europe
This **monthly** newsletter provides production figures for various food and drink sectors, monitors changes in legislation, reports up-to-date news, highlights investment decisions.

Contact details: Pyrabelisk, PO Box 1530, Gillingham, Dorset SP8 5TD, UK. Tel. +44 (0)1747 8389555. Fax +44 (0)1747 838955. Email: pyrabelisk@btinternet.com URL: http://www.pyrabelisk.com/

Cost: £175/$285 pa

Savoury Snacks in Eastern Europe
One of the most potent signs of change in CEE countries is the rapid growth of fast and convenience foods and prepared snacks. This market report (1997), like others from Euromonitor, reviews past trends and developments preparatory to the presentation of likely future development scenarios. The major operators in the sector are profiled. The CEE countries covered are Bulgaria, Czech Republic, Hungary, Poland, Romania, Slovakia.

Contact details: Euromonitor plc, 60-61 Britton Street, London EC1M 5NA, UK. Tel. +44 (0)20 7251 1105. Fax +44 (0)20 7251 0985. URL: http://Euro.imrmall.com/chapters/0129/index.shtml

Cost: £1905/$3900. The country chapters can be purchased separately.

Soft Drinks in Eastern Europe
This market research report (1998) examines developments of the past five years and provides a five-year forecast of likely future market developments. There is strong statistical support. Among the countries included in this review and analysis are Bulgaria, Hungary, Poland, Romania, Slovakia.

Contact details: Euromonitor, 60-61 Britton Street, London EC1M 5NA, UK. Tel. +44 (0)20 7251 1105. Fax +44 (0)20 7251 0985. URL: http://Euro.imrmall.com/chapters/0098/index.shtml

Cost: £1950/$3900. The country chapters can be purchased separately

Tobacco in Eastern Europe
A market research report (1998) which, like all Euromonitor sources, provides a great deal of data and information in compact form. The market is reviewed in regional and country terms, taking into account observed trends and developments. This exercise provides a basis for an assessment of future market prospects. As usual statistics feature prominently.

Contact details: Euromonitor plc, 60-61 Britton Street, London EC1M 5NA, UK. Tel. +44 (0)20 7251 1105. Fax +44 (0)20 7251 0985. URL: http://Euro.imrmall.com/

Cost: £1905/$3900

Healthcare and Medical

OTC Healthcare in Eastern Europe

A market research report (1997) reviewing trends and developments within a rapidly changing sector. The future of the market up to 2001 is outlined. The countries covered include Bulgaria, Czech Republic, Hungary, Poland, Slovakia.

Contact details: Euromonitor plc, 60-61 Britton Street, London EC1M 5NA, UK. Tel. +44 (0)20 7251 1105. Fax +44 (0)20 7251 0985. URL: http://Euro.imrmall.com/chapters/0128/index.shtml

Cost: £1905/$3900. Country chapters can be purchased separately.

Media

Media Map of Eastern Europe 1999

This **annual** reports on the state of 'consumer media' in 15 countries. It 'profiles all the major players and includes their latest financial results, contact details and media interests, plus circulation figures, viewing shares as well as media regulations'. There is a directory of contacts

Contact details: CIT Publications, 3 Colleton Crescent, Exeter, Devon EX2 4DG, UK. Tel. +44 (0)1392 315567. Fax +44 (0)1392 315556. Email: citpubs@eurobell.co.uk URL: http://www.telecoms-data.com/

Cost: £195

European Newspaper Industry Report

This **report** (1998) surveys the newspaper industry throughout Europe, and provides market data for the major players. Among the countries covered in this way are Bulgaria, Czech Republic, Hungary, Poland, Romania, Slovakia.

Contact details: Pira International, Randalls Road, Leatherhead, Surrey KT22 7RU, UK. Tel. +44 (0)1372 802080. Fax +44 (0)1372 802079. Email: publications@pira.co.uk URL: http://newmedia.pira.co.uk/

Cost: £495/$790

Future of Media in Eastern Europe and Russia

This substantial report (1997) describes and evaluates the various markets in Bulgaria, Czech Republic, Hungary, Poland, Romania and the Slovak Republic, among other CEE countries. Technological and financial trends are highlighted, as well as other influential factors – regulatory, political, competitors, for example. Contact data for companies and individuals in each country are provided.

Contact details: Kagan World Media, 524 Fulham Road, London SW6 5NR, UK. Tel. +44 (0)20 7371 88850. Fax +44 (0)20 7371 8715. URL: http://www.pkbaseline.com

Cost: £495/$795

Television in Central and Eastern Europe
This report (1998) reviews the prospects of the sector in a number of CEE countries.

Contact details: FT Media and Telecoms, Maple House, 149 Tottenham Court Road, London W1P 9LL, UK. Tel. +44 (0)20 7896 2721. Fax +44 (0)20 7896 2256. Email: info@ftmedia.com
URL: http://www.ftmedia.com/tv/tve.htm

Cost: £445/$756

Television in Europe to 2007
This **annual** provides 'facts and figures on today's audiences, channels and advertising ... with long-range forecasts of satellite/cable growth'. For each country there is a section of basic data (average daily hours of viewing, satellite and cable penetration, number of TV households, etc.), TV profiles of major channels (household penetration, share of viewing, advertising revenue, etc.), history and forecasts (cable revenues, TV adspend, etc.) and contacts. The CEE countries covered include Bulgaria, Czech Republic, Hungary, Poland, Romania, Slovakia, Slovenia.

Contact details: Zenith Media, Bridge House, 63-65 North Wharf Road, London W2 1LA, UK. Tel. +44 (0)20 7224 8500. Fax +44 (0)20 7255 2187. Email: info@zenithmedia.com
URL: http://www.zenithmedia.com/

Cost: £250/$400

TV East Europe
This **monthly** newsletter reports on developments in all sectors of the television industry including, for example, company news and profiles, advertising expenditure, legal requirements, latest ratings, country pro-files.

Contact details: FT Media & Telecoms, Maple House, 149 Tottenham Court Road, London W1P 9LL, UK. Tel. +44 (0)20 7896 2234. Fax +44 (0)20 7896 2235. Email: info@ftmedia.com URL: http://www.ftmedia.com

Cost: £395/$632 pa

TV East Europe Handbook
This **annual** reference source is often the orientation point for deeper information searches in this sector. CEE countries are profiled in industry terms, with supporting statistics and lists of contacts.

Contact details: FT Media & Telecoms, Maple House, 149 Tottenham Court Road, London W1P 9LL, UK. Tel. +44 (0)20 7896 2234. Fax +44 (0)20 7896 2235. Email: info@ftmedia.com URL: http://www.ftmedia.com

Cost: £99/$158

Packaging and Paper

Database of Pulp, Paper and Board Mills in Central and Eastern Europe
This is a directory of mills in all the CEE countries. The company profiles include locational and contact details, production statistics, investment projections, product capacity, number of employees, turnover, etc.

Contact details: Pyrabelisk Ltd., PO Box 1530, Gillingham, Dorset SP8 5TD, UK. Tel./Fax +44 (0)1747 838955. Email: pyrabelisk@btinternet.com URL: http://www.pyrabelisk.com/

Cost: £300

Packaging in Central/Eastern Europe
This **monthly** monitors events and developments in the sector – production figures for various types of packaging materials, import and export data, company activities, technology developments, new products, consumer information, etc.

Contact details: Pyrabelisk Ltd., PO Box 1530, Gillingham, Dorset SP8 5TD, UK. Tel./Fax +44 (0)1747 838955. Email: pyrabelisk@btinternet.com URL: http://www.pyrabelisk.com/

Cost: £200 pa

Packaging in Eastern Europe
A sectoral reference source (1998). Countries are profiled in economic, demographic, political and social terms. Information and data relating to the industry – production figures, imports and exports, main firms, etc. are provided. Countries covered include Bulgaria, Croatia, Czech Republic, Hungary, Macedonia, Poland, Romania, Serbia and Montenegro, Slovakia, Slovenia.

Contact details: Pira International, Randalls Road, Leatherhead, Surrey KT22 7RU, UK. Tel. +44 (0)1372 802080. Fax +44 (0)1372 802079. Email: publications@pira.co.uk URL: http://newmedia.pira.co.uk/

Cost: £495/$795

Pulp and Paper in Central and Eastern Europe
This **monthly** newsletter monitors events and developments in the industry in standard fashion – statistics, government policies, company news, state of the economy, etc.

Contact details: Pyrabelisk Ltd., PO Box 1530, Gillingham, Dorset SP8 5TD, UK. Tel./Fax +44 (0)1747 838955. Email: pyrabelisk@btinternet.com URL: http://www.pyrabelisk.com/

Cost: £275 pa

Pharmaceuticals

Pharmaceutical and Cosmetic Producers in Central and Eastern Europe
This **annual** directory profiles 2000 chemical, pharmaceutical and cosmetic producers in CEE countries. The details are basic but, generally, up-to-date and useful for first, or mailing, contacts.

Contact details: EXIN, Šeřikova 32, 63700 Brno, Czech Republic. Tel. +420 5 432 36040 1. Fax +420 5 432 36040. Email: exin@exin.cz URL:http://www.exin.cz

Cost: 150 EUR

Pharmaceutical Markets in Central Europe
A report (1998) presenting descriptive, analytical and statistical detail on markets and factors influencing demands for, and supply of, pharmaceutical products.

Contact details: Scrip Reports, Hill Rise, Richmond, Surrey TW10 6UA, UK. Tel. +44 (0)20 8948 6866. Fax +44 (0)20 8948 6866. URL: http://www.pjpubs.co.uk/scriprep/home.html

Cost: £295/$530

Pharmaceuticals in Central and Eastern Europe
A market analysis report (1997) of CEE countries including assessments of local producers and suppliers of pharmaceutical products. The technical analysis is supported by critical assessments of the current economic and political scene and copious statistics.

Contact details: Espicom Business Intelligence, Lincoln House, City Fields Business Park, City Fields Way, Chichester, West Sussex PO20 6FS, UK. URL:http://www.energybase.com/
Espicom Inc., 116 Village Boulevard, Suite 200, Princeton Forrestal Village, Princeton, New Jersey 08540 5799, USA. Tel. 1 609 951 2227. Fax 1 609 734 7428.

Cost: £595/$1070

Retailing

Distribution and Retailing in Eastern Europe

Sold (1998) as the 'first study to provide a clear picture of a notoriously opaque sector'. Others in the field might have a different view. Beyond the hype the compilers have put together a helpful and informative package about the business of moving goods about, and about selecting distributors. The retail sector is analysed and described with the aid of statistics.

Contact details: Economist Intelligence Unit, PO Box 200, Harold Hill, Romford, RM3 8UX, UK. Tel. +44 (0)20 7830 1007. Fax +44 (0)1708 371 850. Email: london@eiu.com URL: http://www.eiu.com

Cost: £365/$595

European Retail Handbook

The coverage of the *Handbook* (1998) includes Bulgaria, Czech Republic, Hungary, Poland, Romania, Slovakia and Slovenia. The individual countries are surveyed to present an overview of the sector. Topics treated include, for example, legal issues, recent developments, list of major retailing groups, analysis of trends.

Contact details: Corporate Intelligence on Retailing, 48 Bedford Square, London WC1B 3DP, UK. Tel. +44 (0)20 7696 9006. Fax +44 (0)20 7696 9004. Email: sales@cior.com URL: http://www.cior.com/

Cost: £60/$95

Retailing Central Europe

The report (1998) 'considers the opportunities open to British retailers in the dynamic markets of Czech Republic, Hungary, Poland, Slovak Republic and Slovenia'. Consumer characteristics and the retailing environment in each country are described, and placed within their political and economic contexts. The message, with all the expected qualifications, is encouraging.

Contact details: DTI Export Publications, Admail 528, London SW1W8YT, UK.Tel. +44 (0)20 7510 0171. Fax +44 (0)20 7510 0197. Can be ordered online – URL: http://www.dti.gov.uk/ots/publications/export_publications_home.html

Cost: £60

Retailing in Central and Eastern Europe

A report (1997) detailing opportunities and risks for potential investors in the retail sector. The political and economic backgrounds of the countries assessed are reviewed, and illustrative case studies presented.

Contact details: FT Retail and Consumer Publishing, Maple House, 149 Tottenham Court Road, London W1P 9ALL, UK. Tel. +44 (0)20 7896 2698. Fax +44 (0)20 7896 2333. URL: http://www.ft.com

Cost: £375/$563

Telecommunications

Communications Markets in Eastern Europe

This report (1998) reviews developments in CEE countries – cable, satellite, mobile, networks, etc. Trends are discussed and future projections offered. The main companies are profiled and an extensive list of industry contacts provided.

Contact details: CIT Publications, 3 Colleton Crescent, Exeter, Devon EX2 4DG, UK. Tel. +44 (0)1392 493444. Fax +44 (0)1392 493626. URL: http://www.telecoms-data.com

Cost: £195

Datafile of Eastern European Communications

This major reference source (1999) is in loose-leaf format. Sections are updated as and when required. The country files include brief descriptions of the general economy, followed by close analyses of various sectors of the industry, detailed company profiles, contacts.

Contact details: CIT Publications, 3 Colleton Crescent, Exeter, Devon EX2 4DG, UK. Tel. +44 (0)1392 493444. Fax +44 (0)1392 493626. URL: http://www.telecoms-data.com

Cost: £585

East European Telecoms Newsletter

A **monthly** monitor of sectoral developments and trends, presented briefly, throughout central and eastern Europe.

Contact details: FT Media & Telecoms, Maple House, 149 Tottenham Court Road, London W1P 9LL, UK. Tel. +44 (0)20 7896 2234. Fax +44 (0)20 7896 2235. Email: info@ftmedia.com URL: http://www.ftmedia.com/tv/tve.htm

Cost: £645/$1097 pa

Eastern Europe Newsletter

This is a **fortnightly** review of events in, and having a bearing on, the telecommunication sectors of CEE countries. Highlights opportunities for investors. It is available in hard copy and via email.

Contact details: FT Media & Telecoms, Maple House, 149 Tottenham Court Road, London W1P 9LL, UK. Tel. +44 (0)20 7896 2721. Fax +44

(0)20 7896 2256. Email: info@ftmedia.com URL: http://
www.ftmedia.com/tv/tve.htm

Cost: £795/$1272 pa

Emerging Telecoms and Wireless Operators in Eastern Europe
This report (1997) reviews 'telecoms service markets in Poland, Hungary,
the Czech Republic, Slovakia, Romania, and Bulgaria'. It analyses the
demand for communication services, current regulatory policies, and 'competitive environments'.

Contact details: Pyramid Research, PO Box 1781, Cambridge, MA 02238,
USA. Tel. +1 617 868 5574. Fax +1 617 868 4725. Email: info@pyr.com
URL: http://www.pyr.com

Cost: $2850

Radio and Television Systems in Central and Eastern Europe
This is a reference source (1998) forming part (volume 3) of a four-volume
set covering Europe generally. Good coverage of such topics as regulatory
laws, privatisation, foreign investment.

Contact details: Observatoire européen de l'audiovisuel, 76 allée de la
Robertsau, F-67000 Strasbourg, France. Tel. +33 (0)388 144404. Fax +33
(0)388 144419. URL: http://www.obs.coe.int/oea/en/index.htm

Cost: £15/$25

Telecom and Wireless Eastern Europe/CIS
This **monthly** newsletter has a useful feature included in its subscription
– a CD-ROM of back-issues updated at **quarterly** intervals. The newsletter itself reports on market developments, changes in regulatory
requirements, technology applications, company activities.

Contact details: Pyramid Research, PO Box 1781, Cambridge, MA
02238, USA. Tel. +1 617 868 5574. Fax +1 617 868 4725.
Email: info@pyr.com URL: http://www.pyr.com

Cost: $795 pa

Telecom Market Report: Russia, Central Europe and Central Asia
The wide geographical coverage of this **monthly** newsletter takes in all
the CEE countries, and beyond. Sectoral news is reported briefly and snap-
pily under country headings; market trends noted; personalities
interviewed; company activities described, etc.

Contact details: ITC Publications, 4340 East West Highway, Suite 1020,
Bethesda MD 20814, USA. Tel. +1 301 907 0060. Fax +1 301 907 6555.
Email: itcorp@itcresearch.com URL: http://www.intl-tech.com

Cost: $795 pa

Telecommunications in Central and Eastern Europe
A two-volume report (1997) analysing the market conditions in 12 CEE countries, with assessments of their potential for foreign investors. Background economic, financial, political and technical information and data are provided.

Contact details: Espicom Business Intelligence, Lincoln House, City Fields Business Park, City Fields Way, Chichester, West Sussex PO20 6FS, UK. URL:http://www.energybase.com/
In the US: Espicom Inc., 116 Village Boulevard, Suite 200, Princeton Forrestal Village, Princeton, New Jersey 08540 5799, USA. Tel. 1 609 951 2227. Fax 1 609 734 7428.

Cost: £495/$885

Textiles

East European Clothing and Textile Industry Directory
This **annual** directory is an essential source for this sector. Company descriptions, in addition to the usual locational and contact data, include fuller accounts of activities and production specialisation than is common.

Contact details: World Textile Publications, 1 Longlands Street, Bradford, West Yorkshire BD1 2TP, UK. Tel. +44 (0)1274 378800. Fax +44 (0)1274 378811. Email: info@worldtextile.com URL: http://www.worldtextile.com/

Cost: £105 (UK)/£120 (Europe)

Textiles Eastern Europe
This **monthly** newsletter reports on all matters having a bearing on the industry – political, economic, technological, investments, trends, production statistics, privatisation progress, for all the CEE countries.

Contact details: World Textile Publications, 1 Longlands Street, Bradford, West Yorkshire BD1 2TP, UK. Tel. +44 (0)1274 37880. Fax +44 (0)1274 37881. Email: info@worldtextile.com URL: http://www.worldtextile.com/

Cost: £200 pa

White Goods

White Goods in Eastern Europe
This report (1997) covers cooking, refrigeration, laundry and dishwashing appliances in terms of key trends and developments, consumer indicators, distribution, market changes. The industry is reviewed and future

prospects analysed. Countries covered include Bulgaria, Czech Republic, Hungary, Poland, Romania and Slovakia.

Contact details: Euromonitor, 60-61 Britton Street, London EC1M 5NA, UK. Tel. +44 (0)20 7251 1105. Fax +44 (0)20 7251 0985. URL: http://Euro.imrmall.com/chapters/0030/index.shtml

Cost: £1950/$3900. Country chapters can be purchased separately.

Legislation

All legitimate business activities are carried on within a legal and regulatory framework. The complexities of CEE business legalities are notorious, as are the often wide discrepancies between the letter, spirit and application of laws, edicts and regulations. These are circumstances in which the advice of legal experts *has* to be sought when final decisions are being taken. However, it is always advisable to acquire a general idea of legal requirements when embarking on exploratory projects, or before engaging legal assistance. Legal information sources exist for the enquiring layman and for the specialists. Examples are:

Central and Eastern European Legal Materials
The legal materials concentrated upon in this compilation are relevant to business, investment and trade activities. The English translations provided are full-text, and cover Albania, Bulgaria, Croatia, Czech Republic, Hungary, Poland, Romania, Slovakia, Slovenia, and others, in 11 volumes. These are updated **ten times a year**.

Contact details: Juris Publishing Inc., Executive Park, 1 Odell Plaza, Yonkers NY 10701, USA. Tel. +1 914 375 3400. Fax +1 914 375 6047. Email: orders@jurispub.com URL: http://www.jurispub.com

Cost: $995 a quarter

East European Business Law
This is a **monthly** newsletter with wide coverage of legal issues. Some legal texts are quoted in full. Readable enough for the non-specialist.

Contact details: FT News Newsletters, Maple House, 149 Tottenham Court Road, London W1P 9LL, UK. Tel. +44 (0)20 7896 2314. Fax +44 (0)20 7896 2274.

Cost: £480 pa (UK); $510 pa (elsewhere)

East European Legislative Monitor
This service reviews legal developments in CEE countries and distributes its results, freely, by email. The number of freely accessible law sites is surprising. The general survey of developments, naturally, encompasses business related legislation. Certainly worth monitoring.

Contact details: URL: http://www.reenic.utexus.edu/reenic/listserv/listservHTMLs/L-00006.html

East/West Executive Guide
This **monthly** reviews legal issues arising from changes in business laws on taxation, banking, foreign investments, etc. Intended, it seems, for non-specialist management.

Contact details: WorldTrade Executive Inc., 2250 Main Street, Suite 100, Concord, MA 01742, USA. Tel. +1 987 287 0301. Fax +1 987 287 0302. Email: info@stexec.com URL: http://www.wtexec.com/

Cost: $656 pa (USA); $706 pa (elsewhere).

Foreign Investment in Central and Eastern Europe
This loose-leaf reference source provides general information about the legal technicalities of doing business in CEE countries. Laws and regulations are described, analysed and provided with explanatory comment. There are annual updates. The countries covered are Bulgaria, Czech Republic, Hungary, Romania, Slovakia.

Contact details: Juris Publishing Inc., Executive Park, 1 Odell Plaza, Yonkers NY 10701, USA. Tel. +1 914 375 3400. Fax +1 914 375 6047. Email: orders@jurispub.com URL: http://www.jurispub.com

Cost: $195

Litigation and Arbitration in Central and Eastern Europe
This report (1998) reviews the progress made in establishing formal, legal, processes for the settlement of commercial disputes. The countries reported on include Hungary, Poland, Czech Republic, Slovakia, Slovenia. A specialist source.

Contact details: Kluwer Law International, PO Box 322, 3300 AH Dordrecht, The Netherlands. Tel. +31 (0)78 654 6454. Fax +31 (0)78 654 6474. Email: sales@kli.wkap.nl

Cost: £78

Survey on East European Law
This **monthly** newsletter monitors and analyses legal developments throughout eastern Europe.

Contact details: Juris Publishing Inc., Executive Park, 1 Odell Plaza, Yonkers NY 10701, USA. Tel. +1 914 375 3400. Fax +1 914 375 6047. Email: orders@jurispub.com URL: http://www.jurispub.com

Cost: $302 pa (USA and Canada); $355 pa (elsewhere)

Taxation and Investment in Central and East European Countries
Legal and tax structures are described for all CEE countries, together with reviews of the business environment – economic developments, political changes, investment climate, etc. There are **three updates a year**.

Contact details: IBFD Publications BV, PO Box 20237, 1000 HE Amsterdam, Netherlands. Tel. +31 20 626 7726. Fax +31 20 622 8658.

Cost: NLG 1700 pa.

Organisations

Organisations, generally with some kind of government connection, exist to advise, assist and inform business people. These operate mainly at the national level. However, there are various agencies with multi-country responsibilities for business information and advice. Business people, sometimes, can be dismissive of such organisations and their efforts to promote business activity. Impatience with the shortcomings of intended bureaucratic assistance is understandable, but the value of the information roles of these agencies, when properly used, is considerable. Some examples are:

British Trade International
This government agency is responsible for providing general export help. Specific country helpdesks are available to provide 'general background material, political and market information, information on tariffs and export regulations'. The helpdesks can be contacted by telephoning (0)20 7215 5000 and 'asking for the Country Helpdesk dealing with your chosen market'. Provision is made for independent research at the Export Market Information Centre (EMIC). EMIC's Internet home page expresses its role in this way – 'EMIC is British Trade International's free self-service library for exporters. We are here to help you identify, select and research the export markets offering the most potential for your products or services'. Opening hours: Monday to Friday 09.00 -20.00, Saturday 09.00 - 17.30.

Contact details: EMIC, Kingsgate House, 66-74 Victoria Street, London SW1E 6SW, UK. Tel. +44 (0)20 7215 5444/5. Fax +44 (0)20 7215 4231. Email: EMIC@xpd3.dti.gov.uk URL: http://www2.dti.gov.uk/ots/emic/index.html

Central and North West European Department: Foreign and Commonwealth Office (FCO)
The FCO 'attaches very high priority to central Europe', i.e. Poland, Czech Republic, Hungary, Slovakia, Slovenia, Romania, Bulgaria and the Baltic

countries. The experts in the Central and North West European Department are 'ready to offer advice to businessmen on political and economic developments in the region as a whole, on individual countries, and would be happy to speak to you on the telephone or see you in our offices'.

Contact details: Central and North West European Department, King Charles Street, London SW1A 2AF, UK. Tel. +44 (0)20 7270 2370. Fax +44 (0)20 7270 2152.

East European Trade Council (EETC)
The EETC has a wide remit to promote business with the countries of central and eastern Europe, central Asia and Transcaucasia. The various activities to this end include, for example, arranging workshops and trade fairs, matching business offers, maintaining a calendar of events, and publishing information sources of different kinds. Among the latter is *East Europe Bulletin* (**bi-monthly**), which reports on an extensive range of business news, government business initiatives, trade offers, statistics, and much else besides. Special lists are also published, such as, for example, *Czech Exporters Looking for UK Customers, Companies to be Sold Off by the State Ownership Fund*. The EETC maintains a library of business sources which is open to the public, but only by appointment. In the early days of fragmenting command economies this library was often the only source for CEE business information and data. Since then, however, the library has lost its lead. Its budget is wholly inadequate for the huge task of keeping abreast of CEE business information developments. It remains a useful first port of call.

Contact details: East European Trade Council, Suite 10, Westminster Palace Gardens, Artillery Row, London SW1P 1RL, UK. Tel. +44 (0)20 7222 7622. Fax +44 (0)20 7222 5359. Email: eetc@easynet.co.uk

EBRD Business Information Centre
The Centre collects 'information relevant to investment in central and eastern Europe and the CIS'. Its resources in terms of 'databases, books, reports, periodicals, newspapers and grey literature ... cannot be found together anywhere else in the world'. The specialist staff have close contacts in CEE countries, and can be used to obtain information and data not readily available through normal channels. The service is available to external subscribers.

Contact details: European Bank for Reconstruction and Development, Business Information Centre, One Exchange Square, London EC2A 2EH, UK. Tel. +44 (0)20 7338 6361. Fax +44 (0)20 7338 6155. Email: kroon@ebrd.com

Vienna Institute for International Economic Studies (WIIW)
The Institute has a long record of comment, analysis and statistics gathering relating to eastern Europe. Among the subscription services available are, for example, *WIIW Annual Database on Eastern Europe* and *WIIW Industrial Database Eastern Europe*. The former is available on the Internet, providing national statistics and information extracted from a variety of current sources. The latter, on CD-ROM, which is updated annually, provides comparative statistics of manufacturing industries in Bulgaria, Czech Republic, Hungary, Poland, Romania, Slovakia and Slovenia. These annual services are complemented by the *WIIW Monthly Database Eastern Europe* in which key economic indicators are employed in comparative fashion to monitor changes in individual countries. The latter include Bulgaria, Croatia, Czech Republic, Hungary, Poland, Romania, Slovakia, Slovenia. Individual services are available to business people on request.

Contact details: Vienna Institute for International Economic Studies, Oppolzergasee 6, A-1010 Austria. Tel: +43 1 533 6610. Fax +43 1 533 6610 50. URL: http://www.wiiw.ac.at/

Chapter 2

Albania

Population 3.2 m. Among the least blessed of CEE countries in economic terms – high unemployment, continuing high inflation, low per capita GDP, substandard communications infrastructure. As one Internet source expresses it – 'an extremely poor country by European standards'. Albania has done little to improve its own situation. Economic reform has made little headway, although the privatisation of the country's extensive mineral resources is promised for 1999. An impoverished country coping with severe economic, political, social and external problems is not likely to encourage outside investors and business operators. Even before the Kosovo crisis Albania attracted the smallest amount of foreign investment of all CEE countries. Recent events have done nothing to improve the country's attractiveness for investors.

The pattern of business information provision reflects the impoverished state of the country. Internally produced English-language sources are sparse. Some categories of information supply are barely represented. To some extent the availability of externally produced sources, especially from the UK and USA, compensates for this deficiency. In addition, the potential of multi-country sources and a variety of Internet sites should be kept in mind.

Overview

The current state of the region (June, 1999) ensures that Albania receives a fair amount of media attention when, normally, it receives very little. Among the surprising number of sources that provide a general overview of developments in the country there are, for example:

Albanews
This Internet site provides a wide range of information about the country, including a review of current events. The site is officially controlled, so information beyond the confirmed factual has to be treated warily. However, for those wishing to gain an understanding of Albanians and Albanian life as a context for a business venture this service could be tried.

Contact details: URL: http://www.albanian.com/main/resources/albanews.html

Albania – Land of Eagles
An informative Internet site. The business advice offered is frank and good sense, for example, 'it is vital that you research the specific field of interest, prior to visiting the country'; 'we would always recommend that the first visit be no shorter than 5 working days'. It also helps to know that 'Albanians nod their heads for NO and shake their heads for YES'; and it may be enough of a warning to be told that Albanian drivers have 'copied the Italian system of driving'. There are pages on the economy, commerce, natural resources, companies, contacts, travel. For business people embarking on Albanian projects this is an excellent first source for local knowledge.

Contact details: URL: http://www.albania.co.uk/main/bus-page.html

Albania On-Line
This Internet site provides general news coverage; a convenient way of keeping in touch with developments.

Contact details: URL: http:www.geocities.com/CapitolHill/Lobby/2610/albania.html

Albanian American Trade and Development Association
AATDA maintains an Internet site which provides, among many other services, pages on doing business in Albania. These pages include, for example, setting up a business, partnerships, limited partnerships, limited liability companies, joint stock companies, ground rules and principal costs. There are also pages about Albania – history, language, religion, climate, politics, economics, trade. Agribusiness Opportunities are highlighted.

Contact details: URL: http:www.albaniabiz.org/

Albanian Home Page
Home pages on the Internet usually provide concise country descriptions, with information and data likely to be useful to business travellers. This home page conforms to the pattern. In May, 1999, visitors were introduced to 'the new Albanian pages on the World Wide Web' – an indication that the site was appealing not only to the 3.3 million living in Albanian, but to the 'seven million Albanians who live in their ancestral land in the Balkans'. In this region politics, history and business are difficult to disentangle. For business use there are, for example, related sites listing companies, regional information, government contacts, organisational contacts but, one suspects, little more than could be found in a well edited business guide.

Contact details: URL: http://www.albanian.com/main/

Business Investment Opportunity Yearbook: Albania
This **annual** covers 'business, investment, export-import, economic and other opportunities in respected countries. Foreign economic assistance projects, sources of financing , strategic government and business contacts, and more...'. The annual publication cycle precludes 'hot' investment news. The series titles, of which this is one, cover numerous countries throughout the world. So much so that it is difficult to know what weight to attach to the description 'respected'.

Contact details: Russian Information and Business Center, PO Box 15343, Washington DC 20003, USA. Tel. +1 202 546 2103. Fax +1 202 546 3275. Email: rusline@erols.com. URL: http://www.rusline.com/

Cost: $89

Country Profile: Albania
This **annual** publication is a standard reference source. Comment, analysis and statistics cover the main industrial sectors, economic policies, political background, population, finance, prices and wages – with remarkable succinctness.

Contact details: Economist Intelligence Unit, 15 Regent Street, London SW1Y 4LR, UK. Tel. +44 (0)20 7830 1000. Fax +44 (0)20 7499 9767. Email: london@eiu.com URL: http://www.eiu.com
In the US: Economist Intelligence Unit, The Economist Building, 111 West 57th Street, NY, NY 10019, USA . Tel. +1 212 554 060/1 800 938 4685 (USA and Canada only). Fax +1 212 586 0248. Email: newyork@eiu.com URL: http://www.eiu.com

Cost: £120/$205

EBRD Country Profiles: Albania
The main headings in this **annually** produced report are – economic survey, investment climate, financial sector, multilateral funding, EBRD activities, contact list. The report is prepared for the Annual Meeting of the European Bank for Reconstruction and Development.

Contact details: Effective Technology Marketing, PO Box 171, Grimsby DN35 0TP, UK. Tel/Fax +44 (0)1472 816660. Email: sales@etmltd.demon.co.uk URL: http://www.etmltd.demon.co.uk

Cost: £10/$17

IMF Staff Country Reports: Albania
The International Monetary Fund monitors the economic and financial affairs of its member countries. A series of reports, updated at irregular intervals, are produced for the consultations and assessments that take place. These appear as reviews of recent economic developments, selected

issues and statistical annexes. The result, for each country surveyed, is a useful source of general and specialised knowledge of the economy, with an emphasis upon financial issues. The reports can be downloaded from the Internet.

Contact details: IMF Publication Services, 700 19th Street, NM, Washington DC 20431, USA. Tel. +1 202 623 7430. Fax +1 202 623 7201. Email: pubweb@imf.org URL: http://www.imf.org/external/pubs/pubs/dist.htm In the UK – The Stationery Office, PO Box 276, London SW8 5DT, UK. Tel. +44 (0)870 600 5522. Fax +44 (0)20 7873 8247. URL: http://www.tso-online.co.uk

Cost: $15

Investment and Business Guide: Albania

This introductory **annual** source provides 'basic information on economy, business and investment climate and opportunities, export-import, industrial development, banking and finance, government and business, contacts'. All from the point of view of those contemplating doing business in the country. Readable and informative.

Contact details: Russian Information and Business Center, PO Box 15343, Washington DC 20003, USA. Tel. +1 202 546 2103. Fax +1 202 546 3275. Email: rusline@erols.com URL: http://www.rusline.com/

Cost: $89

Political Risk Services: Country Reports: Albania

These reports are produced **annually.** They include 'fact sheets' of basic national data, background information, 'eighteen month and five year forecasts' indicating the risks that lie ahead, profiles of individuals likely to influence the business climate. The attendant hype suggests that 'this may be the only site you will ever need for country research'. Arguable, but not too far off the mark. The publishers maintain an especially informative web site.

Contact details: The PRS Group, 6320 Fly Road, Suite 102, East Syracuse, NY 13057-0248, USA. Tel. +1 315 431 0511. Fax +1 315 431 0200. URL: http://www.prsgroup.com/

Cost: $395

Current Developments

With the regional political scene in such a turmoil the importance of sources monitoring current political, economic and business developments is evident. There are a small number of services devoted to Albania, but these can be supplemented by the use of multi-country sources and the Internet.

Albanian Daily News
Broad newspaper coverage provides a convenient way of monitoring the confusing forces now operating upon the country's economy and social fabric. The newspaper may not be easy to obtain, but the publishers also maintain a site on the Internet where summaries of major news items are freely available.

Contact details: IAET, 5 Rruga Hile Mosi, Tirana, Albania. Tel/Fax +355 42 276 39. URL: http://www.AlbanianNews.com/

Cost: $442 pa

Albanian Times
The contents of this Internet site are 'designed for the business reader interested in investing in Albania' by providing 'the most up-to-date information on the economic and political developments in the Albania life as well as the changes in the legal system that reflect or precede all these'. The 'electronic gazette' is updated **weekly**. Faxed and mailed printed versions are available.

Contact details: AlbAmerica Trade and Consulting International, 8578 Gwynedd Way, Springfield, VA 22153, USA URL: http://dns.worldweb.net/~ww1054/company/company.html

Cost: On application.

Country Reports: Albania
The Reports are produced **quarterly.** Each issue describes the political and economic structures, reviews political and economic prospects for the next 12 - 18 months, critically reviews major economic and political issues. Economic trends are illustrated with graphs and tables, and there are a number of statistical appendices.

Contact details: Economist Intelligence Unit, 15 Regent Street, London SW1Y 4LR, UK. Tel. +44 (0)20 7830 1000. Fax +44 (0)20 7499 9767 URL: http://www.eiu.com
In the US: Economist Intelligence Unit, The Economist Building, 111 West 57th Street, NY, NY 10019, USA . Tel. +1 212 554 060/1 800 938 4685 (USA and Canada only). Fax +1 212 586 0248. Email: newyork@eiu.com URL: http://www.eiu.com

Cost: £235/$425 pa. The *Country Profile* **annual** is included in the subscription.

Country RiskLines: Albania
This **monthly,** brief, report (usually 4 pages) rates the risk of trading with the country in terms of earnings and international payment obligations, political and economic stability, investment climate, etc.

Contact details: Dun & Bradstreet, Holmers Farm Way, High Wycombe, Bucks HP12 3BR, UK. Tel. +44 (0)1494 422 000. Fax +44 (0)1494 422 929.

Cost: £35 pa

Companies and Contacts

The paucity of sources under this heading reflects the low economic standing of the country. Company information can be obtained from the Organisations mentioned below, and from some of the Internet sites.

Albanian Yellow Pages Business Directory
Telephone directories, because of their comprehensiveness, provide an efficient and effective method of obtaining company contact details. For countries like Albania they are invaluable. *Yellow Pages* lists all businesses with telephone links. It is free on application.

Contact details: Albanian Yellow Pages, 2322 Arthur Avenue Ste. #10, Bronx, NY 10458, USA. Tel. +1 718 584 1620. Fax +1 718 584 1228.
Email: imjeku@albanianyellow pages.com
URL: http://www.albanianyellowpages.com/frame2.html

Industries and Services

Agriculture is the most important activity, with industrial activities in decline. The United Nations Commission on Sustainable Development, when assessing the state of Albania, had to report that there was no information available for technology or industry. It is no surprise to discover that there are no sectoral sources of significance. Sectoral information problems should be addressed to the government agencies listed below.

Legislation

An observation on the legal system, found on the Albania – Land of Eagles web site, is worth repeating: 'Because the legal profession in Albania is so new and inexperienced there is no interpretation of law. Whatever is published as law is taken as sacrosanct and non-negotiable.'

Authorised translations of the laws are essential for those entering into business transactions.

Albania Law Report
A non-official newsletter reviewing legal developments, including those affecting business. Law translations available for modest fees.

Contact details: Albania Law Report, Rruga Sami Frashëri Pal. 20/1
Shk.1, Apt. 6, Tirana, Albania. Tel. +355 42 49 307.
Email: dgentry@icc.al.eu.org.

Cost: $98 pa

Business Law Handbook: Albania
This *Handbook* is updated **annually** to take account of changes in the laws
and regulations governing business activities generally, and those of foreigners in particular. A readable introduction for the layman.

Contact details: Russian Information and Business Center, PO Box 15343,
Washington DC 20003, USA. Tel. +1 202 546 2103. Fax +1 202 546 3275.
Email: rusline@erols.com URL: http://www.rusline.com/

Cost: $89

Taxation
This is a straightforward compilation of Albanian tax laws translated
into English.

Contact details: Albania Law Report, Rruga Sami Frashëri Pal. 20/1
Shk.1, Apt. 6, Tirana, Albania. Tel. +355 42 49 307.
Email: dgentry@icc.al.eu.org.

Cost: $150

What's Happening
This periodical provides summary English translations and explanations
of the acts passed by the Parliament and published in the official journal.
The English version usually appears after a lapse of a week or so, following the appearance of the official version.

Contact details: Albania Law Report, Rruga Sami Frashëri Pal. 20/1
Shk.1, Apt. 6, Tirana, Albania. Tel. +355 42 49 307.
Email: dgentry@icc.al.eu.org.

Cost: $98 pa

Organisations
All CEE countries have set up agencies to encourage inward foreign investment. Albania has not been backward in this respect. The nature of
the economic regime, still largely controlled, means that these agencies
are often the best, and sometimes the only, sources of needed business
information.

Albanian Centre for Foreign Investment Promotion
One of the Government agencies with a promotional remit. Specialised
staff provide practical support to foreign investors.

Contact details: Albanian Centre for Foreign Investment Promotion,
Bulevardi Zhan D'Ark, Tirana, Albania. Tel. +355 42 28439. Fax +355
42 42133.

Albanian Economic Development Agency
The Agency has the difficult task of encouraging foreign investment. Included in its programme is the publication of the **daily** *Economy*, and the
monthly publication *Newsletter*. Both highlight investment opportunities,
monitor changing legal requirements, follow the progress of privatisation, report on the activities of outside interests. The Agency also produces
a *Guide to Business in Albania,* an informative introduction to the basics of
business life and operations, and *Guide to Financing Investment Projects in
Albania*. The latter indicates sources of finance available to private sector
projects.

Contact details: Albanian Economic Development Agency, Bulevardi
Zhan D'Ark, Tirana, Albania. Tel. +355 42 28439. Fax +355 42 28439.
Email: xhepa@cpfi.tirana.al

American Embassy
Will respond to business enquiries.

Contact details: U.S. Embassy, Rruga E Elbasanit 103, Tirana, Albania.
Tel. +355 42 32 875. Fax +355 42 32 222.

British Embassy
'The British Embassy in Tirana recently expanded its activities in the
areas of commerce and technical assistance. Its Commercial Section offers services to British companies interested in doing business with
Albania (*East Europe Bulletin*, April/May, 1999). Opening hours: Monday, Tuesday, Thursday 17.00-12.00/13.00-16.00. Wednesday, Friday
07.00-13.00.

Contact details: British Embassy, Commercial Section, Rruga
Skënderbeg 12, Tirana, Albania. Tel. +355 42 34973. Fax +355 42 47697.
Email: Mira.Berballa@tirana.mail.fco.gov.uk

Chamber of Commerce of the Republic of Albania
Chambers of Commerce are prominent and active players in the business
information sectors of all CEE countries. Their registers of members are
useful for establishing contact, for providing company details, and for

highlighting business opportunities. The Albania Chamber maintains a register of business opportunities, and will assist foreign investors find suitable partners.

Contact details: Chamber of Commerce of the Republic of Albania, Rruga Kavajes 6, Tirana, Albania. Tel. +355 42 302 83/84. Fax +355 42 279 97.

Embassy of the Republic of Albania: UK
Can be approached on business issues.

Contact details: Embassy of the Republic of Albania, 4th Floor, 38 Grosvenor Gardens, London SW1W 0EB, UK. Tel. +44 (0)20 7730 5709. Fax +44 (0)20 7730 5747.

Embassy of the Republic of Albania: USA
Can be contacted with business enquiries

Contact details: Embassy of the Republic of Albania, 2100 S Street, NW, Washington DC 20008, USA. Tel. +1 202 223 4942. Fax +1 202 628 7342

National Agency For Privatisation
The Government agency responsible for establishing privatisation procedures and for implementing agreed programmes of privatisation. Will respond to enquiries from foreign business interests.

Contact details: National Agency for Privatisation, Tirana, Albania. Tel/Fax +355 42 27933.

Chapter 3

Bosnia-Herzegovina

Population 4.1m. With ethnic problems unresolved, NATO troops still guarding the peace, very high unemployment, IMF threats to tighten purse-strings because so little privatisation has taken place, together with uncertainties and difficulties stemming from the Kosovo crisis, there can be no denying that this is a country with serious problems. Before the conflict some observers found reasons for hope in a quickening tempo of privatisation during 1999, rising industrial production, inflation tamed and falling retail prices. Now all such optimistic assessments have had to be recast downwards.

The supply of English-language business information sources is sparse. Even these few are the products of western information providers. What is available can be supplemented by the use of multi-country sources, and by reference to Internet sites.

Overview

General enquiries are catered for by a few English-language specialist sources and Internet sites, but there are numerous multi-country sources providing adequate coverage.

Business Investment Opportunity Yearbook: Bosnia-Herzegovina
This **annual** covers 'business, investment, export-import, economic and other opportunities in respected countries. Foreign economic assistance projects, sources of financing , strategic government and business contacts, and more...'. The annual publication cycle precludes 'hot' investment news. The series titles, of which this is one, cover numerous countries throughout the world. It is difficult to know what weight to attach to the description 'respected'.

Contact details: Russian Information and Business Center, PO Box 15343, Washington DC 20003, USA. Tel. +1 202 546 2103. Fax +1 202 546 3275. Email: rusline@erols.com
URL: http://www.rusline.com/

Cost: $89

Country Profile: Bosnia and Herzegovina
This **annual** publication is a standard reference source. Comment, analysis and statistics cover the main industrial sectors, economic policies, political background, population, finance, prices and wages – with remarkable succinctness.

Contact details: Economist Intelligence Unit, 15 Regent Street, London SW1Y 4LR, UK. Tel. +44 (0)20 7830 1000. Fax +44 (0)20 7299 9767.
Email: london@eiu.com URL: http://www.eiu.com
In the US: Economist Intelligence Unit, The Economist Building, 111 West 57th Street, NY, NY 10019, USA . Tel. +1 212 554 060/1 800 938 4685 (USA and Canada only). Fax +1 212 586 0248. Email: newyork@eiu.com URL: http://www.eiu.com

Cost: £120/$205

EBRD Country Profiles: Bosnia and Herzegovina
The main headings for this **annually** produced report are: economic survey, investment climate, financial sector, multilateral funding, EBRD activities, contact list. The report is prepared for the Annual Meeting of the European Bank for Reconstruction and Development.

Contact details: Effective Technology Marketing, PO Box 171, Grimsby DN35 0TP, UK. Tel/Fax +44 (0)1472 816660.
Email: sales@etmltd.demon.co.uk URL: http://www.etmltd.demon.co.uk

Cost: £10/$17

IMF Staff Country Reports: Bosnia and Herzegovina
The International Monetary Fund monitors the economic and financial affairs of its member countries. A series of reports, updated at irregular intervals, are produced for the consultations and assessments that take place. These appear as reviews of recent economic developments, selected issues and statistical annexes. The result, for each country surveyed, is a useful source of general and specialised knowledge of the economy, with an emphasis upon financial issues. The reports can be downloaded from the Internet.

Contact details: IMF Publication Services, 700 19th Street, NM, Washington DC 20431, USA. Tel. +1 202 623 7430. Fax +1 202 623 7201.
Email: pubweb@imf.org URL: http://www.imf.org/external/pubs/pubs/dist.htm In the UK – The Stationery Office, PO Box 276, London SW8 5DT, UK. Tel. +44 (0)870 600 5522. Fax +44 (0)20 7873 8247. URL: http://www.tso-online.co.uk

Cost: $15

Investment and Business Guide: Bosnia-Herzegovina
This introductory **annual** source provides 'basic information on economy, business and investment climate and opportunities, export-import, industrial development, banking and finance, government and business, contacts'. All from the point of view of those contemplating doing business in the country. Readable and informative.

Contact details: Russian Information and Business Center, PO Box 15343, Washington DC 20003, USA. Tel. +1 202 546 2103. Fax +1 202 546 3275. Email: rusline@erols.com URL: http://www.rusline.com/

Cost: $89

Trade Point
An Internet site that provides information about the region – geography, history, political, economic. There are hints for business visitors, a section on doing business in the country, and a summary of the business regulatory framework and available investment opportunities.

Contact details: URL: http://www.tradepoint.ba/

Current Developments

English language sources are at a premium.

BIH Press
This is the Internet site of the News Agencz of Bosnia and Heryogovina. Its English language pages include business, economic and statistical reports on a **daily** basis. There are links to other sites.

Contact detailsÉ BIH Press. Tel. +387 71 445336. Fax +387 71 445312. Email: bhpress@bih.net.ba URL: http://www.bihpress.com/ glavna.htm

Country Report: Bosnia and Hercegovina
The *Reports* are produced **quarterly**. Each issue describes the political and economic structures, reviews political and economic prospects for the next 12-18 months, critically reviews major economic and political issues. Economic trends are illustrated with graphs and tables, and there are a number of statistical appendices.

Contact details: Economist Intelligence Unit, 15 Regent Street, London SW1Y 4LR, UK. Tel. +44 (0)20 7830 1000. Fax +44 (0)20 7499 9767 URL:http://www.eiu.com
In the US: Economist Intelligence Unit, The Economist Building, 111 West 57th Street, NY, NY 10019, USA . Tel. +1 212 554 060/1 800 938 4685 (USA and Canada only). Fax +1 212 586 0248. Email: newyork@eiu.com URL: http://www.eiu.com

Cost: £235/$425 pa. The *Country Profile* **annual** is included in the subscription.

Companies and Contacts

In recent years there has been activity in the directory producing sector. The resulting products can be complemented through use of the organisations listed below.

BusinessBiH
This Internet site lists companies alphabetically by name, by activities, and by location.

Contact details: URL: http://www.businessbih.com/pocetna/logo1.htm

Directory of Companies, Institutions and Their Activities in Bosnia and Herzegovina
Over 6000 companies are listed in this directory (1998). The descriptive data are locational, with brief activity statements.

Contact details: Poslovni Informator, Titova 5, Sarajevo 71000, Bosnia-Herzegovina. Tel. +387 71 663964. Fax +387 71 663964.

Cost: DEM 130

Kompass Bosnia and Herzegovina
The first edition of this directory appeared in January, 1999. 2000 companies are listed and described in standard fashion – location, contact, number of employees, brief activity description – with supporting indexes.

Contact details: Kompass UK, Reed Information International, Windsor Court, East Grinstead House, East Grinstead, West Sussex RH19 1XA, UK. Tel. +44 (0)1342 326972. Fax +44 (0)1342 335612.

Cost: On application

Industries and Services

There are few sectoral sources, but those that are available can be supplemented by having recourse to the organisations listed below.

Construction

Facts About Construction Growth in Bosnia
This report (1999) 'contains information about construction activity and forecasts of future trends [focusing on] the civil engineering sector, office and housing, retail and industrial construction trends and includes in-

formation about price levels, vacancy rates and yields'. The socio-economic structure is described, and numerous statistical indicators provided.

Contact details: European Construction Research, Bredgade 35B, DK-1260 Copenhagen K, Denmark. Tel. +45 33 162 100. Fax +45 33 162 900. Email: ecr@cybernet.dk URL: http://www.epi.no/ecr/index.htm

Cost: £295/$495

Finance and Banking

Central Bank of Bosnia and Herzegovina
The Bank produces a freely distributed **monthly** *Bulletin* – a source for banking and monetary data, with selected macroeconomic statistics. The Bank maintains an Internet site which, in addition to providing information about the Bank and its activities, has pages of financial and currency data.

Contact details: Central Bank, Research & Development Sector, 25 Maršala Tita, Sarajevo 71000, Bosnia-Herzegovina. Tel. +387 71 663630. Fax +387 71 786297. Email: contact@cbbh.gov.ba URL: http://www.cbbh.gov.ba/english/aboutcbbh.htm

Investment Guarantee Trust Fund
Details of this support fund are to be found on the web site established by the Multilateral Investment Guarantee Agency (MIGA). The Fund was set up to recompense investors for investments lost or diminished by regional difficulties – civil war, political upheavals, the resurgence of communist ideas, etc. As matters stand there is every chance the Fund will be relied upon heavily.

Contact details: Multilateral Investment Guarantee Agency. Tel. +1 202 473 6831. Fax +1 202 522 2640. URL: http://www.miga.or/special/bosnia.htm

Legislation

There is no great competition to provide English language business law sources.

Business Law Handbook: Bosnia-Herzegovina
This *Handbook* is updated **annually** to take account of changes in the laws and regulations governing business activities generally, and those of foreigners in particular. A readable introduction for the layman.

Contact details: Russian Information and Business Center, PO Box 15343, Washington DC 20003, USA. Tel. +1 202 546 2103. Fax +1 202 546 3275. Email: rusline@erols.com URL: http://www.rusline.com/

Cost: $89

Organisations

The relative lack of publicly available English language sources reinforces the importance of Government and other agencies as business information providers and advice givers.

Agency for Privatization in the Federation of Bosnia and Herzegovina
This is the government agency with the responsibility for administering the privatisation programme. An information provider on request.

Contact details: URL: http://www.apf.com.ba/

American Embassy
Will respond to business enquiries.

Contact details: U.S. Embassy, Alipasina 43, Sarajevo, Bosnia and Herzegovina. Tel. +387 71 445 700. Fax +387 71 659 722. URL: http://www.usis.com.ba

British Embassy
Will provide advice, guidance and support to business people.

Contact details: British Embassy, 8 Tina Vjevica, Sarajevo, Bosnia and Herzegovina. Tel. +387 71 444 429. Fax 387 71 666 131. Commercial/ Know How Fund/Visa: Petrakijina 11, Sarajevo, Bosnia and Herzegovina. Tel. +387 71 204781. Fax +387 71 204780. Email: britcomm@bih.net.ba

Chamber of Economy of Bosnia and Herzegovina
The Chamber 'is a part of the institutional infrastructure of the economic and market system of the BH State with specific activities in the field of foreign economic relations'. It has an informational role towards its own members and potential foreign investors. The Chamber's Internet site is being developed to widen its information potential. Currently the site lists Bosnian companies, industrial projects, trade fairs and exhibitions.

Contact details: Chamber of Economy of Bosnia and Herzegovina, Branislava Đurđeva, 71000 Sarajevo, Bosnia-Herzegovina. Tel. +387 71 663 370. Fax +387 71 663 633. URL: http://www.komorabih.com/ ectoday.htm

Embassy of the Republic of Bosnia-Herzegovina: UK
Can be approached on business issues.

Contact details: Embassy of the Republic of Bosnia-Herzegovina, 4th Floor, Morley House, 314-322 Regent Street, London W1R 5AB, UK. Tel. +44 (0)20 7255 3258. Fax +44 (0)20 7255 3760.

Embassy of the Republic of Bosnia-Herzegovina: USA
The web site of the Embassy of Bosnia and Herzogovina in Washington is a useful source for general background data – historical, geographical, demographical, etc. There are pages of investment news, economic indicators, business contacts, company details.

Contact details: Embassy of Bosnia and Herzegovina, 2109 E Street NW, Washington DC 20037, USA. Tel +1 202 337 1500. Fax +1 202 337 15-02. Email: info@bosnianembassy.org
URL: http://www.bosnianembassy.org/bosnia/index.shtml

Chapter 4

Bulgaria

Population 8.3m. Despite reining in galloping inflation business conditions in Bulgaria remain difficult with, according to most observers, only signs of slow improvement. There is high unemployment, falling productivity, and considerable investor wariness. Privatisation is a slow process, with management buyouts the most favoured, if least effective, method of transforming ownership of state enterprises. Private sector growth is most noticeable in the construction, food and some financial sectors. OECD observers recently commented favourably on the 'prolonged period of economic and social stability that is unprecedented in the transition period'.

The English language business information sector is surprisngly well supplied in a number of categories. Although Bulgarian sources do not figure largely in the provision of overview information, other categories display considerable Bulgarian inputs. Despite substantial improvements in country specific English language provision multi-country compilations remain essential for comprehensive information coverage.

Overview

The good showing of general sources is due largely to the efforts of western business information providers, but Internet sites are available to present local views.

Bulgaria Business
The aim of this Internet service is to be a comprehensive site about Bulgaria. Although still developing there are sections on country information, business, law, politics, news and statistical data. The business section includes information on privatisation and foreign investment, banks, finance and capital markets, social and economic transformation. There is also a Companies Section with details of 'Bulgarian manufacturers willing to establish and maintain relations with foreign partners'.

Contact details: URL: http://www.businessbulgaria.com/

Bulgarian Business Adviser
The *Adviser* is available as a pocket-book, and on the Internet. In its own words it 'provides the most concise presentation of everything you should

know about doing business in Bulgaria, both before you've made your decision and after you start'. This breezy guide has main sections on Why Bulgaria, Why Not Bulgaria, Coming to Bulgaria, The Facts, Setting Up, Business Services, Doing Business, Living in Bulgaria.

Contact details: URL: http://www.bba.bg/

Business Investment Opportunity Yearbook: Bulgaria

This **annual** covers 'business, investment, export-import, economic and other opportunities in respected countries. Foreign economic assistance projects, sources of financing , strategic government and business contacts, and more...'. The annual publication cycle precludes 'hot' investment news. The series titles, of which this is one, cover numerous countries throughout the world. It is difficult to understand what weight to attach to the description 'respected'.

Contact details: Russian Information and Business Center, PO Box 15343, Washington DC 20003, USA. Tel. +1 202 546 2103. Fax +1 202 546 3275. Email: rusline@erols.com URL: http://www.rusline.com/

Cost: $89

Business Operations Report: Bulgaria

This is a **quarterly** analysis of the wide range of local and other factors bearing upon business decisions. Examples of such factors are: labour relations, the expected impact of political changes, assessments of future developments. Lessons are drawn from informative case studies. There are supporting statistics. The *Report* is 'also available through on line databases, direct network feeds and the Internet'.

Contact details: Economist Intelligence Unit, 15 Regent Street, London SW1Y 4LR, UK. Tel. +44 (0)20 7830 1000. Fax +44 (0)20 7499 9767 URL:http://www.eiu.com
In the US: Economist Intelligence Unit, The Economist Building, 111 West 57th Street, NY, NY 10019, USA . Tel. +1 212 554 060/1 800 938 4685 (USA and Canada only). Fax +1 212 586 0248. Email: newyork@eiu.com URL: http://www.eiu.com

Cost: £315 pa

Country Commercial Guide: Bulgaria

Titles in the *Guides* series are published **annually**. They review the country's commercial environment 'using economic, political and market analysis', and 'consolidate various reporting documents prepared for the U.S.Embassies community'. There are informative sections on the investment climate, trade regulations and standards, economic trends and outlook, and useful summary statistics in appendices. A good country introduction. Available on the Internet, in hard copy and as a diskette.

Contact details: URL: http://www.stat-usa.gov/Newstand

Cost: $20 (hard copy)

Country Profile: Bulgaria

This **annual** publication is a standard reference source. Comment, analysis and statistics cover the main industrial sectors, economic policies, political background, population, finance, prices and wages – with remarkable succinctness.

Contact details: Economist Intelligence Unit, 15 Regent Street, London SW1Y 4LR, UK. Tel. +44 (0)20 7830 1000. Fax +44 (0)20 7499 9767 URL:http://www.eiu.com
In the US: Economist Intelligence Unit, The Economist Building, 111 West 57th Street, NY, NY 10019, USA . Tel. +1 212 554 060/1 800 938 4685 (USA and Canada only). Fax +1 212 586 0248. Email: newyork@eiu.com URL: http://www.eiu.com

Cost: £120/$205

Dun & Bradstreet Country Report: Bulgaria

This **annual** report profiles the country in terms of the economy, political situation, financial information, its debts and payment potential, the business climate. There are **monthly** monitoring updates. The report is available on diskette also.

Contact details: Dun & Bradstreet, Holmers Farm Way, High Wycombe, Bucks HP12 3BR, UK. Tel. +44 (0)1494 422 000. Fax +44 (0)1494 422 929.

Cost: £245 (hard copy; diskette); £335 (report + monthly updates).

EBRD Country Profiles: Bulgaria

The main headings for this **annually** produced report are: economic survey, investment climate, financial sector, multilateral funding, EBRD activities, contact list. The report is prepared for the Annual Meeting of the European Bank for Reconstruction and Development.

Contact details: Effective Technology Marketing, PO Box 171, Grimsby DN35 0TP, UK. Tel/Fax +44 (0)1472 816660. Email: sales@etmltd.demon.co.uk URL: http://www.etmltd.demon.co.uk

Cost: £10/$17

Hints to Exporters Visiting Bulgaria

This is one of a series produced by the Department of Trade and Industry. It is pocket-sized (1998) and covers 'preparation for the visit, travel and currency information, economic factors, import and exchange control, import and exchange control regulations, methods of doing business and a wealth of useful contact points'. The titles are introductory, and form a good basis for understanding differences in business approaches. A criticism of the series as a whole is slowness in revising individual titles.

Contact details: DTI Export Publications Orderline, Admail 528, London SW1W 8YT, UK. Tel. +44 (0)870 1502 500. Fax +44 (0)870 1502 333. Can be ordered online – URL: http://www.dti.gov.uk/ots/publications/export_publications_home.html

Cost: £7

IMF Staff Country Reports: Bulgaria

The International Monetary Fund monitors the economic and financial affairs of its member countries. A series of reports, updated at irregular intervals, are produced for the consultations and assessments that take place. These appear as reviews of recent economic developments, selected issues and statistical annexes. The result, for each country surveyed, is a useful source of general and specialised knowledge of the economy, with an emphasis upon financial issues. The reports can be downloaded from the Internet.

Contact details: IMF Publication Services, 700 19th Street, NM, Washington DC 20431, USA. Tel. +1 202 623 7430. Fax +1 202 623 7201. Email: pubweb@imf.org URL: http://www.imf.org/external/pubs/pubs/dist.htm In the UK – The Stationery Office, PO Box 276, London SW8 5DT, UK. Tel. +44 (0)870 600 5522. Fax +44 (0)20 7873 8247. URL: http://www.tso-online.co.uk

Cost: $15

Investment and Business Guide: Bulgaria

This introductory **annual** source provides 'basic information on economy, business and investment climate and opportunities, export-import, industrial development, banking and finance, government and business, contacts'. All from the point of view of those contemplating doing business in the country. Readable and informative.

Contact details: Russian Information and Business Center, PO Box 15343, Washington DC 20003, USA. Tel. +1 202 546 2103. Fax +1 202 546 3275. Email: rusline@erols.com URL: http://www.rusline.com/

Cost: $89

OECD Economic Surveys: Bulgaria 1999
Since the last survey in 1997 'Bulgaria has made remarkable progress'. The latest (1999) of the regular OECD economic surveys is upbeat about the country's prospects. An informative account of the state of the country and its economy seen from a conservative perspective. The main sections assess macroeconomic performance and policy, the revival of commercial banks, privatisation and restructuring in the corporate sector. A lengthy summary of the report is available on the Internet.

Contact details: OECD Paris Centre, 2 rue André-Pascal, 75775 Cedex 16, France. Tel. +33 (0)1 49 104235. Fax +33 (0)1 49 104276. Email: sales@oecd.org. Also – The Stationery Office, PO Box 276, London SW8 5DT, UK. Tel. +44 (0)870 600 5522. Fax +44 (0)20 7873 8247. URL: http://www.tso-online.co.uk

Cost: 150FF

Political Risk Services: Country Reports: Bulgaria
Reports in this series are produced **annually.** They include 'fact sheets' of basic national data, background information, 'eighteen month and five year forecasts' indicating the risks that lie ahead, profiles of individuals likely to influence the business climate. The attendant hype suggests that 'this may be the only site you will ever need for country research'. Arguable, but not too far off the mark. The publishers maintain an especially informative web site.

Contact details: The PRS Group, 6320 Fly Road, Suite 102, East Syracuse, NY 13057-0248, USA. Tel. +1 315 431 0511. Fax +1 315 431 0200. URL: http://www.prsgroup.com/

Cost: $395

Welcome to Bulgaria
This Internet site offers a convenient way of obtaining country information of a general nature – geography, history, demography, travel, news, etc. The site provides links to other Bulgarian sources.

Contact details: URL: http://www.bulgaria.com/

World of Information Country Report: Bulgaria
A concise **annual** report reviewing the economic and political scene, with selected supporting statistics. Ideal for quick familiarisation.

Contact details: Walden Publishing, 2 Market Street, Saffron Walden, Essex CB10 1HZ, UK. Tel. +44 (0)1799 521150. Fax +44 (0)1799 524805.

Cost: £30/$65

Current Developments

Around 75% of English language sources in this category are of Bulgarian origin. There is an increasing number of Internet sites.

bol.bg

This web site hosts a number of business information sources providing, for example, company profiles, details of investment opportunities, legal requirements surrounding business activities.

Contact details: BOL, PO Box 71, Sofia 1164, Bulgaria. Tel. +359 2 980 9666. Email: office@bol.bg URL: http://www.bol.bg/index.html

Bulgaria

A desk reference work providing information about national organisations and public figures. It is updated **monthly.** There is an electronic version which is updated **daily.**

Contact details: Bulgarian News Agency, 49 Tsarigradsko Shosse Blvd., 1124 Sofia, Bulgaria. Tel. +359 2 733 7215. Fax +359 2 802 488.

Bulgaria: Business and Investment Opportunities

Another web site providing a general range of business information – business laws, advice on how to do business, investment opportunities, company profiles, etc.

Contact details: URL: http://www.aubg.bg/proj/bg-bio/

Bulgarian Business News

This is a **weekly** reporting on the economic scene. Its broad range reporting covers, for example, banking, finance, industry, agriculture, business legislation, economic policies. Essential for critical analysis of developments.

Contact details: Bulgarian Business News, 47 Tsarigradsko Shosse Blvd., Sofia 1504, Bulgaria. Tel. +359 2 433 9276. Fax +359 2 433 9340.

Cost: $312 pa (Europe); $364 pa (elsewhere).

Bulgarian Economic Outlook

A **weekly** newsletter reviewing economic and business developments – privatisation, capital and stock markets, economic indicators, future assessments, etc. Also distributed via email.

Contact details: Bulgarian News Agency, 49 Tsarigradsko Shosse Blvd., Sofia 1124, Bulgaria. Tel. +359 2 733 7215. Fax +359 2 802 488.

Cost: $370 pa

Bulgarian Economic Review

The *Bulgarian Economic Review* offers a **fortnightly** commentary and news reports on business and economic issues. The paper version is priced, but the *Review* is freely available on the Internet.

Contact details: ITK Pari Daily, 47A Tsarigradsko Shosse Blvd., 1504 Sofia, Bulgaria. Tel. +359 2 943 3147. Fax +359 2 943 3188. Email: office@pari.bg URL: http://www.pari.bg/doc/BER/berindex.htm

Bulgarian Press Digest

A useful source for monitoring events. The service provides a digest of news from national papers.

Contact details: URL: http://www.capital.bg/bp_digest/main.html

Country Forecasts: Bulgaria

This **quarterly** source presents 'five-year forecasts of political, economic and business trends'. Issues examined include, for example, prospects for political stability, business operating climate, government economic policies, labour market developments, sectoral matters.

Contact details: Economist Intelligence Unit, 15 Regent Street, London SW1Y 4LR, UK. Tel. +44 (0)20 7830 1000. Fax +44 (0)20 7499 9767 URL:http://www.eiu.com
In the US: Economist Intelligence Unit, The Economist Building, 111 West 57th Street, NY, NY 10019, USA . Tel. +1 212 554 060/1 800 938 4685 (USA and Canada only). Fax +1 212 586 0248. Email: newyork@eiu.com URL: http://www.eiu.com

Cost: £450 pa

Country Reports: Bulgaria

The *Reports* are produced **quarterly.** Each issue describes the political and economic structures, reviews political and economic prospects for the next 12-18 months, critically reviews major economic and political issues. Economic trends are illustrated with graphs and tables, and there a number of statistical appendices.

Contact details: Economist Intelligence Unit, 15 Regent Street, London SW1Y 4LR, UK. Tel. +44 (0)20 7830 1000. Fax +44 (0)20 7499 9767 URL:http://www.eiu.com
Cost: £235/$425 pa The *Country Profile* **annual** is included in the subscription.

Country Risk Service: Bulgaria

The *Risk Service* takes a two-year 'forecasting horizon' on a **quarterly** basis when presenting assessments of political, economic and financial risks likely to influence business activities. Future trends of 'over 180 major economic indicators' are presented.

Contact details: Economist Intelligence Unit, 15 Regent Street, London SW1Y 4LR, UK. Tel. +44 (0)20 7830 1000. Fax +44 (0)20 7499 9767 URL: http://www.eiu.com

Cost: £395 pa

Country RiskLines: Bulgaria
This **monthly,** brief, report (usually 4 pages) rates the risk of trading with the country in terms of earnings and international payment obligations, political and economic stability, investment climate, etc.

Contact details: Dun & Bradstreet, Holmers Farm Way, High Wycombe, Bucks HP12 3BR, UK. Tel. +44 (0)1494 422 000. Fax +44 (0)1494 422 929.

Cost: £35 pa

Daily News
An obvious source of current country information is the daily newspaper. The *Daily News* is an English language example with a business bias. It is available via email.

Contact details: Bulgarian News Agency, 49 Tsarigradsko Shosse Blvd., 1124 Sofia, Bulgaria. Tel. +359 2 733 7215. Fax +359 2 802 488.

Cost: $875 pa

PARI Daily
The fast-changing financial and business scene is well captured in this 'the largest and only Bulgarian **daily**' specialising in these sectors. There is an English email service.

Contact details: ITK PARI, 47A Tsarigradsko, Shosse Blvd., 1504 Sofia, Bulgaria. Tel. 359 2 943 3147. Fax +359 2 943 3188. Email: office@pari.bg URL: http://www.pari.bg/doc/ENG/engindex.html

Cost: $50 for 6 months (paper edition); $45 for 6 months (email).

Companies and Contacts

There is a reasonable show of sources here, for example:

Bulgaria Business Catalog
This is a directory of over 14,000 companies on the Internet site Bulgaria.Com. The company details are basic, but it is possible to locate

enterprises not easily found in other ways. Other services available on this site include trade offers and investment possibilities.

Contact details: Bulgaria.Com, 2116 Walsh Avenue, Suite C6, Santa Clara, CA 95050, USA. Tel. +1 408 406 6811. Fax +1 408 378 7219. Email: info@bulgaria.com URL: http://www.bulgaria.com/business/index.html

Bulgarian Small and Medium Sized Enterprises
This source lists over 500 enterprises looking for foreign partners. The company profiles provided include contacts details with brief activity descriptions.

Contact details: Bulgarian Ministry of Industry, 8 Slavyanska Street, Sofia 1000, Bulgaria. Tel. +359 2 870 741.

Directory of Industrial Companies in the Republic of Bulgaria
This **annual** lists over 1500 enterprises. The usual basic company details are provided and, in addition, there are appendices setting out the texts of business laws. A useful bonus.

Contact details: National Centre for Information and Documentation, 52A G M Dimitrov Blvd, 1125 Sofia, Bulgaria. Te. +359 2 719 203. Fax +359 2 710 157.

Cost: $82

Kompass Bulgaria
One of the largest (4th edition, 1999) and most authoritative of the paper-based directories. 9000 firms are listed and described in terms of location, contact data, products and services, annual turnover, trade markets, number of employees, etc.

Contact details: Kompass UK, Reed Information Services, Windsor Court, East Grinstead House, East Grinstead, West Sussex RH19 1XA, UK. Tel. +44 (0)1342 326972. Fax +44 (0)1342 335612.

Cost: £220

PARI Who's Who in Bulgarian Business
This Internet site provided basic contact data and activity descriptions of twenty firms the last time consulted (29/05/99). New companies are being added.

Contact details: http://www.pari.bg/doc/ENG/who-bus.htm

Industries and Services

The financial and banking sources are reasonably represented. Other sectors are developing slowly.

Agriculture

Agricultural Situation and Perspectives in the Central and East European Countries: Bulgaria
This report, from the European Union, 'aims to provide an analysis of the current situation and the medium-term outlook for the agricultural and agri-food industries' in the CEE countries aiming for EU membership – Bulgaria, Czech Republic, Hungary, Poland, Romania, Slovakia, Slovenia. The report is freely available on the Internet.

Contact details: URL: http://www.europa.eu.int/comm/dg06/publi/peco.index-en.htm

Construction

Facts About Construction Growth in Bulgaria
This report (1999) 'contains information about construction activity and forecasts of future trends [focusing on] the civil engineering sector, office and housing, retail and industrial construction trends and includes information about price levels, vacancy rates and yields'. The socio-economic structure is described, and numerous statistical indicators provided.

Contact details: European Construction Research, Bredgade 35B, DK-1260 Copenhagen K, Denmark. Tel. +45 33 162 100. Fax +45 33 162 900. Email: ecr@cybernet.dk URL: http://www.epi.no/ecr/index/htm

Cost: £98/$145

Finance and Banking

Bulgarian National Bank: Monthly Bulletin
The *Bulletin* monitors and explains financial and national policy issues. It is a convenient source of up-to-date statistics for the financial and banking sectors.

Contact details: Bulgarian National Bank Publications Division, 1 Al. Battenberg Square, 1000 Sofia, Bulgaria. Tel. +359 2 886 1351. Fax +359 2 980 2425.

Cost: DEM 135 pa (Europe); DEM 185 pa (elsewhere).

Bulgarian Stock Exchange

The Exchange opened in October, 1997. It has established an active information programme publishing **daily** and **monthly** bulletins of trading data. Details of these are best searched out on the Exchange's web site. The *Rules and Regulations of the Bulgarian Stock Exchange* is essential reading.

Contact details: Bulgarian Stock Exchange, Sofia, Bulgaria. Tel. +359 2 815711. Fax +359 2 875566. Email: bse@bg400.bg URL: http://www.online.bg/bse/

Capital Weekly

Provides comprehensive coverage of banking and financial sectors, as well as the economic and political background. Summaries of past items are available on the Internet.

Contact details: Capital Weekly, 20 Ivan Vazov Street, Sofia 1000, Bulgaria. Tel. +359 2 981 5816. Fax +359 2 980 9439. URL: http://www.capital.bg/

Cost: $135 pa (Europe); $210 pa (USA)

Secondary Market of Government Securities

This is a **monthly** publication of the Bulgarian National Bank. It provides data on the issue and trading of government securities.

Contact details: Bulgarian National Bank, Publications Division, 1 Al. Battenberg Square, 1000 Sofia, Bulgaria. Tel. +359 2 886 1351. Fax +359 2 980 2425

Cost: DEM 85 pa (Europe); DEM 120 pa (elsewhere)

Transparency of the Bulgarian Capital Market

This two-part report (1997, 1998) provides a closely critical analysis of the operational procedures of the Bulgarian stock and securities markets.

Contact details: Economic Policy Institute, 12A Luben Karavelov Street, 1142 Sofia, Bulgaria. Tel/Fax +359 2 980 4740, 980 8489, 980 9268. Email: epi@bulnet.bg URL: http://www.online.bg/epi/

Who's Who in Bulgarian Banking

This Internet site, maintained by ITK Pari, provides details of BalkanBank Ltd., The International Orthodox Bank 'St. Nicholas' Ltd, and the National Privatisation Fund Nadejda JSCo.

Contact details: URL http://www.pari.bg/doc/ENG/who-ban.htm

Legislation

Business law is reasonably covered at a number of levels. Examples are:

Business Law Guide: Bulgaria
This is a guide (1997) intended for general consumption. Following a review of the political and economic background major business related laws are translated into English, with commentaries.

Contact details: Book World Publications, PO Box 11089, EB Den Bosch, NL-5200, Netherlands. Tel. +31 73 599 6260. Fax +31 73 599 4555. Email: info@bwp-mediagroup.com URL: http://www.bwp-mediagroup.com/

Cost: $60

Business Law Handbook: Bulgaria
This *Handbook* is updated **annually** to take account of changes in the laws and regulations governing business activities generally, and those of foreigners in particular. A readable introduction for the layman.

Contact details: Russian Information and Business Center, PO Box 15343, Washington DC 20003, USA. Tel. +1 202 546 2103. Fax +1 202 546 3275. Email: rusline@erols.com URL: http://www.rusline.com/

Cost: $89

Collection of Bulgarian Laws
English language translations of laws relating to business activities can be found in this major compilation of legislation. There are nine volumes in the complete set.

Contact details: Bulgarian Business News, 47 Tsarigradsko Shosse Blvd., 1504 Sofia, Bulgaria. +359 2 433 9265. Fax +359 2 943 3058

Cost: $24 per volume

Commercial and Investment Law: Bulgaria
A full presentation of business related laws from an authoritative US source. It is updated annually.

Contact details: Juris Publishing, Executive Park, 1 Odell Plaza, Yonkers, NY 10701, USA. Tel. +1 914 375 3400. Fax +1 914 375 6047. Email: orders@jurispub.com URL: http://www.jurispub.com

Cost: $125

Foreign Investors' Legal Guide to Bulgaria
Summarises (1998) the main laws applicable to foreign business operators. It covers, for example, the definition of a foreign person, standards of treatment of foreign investors, adverse changes in the law, foreign ex-

change regulations, repatriation of proceedings, tax incentives. A handy compilation. The text is available on the Internet.

Contact details: Economic Policy Institute, 17A Luben Karavelov Street, Sofia, Bulgaria. Tel. +359 2 980 4740. Fax +359 2 980 8489. Email: epi@bulnet.bg URL: http://www.online.bg/epi/

Foreign Investors' Legal Guide to the Bulgarian Securities Market
This guide (1997) is intended for the layman. Business legalities are explained, but the message with regard to trading in securities seems to be – be careful!

Contact details: Economic Policy Institute, 17A Lyuben Karavelov Street, Sofia, Bulgaria. Tel. +359 2 980 4740. Fax +359 2 980 8489. Email: epi@bulnet.bg URL: http://www.online.bg/epi/

Organisations

A useful and active range of organisations offering information, advice and assistance is available. For example:

American Embassy
The Embassy's Commercial Counselor is available for business matters. The Embassy's home page provides general information.

Contact details: U.S. Embassy, 1 Saborna Street, Sofia, Bulgaria. Tel. +359 2 980 5241. Fax +359 2 981 8977. Email: usis@library.bg URL: http://www.usis.bg/

British Embassy
Embassies sometimes receive unflattering notices from business people. In most cases, however, they can be helpful in establishing first contacts and in providing useful background information. Not a source to be ignored.

Office hours: Monday - Thursday 06.30-15.30; Friday 06.30-11.00.

Contact details: British Embassy, Commercial Section, Boulevard Vassil Levski 38, 1000 Sofia, Bulgaria. Tel. +359 2980 1220; +359 2981 7765 (out of hours). Fax +359 2980 1229; +359 2981 7753 (Consular/Visa); +359 2983 3307 (KHF); +359 2988 5362 (Commercial). Email: britembsof@mbox.cit.bg; britembcon@mbox.cit.bg Consular Section); besofia-cs@mbox.cit.bg (Commercial Section).

Bulgarian Chamber of Commerce and Industry (BCCI)
Unlike some of its neighbours, the Bulgarian Chamber 'is based on the principles of voluntary affiliation, autonomy, and self-financing'. Among its promotional activities is the publication of *Infobusiness: Economic News*

from Bulgaria – a **monthly.** This newsletter provides an official account of current business developments and, on occasion, the texts of new business laws. Another source to note is *Trade Directory* – an **annual** listing of 3000 enterprises. A selection of what is published in print form is available on the Internet site maintained by the Chamber. The selection includes, for example, a helpful summary of the legislative framework, business opportunities with member firms of the Chamber, fairs and exhibitions, business news in *Infobusiness Newspaper*, and the highlighting of some of the companies listed in the *Trade Directory*. The publications of the BCCI also include translations of business law, for example, *Law on Commerce, Law on Foreign Investments, Law on Foreigners' Stay in the Republic of Bulgaria*. Basic data that can be acquired cheaply – between $9 and $28 per item. Enquiries from business people are welcomed.

Contact details: BCCI, Information and Publication Bureau, Floor 7, Room 8, 42 Parteviechi St., 1000 Sofia, Bulgaria. Tel. +359 2 987 2631. Fax +359 2 987 3209. Email: bcci@bcci.bg URL: http://212.56.3.2/

Bulgarian Foreign Investment Agency (BIFA)
BIFA has 'close business relations with government institutions, municipalities and numerous business organisations'. Based on this experience the Agency provides free advice and information to potential investors on such issues as privatisation, partnerships and joint ventures, sectoral data, established foreign investments, etc. The Agency's web site carries investment statistics, a business guide, business law, privatisation news, tenders, capital market data, and also provides links to 'key Bulgarian institutions, economic, financial, legal and general information'. A very useful general and special source.

Contact details: Bulgarian Foreign Investment Agency, 3 Sveta Sofia St., 1000 Sofia, Bulgaria. Tel. +359 2 980 0918. Fax +359 2 980 1320. Email: fia@bfia.org URL: http://www.bfia.org/

Bulgarian Privatisation Agency
The process of privatisation is the responsibility of the Agency. Information about enterprises to be privatised, about laws relating to the process, and about developments affecting the process can be found on the Agency's web site.

Further information: URL: http://www.privatisation.online.bg/

Embassy of the Republic of Bulgaria: UK
Provides assistance in furthering business aims.

Contact details: Embassy of the Republic of Bulgaria, Commercial Office, 186-188 Queen's Gate, London SW7 5HL, UK. Tel. +44 (0)20 7584 9400. Fax +44 (0)20 7581 324.

Embassy of the Republic of Bulgaria: USA

The Embassy's web site provides country information and has a section for economy and business.

Contact details: Embassy of the Republic of Bulgaria, 1621 22nd Street, NW, Washington DC 20008, USA. Tel. +1 202 387 7969. Fax +1 202 234 7973. Email: bulgaria@access.digex.net URL: http://www.bulgaria-embassy.org

National Statistical Institute of Bulgaria (NSI)

The NSI publishes a number of English language sources. The most accessible of these is the *Statistical Yearbook*, the standard reference source for national economic data. The latest edition (1998) 'contains final data about demographic and socioeconomic developments of the country and international comparisons for the period 1993-1997'. A summary **annual** version – *Bulgaria* – is a handy portable source. Monitoring developments is possible through the **quarterly** *Statistical News*. However, most of the time series in these publications are freely available on the Internet with, in addition, figures for 1998. An excellent site.

Contact details: National Statistical Institute of Bulgaria, 2, Panajot Volov Str., 1504 Sofia, Bulgaria. Tel. +359 2 818 483. Fax +359 2 879 638. Email: BTodorova@NSI.BG URL: http://195.138.134.12/

Privatisation Agency

The Agency's responsibility for the privatisation programme includes a large amount of information work to answer such questions as: what firms are scheduled for privatisation?, what are the legal constraints on purchasers of firms?, how does new legislation affect foreign investors?, what are the prospects of a specific economic sector? what is the financial standing of an enterprise due for privatisation? These questions and related issues are reported on, at **monthly** intervals, in *Privatisation Agency Information Bulletin*.

Contact details: Privatisation Agency, Marketing OPR, 29 Aksakov Street, 1000 Sofia, Bulgaria. Tel. 359 2 988 2402. Fax +359 2 981 6201. Email: bgpriv@online.bg URL: http://www.privatisation.online.bg/

Chapter 5

Croatia

Population 4.5m. Croatia depends heavily upon foreign investment and tourism to keep its creaking economy going. Reform in critical areas such as banking, capital markets and corporate restructuring is slow. Inflation, although not as rampant as in neighbouring states, remains high, as does the unemployment level. Inter-company debts, much higher than officially recognised, are a persisting problem with no evident sign of a solution. The country has failed to impress the European Union with its required commitment to greater democratisation and liberalisation of the media. The result is a reluctance to renew financial support.

English language provision is largely that offered by major western information producers. Local sources are being produced in greater numbers however, and, as in most other CEE countries, the impact of the Internet is noticeable.

Overview

There is a reasonable number and variety of overview sources, and these can be supplemented by the use of multi-country compilations. All the examples selected below are from outside publishers.

Business Investment Opportunity Yearbook: Croatia
This **annual** covers 'business, investment, export-import, economic and other opportunities in respected countries. Foreign economic assistance projects, sources of financing , strategic government and business contacts, and more ...'. The annual publication cycle precludes 'hot' investment news. The series titles, of which this is one, cover numerous countries throughout the world. In the circumstances it is difficult to know what weight to attach to the description 'respected'.

Contact details: Russian Information and Business Center, PO Box 15343, Washington DC 20003, USA. Tel. +1 202 546 2103. Fax +1 202 546 3275. Email: rusline@erols.com URL: http://www.rusline.com/

Cost: $89

Country Profile: Croatia
This **annual** publication is a standard reference source. Comment, analysis and statistics cover the main industrial sectors, economic policies, political background, population, finance, prices and wages – with remarkable succinctness.

Contact details: Economist Intelligence Unit, 15 Regent Street, London SW1Y 4LR, UK. Tel. +44 (0)20 7830 1000. Fax +44 (0)20 7499 9767. Email: london@eiu.com URL: http://www.eiu.com
In the US: Economist Intelligence Unit, The Economist Building, 111 West 57th Street, NY, NY 10019, USA . Tel. +1 212 554 060/1 800 938 4685 (USA and Canada only). Fax +1 212 586 0248. Email: newyork@eiu.com URL: http://www.eiu.com

Cost: £120/$205

Doing Business In Croatia
One of a series (1998) produced by the CBI as introductions to business practices and environments in CEE countries. Titles are produced to a standard format covering the business context, market potential, business development and building an organisation. Appendices include useful contacts. The advice offered is middle of the road – sensible and with risk avoidance as a priority.

Contact details: VP International, Red Hill House, Hope Street, Chester CH4 8BU, UK. Tel. +44 (0)1244 681619. Fax +44 (0)1244 681617. Email: helen@vpinternational.com URL: hrrp://www.vpinternational.com/

Cost: £30

Dun & Bradstreet Country Report: Croatia
This **annual** report profiles the country in terms of the economy, political situation, financial information, its debts and payment potential, the business climate. There are **monthly** monitoring updates. The report is available on diskette also.

Contact details: Dun & Bradstreet, Holmers Farm Way, High Wycombe, Bucks HP12 3BR, UK. Tel. +44 (0)1494 422 000. Fax +44 (0)1494 422 929.

Cost: £245 (hard copy; diskette); £335 (report + monthly updates).

EBRD Country Profiles: Croatia
The main headings for this **annually** produced report are: economic survey, investment climate, financial sector, multilateral funding, EBRD activities, contact list. The report is prepared for the Annual Meeting of the European Bank for Reconstruction and Development.

Contact details: Effective Technology Marketing, PO Box 171, Grimsby DN35 0TP, UK. Tel/Fax +44 (0)1472 816660.
Email: sales@etmltd.demon.co.uk
URL: http://www.etmltd.demon.co.uk

Cost: £10/$17

Hints to Exporters Visiting Croatia
This is one of a series produced by the Department of Trade and Industry. It is pocket-sized (1998) and covers 'preparation for the visit, travel and currency information, economic factors, import and exchange control, import and exchange control regulations, methods of doing business and a wealth of useful contact points'. The titles are introductory, and form a good basis for understanding differences in business approaches. A criticism of the series as a whole is slowness in revising individual titles.

Contact details: DTI Export Publications Orderline, Admail 528, London SW1W 8YT, UK. Tel. +44 (0)870 1502 500. Fax +44 (0)870 1502 333. Can be ordered online – URL: http://www.dti.gov.uk/ots/publications/export_publications_home.html

Cost: £7

IMF Staff Country Reports: Croatia
The International Monetary Fund monitors the economic and financial affairs of its member countries. A series of reports, updated at irregular intervals, are produced for the consultations and assessments that take place. These appear as reviews of recent economic developments, selected issues and statistical annexes. The result, for each country surveyed, is a useful source of general and specialised knowledge of the economy, with an emphasis upon financial issues. The reports can be downloaded from the Internet.

Contact details: IMF Publication Services, 700 19th Street, NM, Washington DC 20431, USA. Tel. +1 202 623 7430. Fax +1 202 623 7201. Email: pubweb@imf.org URL: http://www.imf.org/external/pubs/pubs/dist.htm In the UK – The Stationery Office, PO Box 276, London SW8 5DT, UK. Tel. +44 (0)870 600 5522. Fax +44 (0)20 7873 8247. URL: http://www.tso-online.co.uk

Cost: $15

Investment and Business Guide: Croatia
This introductory **annual** source provides 'basic information on economy, business and investment climate and opportunities, export-import, industrial development, banking and finance, government and business, contacts'. All from the point of view of those contemplating doing business in the country. Readable and informative.

Contact details: Russian Information and Business Center, PO Box 15343, Washington DC 20003, USA. Tel. +1 202 546 2103. Fax +1 202 546 3275. Email: rusline@erols.com URL: http://www.rusline.com/

Cost: $89

Political Risk Services: Country Reports: Croatia
Reports in this series are produced **annually.** They include 'fact sheets' of basic national data, background information, 'eighteen month and five year forecasts' indicating the risks that lie ahead, profiles of individuals likely to influence the business climate. The attendant hype suggests that 'this may be the only site you will ever need for country research'. Arguable, but not too far off the mark. The publishers maintain an especially informative web site.

Contact details: The PRS Group, 6320 Fly Road, Suite 102, East Syracuse, NY 13057-0248, USA. Tel. +1 315 431 0511. Fax +1 315 431 0200. URL: http://www.prsgroup.com/

Cost: $395

Current Developments

There is no difficulty in following current events in Croatia through English language sources. Many of the current sources mentioned in the opening general category also report on current business and political events in the country.

Business Operations Report: Croatia
This is a **quarterly** analysis of the wide range of local and other factors bearing upon business decisions. Examples of such factors are: labour relations, the expected impact of political changes, assessments of future developments. Lessons are drawn from informative case studies. There are supporting statistics. The *Report* is 'also available through on line databases, direct network feeds and the Internet'.

Contact details: Economist Intelligence Unit, 15 Regent Street, London SW1Y 4LR, UK. Tel. +44 (0)20 7830 1000. Fax +44 (0)20 7499 9767 URL: http://www.eiu.com

Cost: £315 pa

Country Reports: Croatia
The *Reports* are produced **quarterly.** Each issue describes the political and economic structures, reviews political and economic prospects for the next 12 - 18 months, critically reviews major economic and political issues. Economic trends are illustrated with graphs and tables, and there are a number of statistical appendices.

Contact details: Economist Intelligence Unit, 15 Regent Street, London SW1Y 4LR, UK. Tel. +44 (0)20 7830 1000. Fax +44 (0)20 7499 9767 URL:http://www.eiu.com
In the US: Economist Intelligence Unit, The Economist Building, 111 West 57th Street, NY, NY 10019, USA . Tel. +1 212 554 060/1 800 938 4685 (USA and Canada only). Fax +1 212 586 0248. Email: newyork@eiu.com URL: http://www.eiu.com

Cost: £235/$425 pa The *Country Profile* **annual** is included in the sub-scription.

Country Risk Service: Croatia
The *Risk Service* takes a two-year 'forecasting horizon' on a **quarterly** basis when presenting assessments of political, economic and financial risks likely to influence business activities. Future trends of 'over 180 major economic indicators' are presented.

Contact details: Economist Intelligence Unit, 15 Regent Street, London SW1Y 4LR, UK. Tel. +44 (0)20 7830 1000. Fax +44 (0)20 7499 9767 URL: http://www.eiu.com

Cost: £395 pa

Country RiskLines: Croatia
This **monthly**, brief, report (usually 4 pages) rates the risk of trading with the country in terms of earnings and international payment obligations, political and economic stability, investment climate, etc.

Contact details: Dun & Bradstreet, Holmers Farm Way, High Wycombe, Bucks HP12 3BR, UK. Tel. +44 (0)1494 422 000. Fax +44 (0)1494 422 929.

Cost: £35 pa

Croatian News Agency
The Agency provides English language news items on a **daily** basis. The coverage is general. It is available on the Internet, by mail, and fax.

Contact details: Croatian News Agency, Maruličev trg. 16, 10000 Zagreb, Croatia. Tel. +385 1 480 8700. Fax +385 1 480 8820. Email: almanah@hina.hr URL: http://www.hina.hr

Cost: On application.

Monitor: Croatian Economic Indicators
This **monthly** service re-presents the statistical material supplied by the official data gathering agencies. The value-added component is the criti-cal interpretation provided.

Contact details: Data Press, Cvijete Zuzorić 37, 10000 Zagreb, Croatia. Tel/Fax +385 1 66 00 763. Email: sanja.rapaic@zg.tel.hr

Cost: DEM220 pa

Companies and Contacts

In this sector of information provision local producers have made a significant impact with competing products and use of the Internet.

Croatian Almanac
This **annual** directory provides sectoral lists of selected companies, as well a general review of the economy and of developments in the financial sector. It is available in print, in CD-ROM format, and on the Internet.

Contact details: Croatian News Agency, Maruličev trg. 16, 10000 Zagreb, Croatia. Tel. +385 1 480 8700. Fax +385 1 480 8820. Email: almanah@hina.hr URL: http://www.hina.hr

Cost: $35 (print); $35 (CD-ROM); £25 (Internet).

Croatian Business Directory 1997
This **annual** profiles over 15,000 companies. Company data include addresses, phone/fax numbers, names of top personnel, number of employees, product/service descriptions. There are supporting indexes. It is available in print, in CD-ROM format, and on the Internet.

Contact details: Masmedia, 13 Ulica baruna Trenka, 10000 Zagreb, Croatia. Tel. +385 1 457 7400. Fax +385 1 457 7769. Email: masmedia@zg.tel.hr URL: http://www.tel.hr/masmedia

Cost: $140 (hard copy); $200 (CD-ROM); $150 (Internet).

Croatian Business Pages
This Internet site, maintained by Abacus Varazdin, lists Croatian companies and organisations. The data are basically descriptive, with promotional intent; enough for initial contacts.

Contact details: URL: http://www.hrvatska.com/company.html

Kompass Croatia
One of the major directories (5th edition, 1999) listing details of over 16,000 companies. Company profiles include, for example, names of top personnel, addresses and other contact data, number of employees, annual turnover, activity descriptors, trade marks. There are supporting indexes.

Contact details: Kompass UK, Reed Information Services, Windsor Court, East Grinstead House, East Grinstead, West Sussex RH19 1XA, UK. Tel. +44 (0)1342 326 972. Fax +44 (0)1342 335 612.

Cost: £300

Industries and Services

Apart from the financial and banking sector there are no sectoral sources worthy of note. Sectoral information has to be sought from the agencies listed under Organisations below.

Finance and Banking

Banka Magazine

This **bi-monthly** magazine produced by Zagrebacka Bank reports on banking, finance, capital markets and foreign investment issues. There are also more general items of business news.

Contact details: Zagrebacka Bank, Savska 62, Zagreb 10000, Croatia.Tel. +385 1 611 7561. Fax +385 1 611 7657. URL: http://www.banka-mzb.tel.hr/banka-mzb/

Cost: DEM 144 pa.

Insurance and Reinsurance Companies in the Republic of Croatia

This directory (1998) is a sectoral listing providing locational data and activities information.

Contact details: Croatian Insurance Bureau, 73 Marticeva Street, 10000 Zagreb, Croatia. Tel. +385 1 461 6755. Fax +385 1 461 6757.

Cost: Free on application

National Bank of Croatia

The Bank publishes a **quarterly** *Bulletin* which surveys developments in the banking and financial sectors, and other monetary institutions. A range of general economic statistics are also provided.

Contact details: National Bank of Croatia, trg Burze 3, 10000 Zagreb, Croatia. Tel. +385 1 456 4555. Fax +385 1 461 0591. URL: http://www.nbh.hr/

Zagreb Stock Exchange

The Stock Exchange now has a web site with pages of daily reports, basic information for foreign investors, legislation (*Securities Act* and *Investment Funds Act*), banking and finance news, CROBEX – the Zagreb Stock Exchange share price index, information about the Zagreb Stock Exchange. There are links to other sources of information about Croatia.

Contact details: URL: http://www.zse.hr/

Legislation

English translations of business laws are accessible. Problems can usually be solved by application to the Institute of Public Finance and/or the various agencies mentioned below.

Business Law Handbook: Croatia

This *Handbook* is updated **annually** to take account of changes in the laws and regulations governing business activities generally, and those of foreigners in particular. A readable introduction for the layman.

Contact details: Russian Information and Business Center, PO Box 15343, Washington DC 20003, USA. Tel. +1 202 546 2103. Fax +1 202 546 3275. Email: rusline@erols.com URL: http://www.rusline.com/

Cost: $89

Croatian Income Tax and Profit Tax Acts

The two acts, in English translation, have an obvious bearing upon business activities. Published in 1997.

Contact details: Institute of Public Finance, ul Kantančićeva 5, 10000 Zagreb, Croatia. Tel. +385 1 459 1227. Fax +385 1 481 9365. URL: http://www.iff.hr/

Cost: DEM 45

Croatian Value Added Tax Act

The full text of this Act is translated into English and German.

Contact details: Institute of Public Finance, ul Kantančićeva 5, 10000 Zagreb, Croatia. Tel. +385 1 459 1227. Fax +385 1 481 9365. URL: http://www.iff.hr/

Cost: DEM 30.

Organisations

There are a number of organisations willing to assist business people, but the prime source is the Chamber of Economy. All enterprises have to be members of this body – a requirement that is a hangover from the 'old' days and has more to do with control rather than the furthering of business efficiency.

American Embassy

Will respond to enquiries. A newsy Internet site.

Contact details: U.S. Embassy, Andrije Hebranga 2, 10000 Zagreb, Croatia. Tel. +385 1 455 5500. Fax +385 1 440 235. URL: http://www.usembassy.hr

British Embassy
Provides advice, guidance and support when asked. Office hours: Summer: Monday to Thursday 06.30-15.00. Friday 06.00-112.00. Winter: Monday to Friday 08.00-16.00.

Contact details: British Embassy, Vlaska 121/III Floor, PO Box 454, 10000 Zagreb, Croatia. Tel. +385 1 455 5310. Fax +385 1 455 1685, +385 1 449 834. Email: british-embassy@zg.tel.hr

Central Bureau of Statistics
The Bureau publishes a wide range of statistics. Among the most useful titles are, for example, *Statistical Yearbook* and *Monthly Statistical Reports*. For travellers there is the concise pocket-sized *Statistical Information*. The Bureau's informative Internet site provides details of all its publications. The Bureau welcomes enquiries for data not available in its summarising publication.

Contact details: CBS, Ilica 3, POB 671, 10000 Zagreb, Croatia. Tel. +385 1 455 4422. Fax +385 1 429 413. Email: markovicl@dzs.hr URL: http://www.dzs.hr/Eng/Default.htm

Croatian Chamber of Economy
The result of compulsory membership is a Business Register with well over a 100,000 companies. The Register is not available for public scrutiny. It can be accessed only through the Chamber. It makes sense, therefore, to direct initial company enquiries to the Chamber. Such approaches are welcomed. In its promotional armoury is the **monthly** *Croatian Outlook* which reviews business, financial and economic developments in, generally, a hopeful light. Probably the most helpful source is *How To Do Business In Croatia*, freely available on the Chamber's Internet site. The pages cover, for example, country background information, economic data, business laws, the position of foreign investors, incentives to invest.

Contact details: Croatian Chamber of Commerce, Rooseveltov trg. 2, 10000 Zagreb, Croatia. Tel. +385 1 456 1555. Fax +385 1 448 618. URL: http://www.hgk.hr

Croatian Privatisation Fund
Formed in 1994 from a merger of two previously separate promotional and development agencies. The Fund will accept enquiries from foreign business people with an interest in properties and businesses likely to be privatised.

Contact details: Croatian Privatisation Fund, Gajeva 30A, 10000 Zagreb, Croatia. Tel. +385 1 469 168. Fax +385 1 469 138.

Croatian Ministry of Finance

The Ministry publishes *Monthly Statistical Review*. It carries analyses of developments in national taxation and government finances, as well as providing a range of macroeconomic indicators. Some statistics are available on the Ministry's Internet site.

Contact details: Ministry of Finance, ul Kantančićeva 5, 10000 Zagreb, Croatia. Tel. +385 1 459 1392. Fax +385 1 459 1393. URL: http://www.mfin.her/stat

Cost: On application.

Embassy of the Republic of Croatia: UK

Can be approached on business issues.

Contact details: Embassy of the Republic of Croatia, 21 Conway Street, London W1P 5HL, UK. Tel. +44 (0)20 7387 1790. Fax +44 (0)20 7387 3269.

Embassy of the Republic of Croatia: USA

The Embassy's web site provides country information, news and a section on Business and Economy.

Contact details: Embassy of the Republic of Croatia, 2343 Massachusetts Avenue, NW, Washington DC 20008, USA. Tel. +1 202 588 5899. Fax +1 202 588 8936. Email: webmaster@croatiaemb.org URL: http://croatiaemb.org

Chapter 6

Czech Republic

Population 10.3m. Earlier promising economic developments have slowed down. A flat economy, with no growth predicted for 1999, and rising unemployment have diminished optimism. Inflation, although falling, is still high. The banking sector awaits fundamental reform. However, most analysts predict a brighter future for this, one of the better organised CEE economies and among the first six applicant countries now negotiating for accession to the European Union.

The business information pattern reflects the relative economic progressiveness of the country. For example, there are numerous Internet sites, while the provision of company information is more extensive than is found in the majority of CEE countries. The range of business information sources, produced internally and externally, is wide and varied, with all the signs of high levels of competition. The array of statistical data is impressive and improving rapidly in methodological terms. These observations apply to the English language sector; the parallel Czech language sector is even better provided for.

Overview

Country information is available in abundance, and from widely different types of information sources. In all CEE countries there is growing use of the Internet to provide general information and data that contribute to improved awareness of the cultural, historical and political influences that have shaped the current business environment. Insensitivity to such factors can antagonise, as numerous early experiences of over-eager western business people discovered to their cost. The country information sources listed below are a selection only. Any one should produce enough relevant information to prepare for business trips to the Czech Republic. For those averse to print-on-paper, the use of Internet services should gather in masses of information in a short time.

Business Investment Opportunity Yearbook: Czech Republic
This **annual** covers 'business, investment, export-import, economic and other opportunities in respected countries. Foreign economic assistance projects, sources of financing , strategic government and business contacts, and more ...'. The annual publication cycle precludes 'hot' investment

news.The series titles, of which this is one, cover numerous countries throughout the world. In the circumstances it is difficult to know what weight to attach to the description 'respected'.

Contact details: Russian Information and Business Center, PO Box 15343, Washington DC 20003, USA. Tel. +1 202 546 2103. Fax +1 202 546 3275. Email: rusline@erols.com URL: http://www.rusline.com/

Cost: $89

Country Commercial Guide: Czech Republic
Titles in the *Guides* series are published annually. They review the country's commercial environment 'using economic, political and market analysis', and 'consolidate various reporting documents prepared for the U.S.Embassies community'. There are informative sections on the investment climate, trade regulations and standards, economic trends and outlook, and useful summary statistics in appendices. A good country introduction. Available on the Internet, in hard copy and as a diskette.

Contact details: URL: http://www.stat-usa.gov/Newstand

Cost: $20 (hard copy)

Country Profile: Czech Republic
This **annual** publication is a standard reference source. Comment, analysis and statistics cover the main industrial sectors, economic policies, political background, population, finance, prices and wages – with remarkable succinctness.

Contact details: Economist Intelligence Unit, 15 Regent Street, London SW1Y 4LR, UK. Tel. +44 (0)20 7830 1000. Fax +44 (0)20 7499 9767. Email: london@eiu.com URL: http://www.eiu.com
In the US: Economist Intelligence Unit, The Economist Building, 111 West 57th Street, NY, NY 10019, USA . Tel. +1 212 554 060/1 800 938 4685 (USA and Canada only). Fax +1 212 586 0248. Email: newyork@eiu.com URL: http://www.eiu.com

Cost: £120/$205

Czech Business Navigator
An extensive web site with links to a further 800. The Business Section includes financial, stock market, export-import, sectoral information.

Contact details: URL: http://dvorak.mcs.cz/navig

Czech Happenings
An Internet site with information on all aspects of Czech life – summaries of press reports, trading on the Prague Stock Exchange, cultural news,

economic reports, political developments. There are links to other relevant sites.

Contact details: URL: http://www.ctknews.com/index/html

Czech International Market
An expansive Internet site covering, for example, real estate, banking, taxes and auditing, culture, health care, history.

Contact details: URL: http://www.russia.cz/iii/

Czech Welcome Page
This Internet site provides an introduction to the country for business people and general enquirers.

Contact details: URL: http://www.czech.cz/

Dun & Bradstreet Country Report: Czech Republic
This **annual** report profiles the country in terms of the economy, political situation, financial information, its debts and payment potential, the business climate. There are **monthly** monitoring updates. The report is available on diskette also.

Contact details: Dun & Bradstreet, Holmers Farm Way, High Wycombe, Bucks HP12 3BR, UK. Tel. +44 (0)1494 422 000. Fax +44 (0)1494 422 929.

Cost: £245 (hard copy; diskette); £335 (report + monthly updates).

EBRD Country Profiles: Czech Republic
The main headings for this **annually** produced report are – economic survey, investment climate, financial sector, multilateral funding, EBRD activities, contact list. The report is prepared for the Annual Meeting of the European Bank for Reconstruction and Development.

Contact details: Effective Technology Marketing, PO Box 171, Grimsby DN35 0TP, UK. Tel/Fax +44 (0)1472 816660. Email: sales@etmltd.demon.co.uk URL: http://www.etmltd.demon.co.uk

Cost: £10/$17

IMF Staff Country Reports: Czech Republic
The International Monetary Fund monitors the economic and financial affairs of its member countries. A series of reports, updated at irregular intervals, are produced for the consultations and assessments that take place. These appear as reviews of recent economic developments, selected issues and statistical annexes. The result, for each country surveyed, is a useful source of general and specialised knowledge of the economy, with an emphasis upon financial issues. The reports can be downloaded from the Internet.

Contact details: IMF Publication Services, 700 19th Street, NM, Washington DC 20431, USA. Tel. +1 202 623 7430. Fax +1 202 623 7201. Email: pubweb@imf.org URL: http://www.imf.org/external/pubs/pubs/dist.htm In the UK – The Stationery Office, PO Box 276, London SW8 5DT, UK. Tel. +44 (0)870 600 5522. Fax +44 (0)20 7873 8247. URL: http://www.tso-online.co.uk

Cost: $15

Investment and Business Guide: Czech Republic
This introductory **annual** source provides 'basic information on economy, business and investment climate and opportunities, export-import, industrial development, banking and finance, government and business, contacts'. All from the point of view of those contemplating doing business in the country. Readable and informative.

Contact details: Russian Information and Business Center, PO Box 15343, Washington DC 20003, USA. Tel. +1 202 546 2103. Fax +1 202 546 3275. Email: rusline@erols.com URL: http://www.rusline.com/

Cost: $89

Political Risk Services: Country Reports: Czech Republic
Reports in this series are produced **annually.** They include 'fact sheets' of basic national data, background information, 'eighteen month and five year forecasts' indicating the risks that lie ahead, profiles of individuals likely to influence the business climate. The attendant hype suggests that 'this may be the only site you will ever need for country research'. Arguable, but not too far off the mark. The publishers maintain an especially informative web site.

Contact details: The PRS Group, 6320 Fly Road, Suite 102, East Syracuse, NY 13057-0248, USA. Tel. +1 315 431 0511. Fax +1 315 431 0200. URL: http://www.prsgroup.com/

Cost: $395

World of Information Country Report: Czech Republic
A concise **annual** report reviewing the economic and political scene, with selected supporting statistics. Ideal for quick familiarisation.

Contact details: Walden Publishing, 2 Market Street, Saffron Walden, Essex CB10 1HZ, UK. Tel. +44 (0)1799 521150. Fax +44 (0)1799 524805.

Cost: £30/$65

Current Developments

This is a lively sector with numerous competing sources and a strong local presence.

Business Operations Report: Czech Republic
This is a **quarterly** analysis of the wide range of local and other factors bearing upon business decisions. Examples of such factors are: labour relations, the expected impact of political changes, assessments of future developments. Lessons are drawn from informative case studies. There are supporting statistics. The *Report* is 'also available through on line databases, direct network feeds and the Internet'.

Contact details: Economist Intelligence Unit, 15 Regent Street, London SW1Y 4LR, UK. Tel. +44 (0)20 7830 1000. Fax +44 (0)20 7499 9767 URL: http://www.eiu.com

Cost: £315 pa

Country Forecasts: Czech Republic
This **quarterly** source presents 'five-year forecasts of political, economic and business trends'. Issues examined include, for example, prospects for political stability, business operating climate, government economic policies, labour market developments, sectoral matters.

Contact details: Economist Intelligence Unit, 15 Regent Street, London SW1Y 4LR, UK. Tel. +44 (0)20 7 830 1000. Fax +44 (0)20 7 499 9767 URL: http://www.eiu.com

Cost: £450 pa

Country Reports: Czech Republic
The *Reports* are produced **quarterly.** Each issue describes the political and economic structures, reviews political and economic prospects for the next 12 - 18 months, critically reviews major economic and political issues. Economic trends are illustrated with graphs and tables, and there a a number of statistical appendices.

Contact details: Economist Intelligence Unit, 15 Regent Street, London SW1Y 4LR, UK. Tel. +44 (0)20 7830 1000. Fax +44 (0)20 7499 9767 Email: london@eiu.com URL:http://www.eiu.com
In the US: Economist Intelligence Unit, The Economist Building, 111 West 57th Street, NY, NY 10019, USA . Tel. +1 212 554 060/1 800 938 4685 (USA and Canada only). Fax +1 212 586 0248. Email: newyork@eiu.com URL: http://www.eiu.com

Cost: £235/$425 pa. The *Country Profile* annual is included in the subscription.

Country Risk Service: Czech Republic

The *Risk Service* takes a two-year 'forecasting horizon' on a **quarterly** basis when presenting assessments of political, economic and financial risks likely to influence business activities. Future trends of 'over 180 major economic indicators' are presented.

Contact details: Economist Intelligence Unit, 15 Regent Street, London SW1Y 4LR, UK. Tel. +44 (0)20 7830 1000. Fax +44 (0)20 7499 9767 Email: london@eiu.com URL:http://www.eiu.com
In the US: Economist Intelligence Unit, The Economist Building, 111 West 57th Street, NY, NY 10019, USA . Tel. +1 212 554 060/1 800 938 4685 (USA and Canada only). Fax +1 212 586 0248. Email: newyork@eiu.com URL: http://www.eiu.com

Cost: £395/$565 pa

Country RiskLines: Czech Republic

This **monthly,** brief, report (usually 4 pages) rates the risk of trading with the country in terms of earnings and international payment obligations, political and economic stability, investment climate, etc.

Contact details: Dun & Bradstreet, Holmers Farm Way, High Wycombe, Bucks HP12 3BR, UK. Tel. +44 (0)1494 422 000. Fax +44 (0)1494 422 929.

Cost: £35 pa

Czech A.M.

This is a **daily** news digest. The coverage, in the briefest form, is general, taking in business, politics, the economy, significant domestic news, the stock exchange. Available by fax or email.

Contact details: VP International, Red Hill House, Hope Street, Chester CH4 8BU, UK. Tel +44 (0)1244 681619. Email: helen@vpinternational.com URL: http://www.vpinternational.com/

Cost: £495 pa

Czech Info Centre

This web site has a substantial business directory reporting current commercial and economic issues, highlighting selected companies and their activities, etc. It also has a great deal of data and information about the Republic.

Contact details: URL: http://www.muselik.com/czech/frame.html

Fleet Sheet

For business people who have little time to read this could be the answer – business and political news abstracted from major Czech newspapers, translated into English, and summarised on to a single page. It is a **daily** fax service.

Contact details: E.S.Best, Opletalova 39, 13011 Prague, Czech Republic. Tel. +420 2 2210 5515. Fax +420 2 2422 1580.

Cost: Varies according to delivery time – 9a.m. delivery costs 89CzK.

Investing, Licensing and Trading: Czech Republic
This service consists of 'one main report and an updater six months later'. It is a guide to operating conditions covering such topics as foreign trade regulations, the legal requirements when setting up a company, the licensing of trading activities, private and personal taxation, labour laws and practices. The report is available in print format and is also 'available through online databases, direct network feeds and the Internet'.

Contact details: Economist Intelligence Unit, 15 Regent Street, London SW1Y 4LR, UK. Tel. +44 (0)20 7830 1000. Fax +44 (0)20 7499 9767 URL: Email: london@eiu.com http://www.eiu.com
In the US: Economist Intelligence Unit, The Economist Building, 111 West 57th Street, NY, NY 10019, USA . Tel. +1 212 554 060/1 800 938 4685 (USA and Canada only). Fax +1 212 586 0248. Email: newyork@eiu.com URL: http://www.eiu.com

Cost: £225/$310 pa

Prague Business Journal
This **weekly** source monitors economic and financial developments, provides sectoral and stock exchange news, as well as general news with a bearing upon business operations and foreign investments.

Contact details: VP International, Red Hill House, Hope Street, Chester, CH4 8BU, UK. Tel. +44 (0)1244 681619. Fax +44 (0)1244 681617. Email: helen@vpinternational.com URL: http://www.vpinternational.com

Cost: £130 pa (UK) ; $195 pa (Europe); $205 pa (elsewhere).

Prague Post
This **weekly** newspaper reports on all aspects of Czech life, and is strong on monitoring commercial, industrial and financial event. Available online on the online host service GENIOS.

Contact details: Prague Post, Na Pǒříčí 12, 11530 Prague 1, Czech Republic. Tel. +420 2 2487 5000. Fax +420 2 2487 5050.

Cost: $105 pa (Europe); $150 pa (elsewhere).

Companies and Contacts

This is another well-supplied sector with a very strong contingent of locally produced sources.

Albertina Company Register

This database on CD-ROM lists all registered companies in the Czech Republic and Slovakia, not far off 2 million enterprises in all. Company data consists of contact details, legal status, business activity, annual turnover, 'records of companies that owe money'. The CD-ROM has search and printing facilities. **Monthly** updates are available.

Contact details: Albertina Data, Malé náměsti 3, 110 01 Prague 1, Czech Republic. Tel. +420 2 260 217. Fax +420 2 264 602. URL: http://www.albertina.cz

Cost: 2500Kc.

Albertina Financial Profiles

This is a database of over 6000 annual balance sheets and accounts of Czech companies. There are **monthly** updates.

Contact details: Albertina Data, Malé náměsti 3, 110 01 Prague 1, Czech Republic. Tel. +420 2 260 217. Fax +420 2 264 602. URL: http://www.albertina.cz

Cost: 2500Kc

Czech Business Directory

A promotional Internet site with descriptions of a limited range of companies. The latter are broadly classified – car rental companies, computer networking companies, heating systems, real estate companies.

Contact details: URL: http://muselik.com/czech/business/directory

Czech Company Profiles (CFR)

The profiles are compiled by Inform Katalog and made available online on GENIOS, the German online host. The details do not include financial data, but cover locational and contact data, legal form, management names, legal form, foundation date, product descriptions and activities.

Contact details: GENIOS Wirtschaftsdatenbanken, Postfach 101102, Dusseldorf, D-40002 Germany. Tel. +49 211 887 1524. Fax +49 211 887 1520. Email: info@genios.de URL: http://www.genios.de/

Cost: On application.

Czech Exporters 1999

This **annual** profiles around 2000 companies. The detail is basic, enough for intitial contact. It is available in hard copy, on the Internet and as a CD-ROM.

Contact details: Inform Katalog, Šumavská 31, 612 54 Brno, Czech Republic. Tel. +420 5 4121 1428. Fax +420 5 4121 3658. URL: http://www.inform.cz/

Cost: On application

Czech Information Centre

The Centre maintains an Internet site which includes a *Business Directory* – a sectoral list of companies. The detail available is of the telephone directory type – names, address, contact numbers.

Contact details: URL: http://www.muselik.com/czech/cbd.html

Foreign Companies in Emerging Markets Yearbook: Czech Republic

This **annual** lists the numerous foreign companies operating in the Republic, highlighting their potential as buyers and suppliers. The company details are standard including, for example, contact data, business activity descriptions, sales volumes. Available in hard copy and CD-ROM formats.

Contact details: Business Monitor International, 179 Queen Victoria Street, London EC4V 4DU, UK. Tel. +44 (0)20 7248 0468. Fax +44 (0)20 7248 0467. URL: http://www.businessmonitor.com

Cost: £240/$390 (print); £390/$650 (CD-ROM)

Inform Base: Czech Republic

Over 17,000 companies are listed in this CD-ROM. The company information is basic, but the value of this type of source is in its print facilities. The CD-ROM can be purchased for viewing only; but it can be purchased in a version that prints labels; or, if needed, in a version that, additonally, prints complete company profiles. The cost will vary according to specification.

Contact details: VP International, Red Hill House, Hope Street, Chester CH4 8BU, UK. Tel. +44 (0)1244 681619. Fax +44 (0)1244 681617. Email: helen@vpinternational.com URL: hrrp://www.vpinternational.com/

Cost: £75/$115 (view only – Europe), $125 (view only – outside Europe); £150/$225 (print labels – Europe), $235 (print labels – outside Europe); £270/$405 (company profiles – Europe), $415 (company profiles – outside Europe).

Inform Katalog: Czech Republic
One of the most extensive **annual** directories. Over 20,000 firms are pro-filed in terms of locational, personal contact and activites data. The *Katalog* comes in two volumes. The first is an alphabetical listing, the second has enterprises grouped by the standard industrial classification. Available in hard copy and CD-ROM formats, and online through GENIOS. A larger number of companies is listed on Inform Katalog's Internet site.

Contact details: VP International, Red Hill House, Hope Street, Chester CH4 8BU, UK. Tel. +44 (0)1244 681619. Fax +44 (0)1244 681617. Email: helen@vpinternational.com URL: hrrp://www.vpinternational.com/

Cost: £70/$105 (Europe); $115 (elsewhere)

Inform Katalog Export 1998/1999
Over 4000 exporting and importing firms are listed and described in ba-sic contact data style.

Contact details: VP International, Red Hill House, Hope Street, Chester CH4 8BU, UK. Tel. +44 (0)1244 681619. Fax +44 (0)1244 681617. Email: helen@vpinternational.com URL: hrrp://www.vpinternational.com/

Cost: £50/$75 (Europe); $85 (elsewhere).

Kompass Czech Republic
A major listing (8th edition, 1999) of over 15,000 firms. The company profiles consist of contact details, names of top personnel, number of em-ployees, bank details, annual turnover, products and activities. Trade marks are listed.

Contact details: Kompass UK, Reed Information International, Windsor Court, East Grinstead House, East Grinstead, West Sussex RH19 1XA, UK. Tel. +44 (0)1342 326972. Fax +44 (0)1342 335612.

Cost: £305

Prague Business Journal Book of Lists
This **annual** profiles over 2000 companies, and is updated at quarterly intervals. The data provided are basic for contact purposes.

Contact details: VP International, Red Hill House, Hope Street, Chester, CH4 8BU, UK. Tel. +44 (0)1244 681619. Fax +44 (0)1244 681617. Email: helen@vpinternational.com URL: http://www.vpinternational.com

Cost: $29.95

Prague Post Book of Business Lists
This **annual** lists over 1500 companies in broad classified groups. The company data provided are basic locational and contact, with number of employees, activity descriptions and latest turnover figures.

Contact details: The Prague Post, Na Poříčí 12, 115 30 Prague 1, Czech Repubic. Tel. +420 2 2487 5000. Fax +420 2 2487 5050. Email: subscriptions@praguepost.cz

Cost: £19.95

Resources 1000
This **annual** directory lists the top 1000 companies assessed on profits, number of employees and revenue. The company profiles include contact details of top personnel, locational data, and statistics to support and explain their ratings. There are updating arrangements. A CD-ROM is also available.

Contact details: Resources, Ječná 39, 12000 Prague, Czech Republic. Tel. +420 2 2494 1800. Fax +420 2 2494 3084. URL: http://www.resources.cz/

Cost: $95 (directory only); $175 (directory + 3 updates); $270 (CD-ROM); $520 (CD-ROM + 4 updates)

Industries and Services
The provision of English language sectoral sources has developed quickly. Examples are:

Agriculture
Agricultural Situation and Perspectives in the Central and East European Countries: Czech Republic
This report, from the European Union, 'aims to provide an analysis of the current situation and the medium-term outlook for the agricultural and agri-food industries' in the CEE countries aiming for EU membership – Bulgaria, Czech Republic, Hungary, Poland, Romania, Slovakia, Slovenia. The report is freely available on the Internet.

Contact details: URL: http://www.europa.eu.int/comm/dg06/publi/peco.index-en.htm

Automotive
Czech and Slovak Automotive Industries
Reviews (1997) and analyses the activities and performance of the major companies in the sector in comparative fashion. There is a directory of addresses and contacts of the main operators.

Contact details: FT Automotive, Maple House, 149 Tottenham Court Road, London W1P 9LL, UK. Tel. +44 (0)20 7896 2241. Fax +44 (0)20 7896 2275. URL: http://www.ftauto.com/

Cost: £395/$672

Chemicals

Czech Chemical Guide
This provides profiles of over 2300 enterprises, providing locational and contact data, activity descriptions, turnover, profit and sales figures. Also includes more than 900 foreign firms, a classification index of 123 product groups and 9 additional indexes. There are diskette and CD-ROM versions with search and print facilities.

Contact details: EXIN, Šeřikova 32, 63700 Brno, Czech Republic. Tel. +420 5 4323.6040 1. Fax +420 5 4122 0005. Email: exin@exin.cz URL: http://www.exin.cz/

Cost: 50 EUR (hard copy); 140 EUR (diskette/CD-ROM)

Czech Plastics and Rubber Guide
This **annual** profiles almost 1900 enterprises, and lists more than 440 foreign firms. Locational and contact data are given, together with brief descriptive detail. Available on diskette or CD-ROM with search and printing facilities.

Contact details: EXIN, Šeřikova 32, 63700 Brno, Czech Republic. Tel. +420 5 4323.6040 1. Fax +420 5 4122 0005. Email: exin@exin.cz URL: http://www.exin.cz/

Cost: 50 EUR (hard copy); 140 EUR (diskette/CD-ROM)

Construction

Czech and Slovak Construction Journal
This **monthly** is a standard monitoring and reporting source for the field, covering all aspects of the construction industry including, for example, building regulations, stock market movements, land purchases.

Contact details: Roberts Publishing, Husenická 33, 13000 Prague 3, Czech Republic. Tel. +420 2 628 4348. Fax +420 2 627 8643. Email: mclean@ini.cz

Czech Construction: Sector Analysis Report
An **annual** report, one of a series compiled by Aspekt Kilcullen. The main companies in the sector are analysed, with close attention to financial data – balance sheets, profit and loss statements, audit results, returns on equity, financial liquidity, profit margins, etc. Individual company analyses are related to likely future scenarios.

Contact details: VP International, Red Hill House, Hope Street, Chester, CH4 8BU, UK. Tel. +44 (0)1244 681619. Fax +44 (0)1244 681617. Email: helen@vpinternational.com URL: http://www.vpinternational.com

Cost: £299/$450

Facts About Construction Growth in Czech Republic
This report (1999) 'contains information about construction activity and forecasts of future trends [focusing on] the civil engineering sector, office and housing, retail and industrial construction trends and includes information about price levels, vacancy rates and yields'. The socio-economic structure is described, and numerous statistical indicators provided.

Contact details: European Construction Research, Bredgade 35B, DK-1260 Copenhagen K, Denmark. Tel. +45 33 162 100. Fax +45 33 162 900. Email: ecr@CYBERNET.DK URL: http://www.epi.no/ecr/index.htm

Cost: £98/$145

Engineering

Czech Engineering: Sector Analysis Report
An **annual** report, one of a series compiled by Aspekt Kilcullen. The main companies in the sector are analysed, with close attention to financial data – balance sheets, profit and loss statements, audit results, returns on equity, financial liquidity, profit margins, etc. Individual company analyses are related to likely future scenarios.

Contact details: VP International, Red Hill House, Hope Street, Chester CH4 8BU, UK. Tel. +44 (0)1244 681619. Fax +44 (0)1244 681617. Email: helen@vpinternational.com URL: http://www.vpinternational.com

Cost: £299/$450 (Europe); $460 (elsewhere).

Finance and Banking

Akcie.cz
This Internet site monitors changes in the capital markets, and provides company information.

Contact details: URL: http://www.akcie.cz/default.asp?LV=2

CSOB Newsletter
This **quarterly** is a bank publication with gravitas. Financial and investment issues are discussed at some length. The brief, breathless, alerting style of the standard newsletter is not attempted.

Contact details: Československá Obchodní Banka, Department of Communication, Na Příkopě 14, 115-20 Prague 1, Czech Republic. Tel. +42 02 2411 2126. Fax +42 02 2411 2240.

Cost: Free on application.

Czech National Bank
The Bank's Internet site provides general country information, monetary indicators and banking sector data.

Contact details: URL: http://www.cnb.cz/en/index.html

The Czech Stock Market Guide and Directory
A convenient **annual** source for data about the Prague Stock Exchange. Top traded companies are profiled, as are important managers and financial personnel. It is updated three times a year.

Contact details: Aspekt Kilcullen, Mikulandská 10, 11000 Prague 1, Czech Republic. Tel. +420 2 2491 4333. Fax +420 2 2491 5677. Email: aspekt@aspekt.cz URL: http://www.aspekt.cz/

Cost: £50

Financing Operations: Czech Republic
This service offers a **quarterly** review of financial conditions reporting on, for example, national monetary policy, banks and other financial institutions, investment incentives, trade financing, various financing techniques. *Financing Operations* is also 'available through on line databases, direct network feeds and the Internet'.

Contact details: Economist Intelligence Unit, 15 Regent Street, London SW1Y 4LR, UK. Tel. +44 (0)20 7830 1000. Fax +44 (0)20 7499 9767 URL: http://www.eiu.com

Cost: £245 pa.

Prague Stock Exchange
Prague Stock Exchange is the **monthly**, free, official information organ of the Stock Exchange. It keeps readers abreast of legislative changes, membership changes, rules of operating, etc. It is distributed by mail and email. With Warsaw the Prague Exchange is regarded as an example of the better run CEE stock exchanges.

Contact details: Prague Stock Exchange, Rybná 14, 11000 Prague 1, Czech Republic. Tel. +420 2 2183 2166. Fax +420 2 2183 3029.

Pharmaceuticals

Czech and Slovak Pharmaceutical Guide
This **annual** lists 1820 enterprises, including individual pharmacies, as well as more than 1150 foreign firms. The company details are basic. Also available on diskette and CD-ROM.

Contact details: EXIN, Šeřikova 32, 63700 Brno, Czech Republic. Tel. +420 5 4323.6040 1. Fax +420 5 4122 0005. Email: exin@exin.cz URL: http://www.exin.z/

Cost: 65 EUR (hard copy); 160 EUR (diskette/CD-ROM)

Czech Pharmaceuticals, Chemicals and Rubber: Sector Analysis Report
This report (1998), produced by Aspekt Kilcullen, provides a list of companies operating in the sectors. It is more than a directory however; for example, it analyses financial ratios of individual companies, examines financial results, compares companies by ratios, assesses the outlook for privatisation.

Contact details: VP International, Red Hill House, Hope Street, Chester CH4 8BU, UK. Tel. +44 (0)1244 681619. Fax +44 (0)1244 681617. Email: helen@vpinternational.com URL: http://www.vpinternational.com

Cost: £299/$450 (Europe); $460 (elsewhere).

Telecommunications

Czech Telecom Weekly
A newsletter that monitors sectoral developments as these appear in the national general and specialist press. It is available in hard copy, email, and fax.

Contact details: VP International, Red Hill House, Hope Street, Chester CH4 8BU, UK. Tel. +44 (0)1244 681619. Fax +44 (0)1244 681617. Email: helen@vpinternational.com URL: http://www.vpinternational.com

Legislation

There's no excuse for being ignorant of Czech business law. English language sources are available in numbers. Examples are:

Accounting Legislation 1998
Contains the *Accounting Act, Chart of Accounts, Accounting Procedures*, translated into English and with a commentary by KPMG. From Trade Links, available through UK agency.

Contact details: VP International, Red Hill House, Hope Street, Chester, CH4 8BU, UK. Tel. +44 (0)1244 681619. Fax +44 (0)1244 681617. Email: helen@vpinternational.com URL: http://www.vpinternational.com

Cost: £40

Bankruptcy and Composition Act, Trades Licensing Act, Act on Prices
The Acts (1998) are fully translated and provided with detailed commentaries. From Trade Links.

Contact details: VP International, Red Hill House, Hope Street, Chester, CH4 8BU, UK. Tel. +44 (0)1244 681619. Fax +44 (0)1244 681617. Email: helen@vpinternational.com URL: http://www.vpinternational.com

Cost: £40

Business Law Handbook: Czech Republic
This *Handbook* is updated **annually** to take account of changes in the laws and regulations governing business activities generally, and those of foreigners in particular. A readable introduction for the layman.

Contact details: Russian Information and Business Center, PO Box 15343, Washington DC 20003, USA. Tel. +1 202 546 2103. Fax +1 202 546 3275. Email: rusline@erols.com URL: http://www.rusline.com/

Cost: $89

Commercial and Investment Law: Czech Republic
A comprehensive compilation of business related laws including, for example, company law, foreign investment regulations, taxation laws. It is updated annually.

Contact details: Juris Publishing, Executive Park, 1 Odell Plaza, Yonkers, NY 10701, USA. Tel. +1 914 375 3400. Fax +1 914 375 6047. Email: orders@jurispub.com URL: http://www.jurispub.com

Cost: $165

Czech Businesses and the EU Law Focus
A booklet (1997) for the layman produced by Cameron McKenna, a law firm with interests in CEE countries. Attention is concentrated upon important legal issues arising from the enlargement of the European Union.

Contact details: Cameron McKenna, Mitre House, 160 Aldersgate Street, London EC1A 4DD, UK. Tel. +44 (0)20 7367 3000. Fax +44 (0)20 7367 2000. Email: info@cmck.com URL: http://www.cmck.com/pub23.htm

Cost: Free on application.

Czech Commercial Code
The Code 'regulates the formation and structure of companies, partnerships, and cooperatives, the business activity of foreign persons, and commercial contracts'. The translation includes a commentary. From Trade Links.

Contact details: VP International, Red Hill House, Hope Street, Chester, CH4 8BU, UK. Tel. +44 (0)1244 681619. Fax +44 (0)1244 681617. Email: helen@vpinternational.com URL: http://www.vpinternational.com

Cost: £45

Czech Financial Services Legislation 1998
This is a compilation consisting of full translations of 12 Acts relating to the financial sector. Among the Acts included are – *Money Laundering Act, Banking Act, Foreign Exchange Act.* From Trade Links.

Contact details: VP International, Red Hill House, Hope Street, Chester, CH4 8BU, UK. Tel. +44 (0)1244 681619. Fax +44 (0)1244 681617. Email: helen@vpinternational URL: http://www.vpinternational.com

Cost: £40

Czech Taxation 1999
All the major legal enactments are fully translated, with introductory commentaries. Among the Acts presented are, for example, *Income Taxes Act, Value Added Tax Act, Act on Reserves.* From Trade Links.

Contact details: VP International, Red Hill House, Hope Street, Chester, CH4 8BU, UK. Tel. +44 (0)1244 681619. Fax +44 (0)1244 681617. Email: helen@vpinternational.com URL: http://www.vpinternational.com

Cost: £45

Environmental Legislation
There are numerous acts aimed at protecting the environment, an increasingly important aspect of business management. Examples are – *Air Protection Act, Act on Waste Dumping Fees, Waste Disposal Act* – only a few of the many. This compilation provides full translations. From Trade Links.

Contact details: VP International, Red Hill House, Hope Street, Chester, CH4 8BU, UK. Tel. +44 (0)1244 681619. Fax +44 (0)1244 681617. Email: helen@vpinternational URL: http://www.vpinternational.com

Cost: £45

Foreign Residents in the Czech Republic
The laws and regulations governing the lives of foreign residents are set out. The compilation (1998) includes the *Act on Foreigners' Stay and Residence*, with information about residents and work permits, business legislation, and extracts from a number of other relevant laws. From Trade Links.

Contact details: VP International, Red Hill House, Hope Street, Chester, CH4 8BU, UK. Tel. +44 (0)1244 681619. Fax +44 (0)1244 681617. Email: helen@vpinternational URL: http://www.vpinternational.com

Cost: £40

Legal Guide: Czech Republic
A layman's guide, from the Department of Trade and Industry, to the more important aspects of business law concentrating especially on the processes of establishing a business. A helpful and informative introduction.

Contact details: DTI, Admail 528, London SW1W 8YT, UK. Tel. +44 (0)171 510 0171. Fax +44 (0)20 7510 0197. URL: http://www.dti.gov.uk/ots/publications

Cost: £12

Real Estate Legislation and the Building Code
Owning land and property, renting accommodation and building are closely governed activities. The laws applying to these activities are set out in this compilation (1999). Some of the operational acts are: *Act on Ownership of Flats, Land Act, Act on Entries of Ownership, Act on Lease and Sub-Lease of Non-Residential Premises.* There is more, of course. From Trade Links.

Contact details: VP International, Red Hill House, Hope Street, Chester, CH4 8BU, UK. Tel. +44 (0)1244 681619. Fax +44 (0)1244 681617. Email: helen@vpinternational URL: http://www.vpinternational.com

Cost: £45

Organisations

The Czech Republic is well organised in the promotional sense with a number of agencies active in encouraging the interest of potential investors. Examples are:

American Embassy
One of the aims of the US Embassy is to 'promote the sale of American goods and services'. It does this by providing information on the Czech market, locating agents and distributors, providing trade leads and counselling on business opportunities, trade barriers and business prospects. The Embassy's Internet site is informative on these and other issues.

Contact details: U.S. Embassy, Commercial Service, Trziste 15, 118 01 Prague, Czech Republic. Tel. +420 2 5753 1162. Fax +420 2 5753 1165. Email: oprague@cs.doc.gov URL: http://www.usis.cz/

British Embassy
Provides advice and information. Office hours: end March to end September 06.30-15.00. End September to end March 07.30-16.00.

Contact details: British Embassy, Thunovská 14, 118 00 Prague 1, Czech Republic. Tel. +420 2 5732, +420 2 536737 (Consular Section). Fax +420

2 5732 1023. Email: info@britain.cz URL: http://www.britain.cz/
Commercial Section: Palac Myslbek, Na Příkopě 21, 117 19 Prague 1,
Czech Republic. Tel. +420 2 2224 0021/2/3. Fax +420 2 2224 3625.

Czech Business Links
The services offered by this organisation include establishing contacts
with Czech companies, providing basic descriptions of companies, in-
depth company reports, market research.

Contact details: Czech Business Links, 48 Courthope Road, London
NW3 2LD, UK. Tel/Fax +44 (0)20 7428 0608. Email:
Maria.jarmila.hughes@dial.pipex.com

Czech Ministry of Industry and Trade
The Ministry is active in promoting the virtues of the Czech Republic as a
profitable destination for outside investors. Among the informative promotional materials which it supports is the quarterly *Czech Business and
Trade*. This is useful in outlining national policy trends, and in presenting
results of regional market and sectoral surveys. There is also advice on
how to do business in the country. The Ministry maintains an Internet
site providing information and data about the economy, as well as links
to other sites with Czech business interests.The Ministry responds to
business enquiries.

Contact details: For *Czech Business and Trade* -PP Agency, V. Jirchářích 8,
11000 Prague 1, Czech Republic. Tel. +420 2 2491 9041. Fax +420 2 2491
2355. Fax +420 2 2491 2355. Email: orders@ppagency.cz URL: http://
www.ppagency.cz/english/home.htm

For the Ministry's Internet site – URL: http://www.mpo.cz/english/
impo_uk.htm

Czech Statistical Office
Almost all CEE statistical offices have web sites; this is one of the more
informative. For details of the full range of sources available in English it
is advisable to consult the *Topical Information* and *CSO Services* sections.
Examples of published sources are *Statistical Yearbook of the Czech Republic Czech Republic in Figures, Monthly Statistics of the Czech Republic, Quarterly
Statistical Bulletin*. Selected statistics are available on the site.

Contact details: CSO, Sokolovská no.142, Prague 8, 186 04, Poland. Tel.
+420 2 6604 2765. Fax +420 2 683 6391. URL: http://www.czso.cz/
eng/angl.htm

CzechInvest
This is a government agency, one of a number, with the task of encouraging foreign investment, and offering advice and guidance to likely

investors. Its promotional material is very good. An example is *CzechInvest: Factsheets*. This is a handy, and free, introductory information pack. It consists of fact sheets of different lengths covering 10 business topics – for example, foreign direct investment, stock exchange, taxation, real estate. The information is updated when necessary. The agency is a source of business advice.

Contact details: CzechInvest, Politickyôch Vězňů 20, 112 49, Prague 1, Czech Republic.Tel. +420 2 2422 1540. Fax +420 2 2422 1804. Email: czechinvest:czechinvest.com URL: http://www.czechinvest.com/index.html

CzechTrade (UK)
CzechTrade 'is a specialised agency of the Czech Ministry of Industry and Trade' with the aim of 'bringing together potential British importers and Czech exporters, as well as spotting for UK business opportunities for Czech firms'. The agency welcomes enquiries from business interests.

Contact details: CzechTrade (UK), 95 Great Portland Street, London W1N 5RA. Tel. +44 (0)20 7291 9924. Fax +44 (0)20 7436 8300.

Economic Chamber of the Czech Republic
Active in disseminating business information and in facilitating business relations. The Chamber has a large institution and company membership of around 20,000. A web site is being developed. Although incomplete it already includes a number of latest business offers.

Contact details: Economic Chamber of the Czech Republic, Argentinská 38, 170 05 Prague 7, Czech Republic.Tel. +420 2 6679 4939. Fax +420 2 875438. URL: http://www.hkcr.cz/

Embassy of the Czech Republic: UK
Assists in establishing business contacts, provides business information.

Contact details: Czech Embassy, Commercial Section, 26 Kensington Palace Gardens, London W8 4QY, UK. Tel. +44 (0)20 7243 1115. Fax +44 (0)20 7727 9654.

Embassy of the Czech Republic: USA
This Embassy's web site carries information on how to conduct business, aspects of business law including tariff regulations, list of Czech companies looking for partners, details of major companies.

Contact details: URL: http://www.czech.cz/washington/ekon/ekon.htm

Chapter 7

Hungary

Population 10.1m. Hungary has attracted a large share of foreign investment, and is still seen as a relatively favourable destination for foreign funds. Over 75% of the economy is now in private hands, even the banking and financial sectors have been largely privatised with substantial foreign holdings. Unemployment and inflation, the standard economic ills of most CEE countries, are not absent, but Hungary is one of the top candidates for inclusion in the European Union.

The English language business information sector is relatively well-developed. Interest in the country's business potential is sufficient to support the information producing activities of all the main western providers in the sector, as well as encouraging local initiatives. Internet entrepreneurs are numerous.

Overview

There are no problems in gaining access to background country and economy information. Some examples of the numerous sources available, without including the multi-country compilations, are:

About the Republic of Hungary
This is an Internet site produced and maintained by USIS Budapest. It provides a quick approach to descriptive national data – basic facts about the country, statistical data, government details, political parties, news items.

Contact details: URL: http://www.usis.hu/huinfo.htm

Access Hungary
Guide to news and business information in Hungary. Covers politics and the economy, stock market, and has a section of market analysis. Sponsors include Cameron McKenna Ormai, PricewaterhouseCoopers, Citibank, HVG Magazine, Hungary Around the Clock.

Contact details: Email: info@access-hungary.hu
URL: http://www.access-hungary.hu/index.html

Business in Hungary: The Essential Guide

The information on this Internet site 'is meant to be useful for anyone interested in the local market [and] to eliminate confusion and reduce risks'. The site provides an overview of the economy, a 'survival guide for those trying to enter and navigate the Hungarian business world', profiles of all the companies listed on the Budapest Stock Exchange (45 in all), sectoral reviews, a lengthy list of contacts, a forum for buying and selling. An informative and lively site.

Contact details: URL: http://www.isys.hu/business/0.0home_e.html

Business Investment Opportunity Yearbook: Hungary

This **annual** covers 'business, investment, export-import, economic and other opportunities in respected countries. Foreign economic assistance projects, sources of financing , strategic government and business contacts, and more...'. The annual publication cycle precludes 'hot' investment news. The series titles, of which this is one, cover numerous countries throughout the world. In the circumstances it is difficult to know what weight to attach to the description 'respected'.

Contact details: Russian Information and Business Center, PO Box 15343, Washington DC 20003, USA. Tel. +1 202 546 2103. Fax +1 202 546 3275. Email: rusline@erols.com URL: http://www.rusline.com/

Cost: $89

Country Commercial Guide: Hungary

Titles in the *Guides* series are published **annually**. They review the country's commercial environment 'using economic, political and market analysis', and 'consolidate various reporting documents prepared for the U.S.Embassies community'. There are informative sections on the investment climate, trade regulations and standards, economic trends and outlook, and useful summary statistics in appendices. A good country introduction. Available on the Internet, in hard copy and as a diskette.

Contact details: URL: http://www.stat-usa.gov/Newstand

Cost: $20 (hard copy)

Country Profile: Hungary

This **annual** publication is a standard reference source. Comment, analysis and statistics cover the main industrial sectors, economic policies, political background, population, finance, prices and wages – with remarkable succinctness.

Contact details: Economist Intelligence Unit, 15 Regent Street, London SW1Y 4LR, UK. Tel. +44 (0)20 7830 1000. Fax +44 (0)1708 371 850. Email: london@eiu.com URL: http://www.eiu.com

In the US: Economist Intelligence Unit, The Economist Building, 111 West 57th Street, NY, NY 10019, USA. Tel. +1 212 554 060/1 800 938 4685 (USA and Canada only). Fax +1 212 586 0248. Email: newyork@eiu.com URL:http://www.eiu.com
Cost: £120/$205

Doing Business in Hungary

A good example (1997) of the brief, informative, booklets produced by accountancy and law firms operating in CEE countries. This introduction explains issues arising when setting up, or doing, business in this country.

Contact details: Cameron McKenna, Mitre House, 160 Aldersgate Street, London EC1A 4DD, UK. Tel. +44 (0)20 7367 3000. Fax +44 (0)20 7367 2000. Email: info@cmck.com URL: http://www.cmck.com/pub23.htm

Cost: Free on application

Doing Business in Hungary

This informative Internet site is maintained by the Singapore Trade Development Board. Its various sections include, for example, a country profile, latest figures of the economy, organisations to assist potential investors, government information, descriptions of cities, international business practices in Hungary.

Contact details: URL: http://www.tdb.gov.sg/country/hungary/bizhun.htm

Dun & Bradstreet Country Report: Hungary

This **annual** report profiles the country in terms of the economy, political situation, financial information, its debts and payment potential, the business climate. There are **monthly** monitoring updates. The report is available on diskette also.

Contact details: Dun & Bradstreet, Holmers Farm Way, High Wycombe, Bucks HP12 3BR, UK. Tel. +44 (0)1494 422 000. Fax +44 (0)1494 422 929.

Cost: £245 (hard copy; diskette); £335 (report + monthly updates).

EBRD Country Profiles: Hungary

The main headings for this **annually** produced report are: economic survey, investment climate, financial sector, multilateral funding, EBRD activities, contact list. The report is prepared for the Annual Meeting of the European Bank for Reconstruction and Development.

Contact details: Effective Technology Marketing, PO Box 171, Grimsby DN35 0TP, UK. Tel/Fax +44 (0)1472 816660. Email: sales@etmltd.demon.co.uk URL: http://www.etmltd.demon.co.uk

Cost: £10/$17

Hungary: A Business and Investment Guide

A concise introduction to the history and economy of the country, with strong sections on business conditions, practices and developments. A good starting point.

Contact details: PricewaterhouseCoopers, Plum Tree Court, London EC4A 4HI, UK. Tel. +44 (0)20 7212 4100. Fax +44 (0)20 7212 4995.

Cost: Free on application

Hungary 1999

This is a title in the *Annual Country Forecasts* series produced by Business Monitor International. It is a reference source for a wide range of economic statistics and summary views of the near future of the business environment, political and economic expectations, risk factors with a bearing upon business activities.

Contact details: Business Monitor International, 179 Queen Victoria Street, London EC4V 4DU, UK. Tel. +44 (0)20 7248 0468. Fax +44 (0)20 7248 0467. URL: http://www.businessmonitor.com

Cost: £295/$485

HVG Online

This web site carries general news with strong emphasis upon business issues in its *Newsline* file.

Contact details: URL: http://www.hvg.hu/new/cimlap_eng.htm

IMF Staff Country Reports: Hungary

The International Monetary Fund monitors the economic and financial affairs of its member countries. A series of reports, updated at irregular intervals, are produced for the consultations and assessments that take place. These appear as reviews of recent economic developments, selected issues and statistical annexes. The result, for each country surveyed, is a useful source of general and specialised knowledge of the economy, with an emphasis upon financial issues. The reports can be downloaded from the Internet.

Contact details: IMF Publication Services, 700 19th Street, NM, Washington DC 20431, USA. Tel. +1 202 623 7430. Fax +1 202 623 7201. Email: pubweb@imf.org URL: http://www.imf.org/external/pubs/pubs/dist.htm In the UK – The Stationery Office, PO Box 276, London SW8 5DT, UK. Tel. +44 (0)870 600 5522. Fax +44 (0)20 7873 8247. URL: http://www.tso-online.co.uk

Cost: $15

Investment and Business Guide: Hungary
This introductory **annual** source provides 'basic information on economy, business and investment climate and opportunities, export-import, industrial development, banking and finance, government and business, contacts'. All from the point of view of those contemplating doing business in the country. Readable and informative.

Contact details: Russian Information and Business Center, PO Box 15343, Washington DC 20003, USA. Tel. +1 202 546 2103. Fax +1 202 546 3275. Email: rusline@erols.com URL: http://www.rusline.com/

Cost: $89

OECD Economic Surveys: Hungary 1999
One of a series (1999) summarising the state of the country from the viewpoint of the Economic and Development Review Committee of the OECD. As is the practice with these surveys, the consideration of recent trends, prospects and economic policies is followed by reviews of specific issues, in this case structural review of the healthcare system. A highly useful source for those wanting a concise overview supported by helpful descriptive statistics.

Contact details: OECD Paris Centre, 2 rue André-Pascal, 75775 Cedex 16, France. Tel. +33 (0) 1 49 104235. Fax +33 (0) 1 49 104276. Email: sales@oecd.org. Also – The Stationery Office, PO Box 276, London SW8 5DT. Tel. +44 (0) 870 5522. Fax +44 (0) 207 873 8247. URL: http://www.tso-online.co.uk

Political Risk Services: Country Reports: Hungary
Reports in this series are produced **annually.** They include 'fact sheets' of basic national data, background information, 'eighteen month and five year forecasts' indicating the risks that lie ahead, profiles of individuals likely to influence the business climate. The attendant hype suggests that 'this may be the only site you will ever need for country research'. Arguable, but not too far off the mark. The publishers maintain an especially informative web site.

Contact details: The PRS Group, 6320 Fly Road, Suite 102, East Syracuse, NY 13057-0248, USA. Tel. +1 315 431 0511. Fax +1 315 431 0200. URL: http://www.prsgroup.com/

Cost: $395

Portrait of the Regions: Volume 5: Hungary
An economic, demographic and social survey (1997) of all the regions of Hungary. A very good source of background information.

Contact details: Office for Official Publications of the European Commission, 2 rue Mercier, L-2985 Luxembourg. Tel. +352 29291. Fax +352 2929 42658. URL: http://eur-op.eu.int/_en/general/s-ad.htm

Virtual Hungary
A subject directory with links to other relevant sites. There is a business section.

Contact details: URL: http://VirtualHungary.com/

World of Information Country Report: Hungary
A concise **annual** report reviewing the economic and political scene, with selected supporting statistics. Ideal for quick familiarisation.

Contact details: Walden Publishing, 2 Market Street, Saffron Walden, Essex CB10 1HZ, UK. Tel. +44 (0)1799 521150. Fax +44 (0)1799 524805.

Current Developments

A well populated sector offering plenty of choice and assistance in keeping abreast of developments. Examples are:

Budapest Business Journal
This **weekly** source monitors economic and financial developments, provides sectoral and stock exchange news, as well as general news with a bearing upon business operations and foreign investments.

Contact details: VP International, Red Hill House, Hope Street, Hope House, Chester CH4 8BU, UK. Tel. +44 (0)1244 681619. Fax +44 (0)1244 681617. Email: helen@vpinternational.com URL: http://www.vpinternational.com/

Cost: £130/$195 pa (Europe): $205 pa (elsewhere).

Business Operations Report: Hungary
This is a **quarterly** analysis of the wide range of local and other factors bearing upon business decisions. Examples of such factors are: labour relations, the expected impact of political changes, assessments of future developments. Lessons are drawn from informative case studies. There are supporting statistics. The *Report* is 'also available through on line databases, direct network feeds and the Internet'.

Contact details: Economist Intelligence Unit, 15 Regent Street, London SW1Y 4LR, UK. Tel. +44 (0)20 7830 1000. Fax +44 (0)20 7499 9767 Email: london@eiu.com URL: http://www.eiu.com

Cost: £315 pa

Country Reports: Hungary

The *Reports* are produced **quarterly.** Each issue describes the political and economic structures, reviews political and economic prospects for the next 12 - 18 months, critically reviews major economic and political issues. Economic trends are illustrated with graphs and tables, and there are a number of statistical appendices.

Contact details: Economist Intelligence Unit, 15 Regent Street, London SW1Y 4LR, UK. Tel. +44 (0)20 7830 1000. Fax +44 (0)20 7499 9767 Email: london@eiu.com URL: http://www.eiu.com

Cost: £235/$425 pa. The *Country Profile* **annual** is included in the subscription.

Country Risk Service: Hungary

The *Risk Service* takes a two-year 'forecasting horizon' on a **quarterly** basis when presenting assessments of political, economic and financial risks likely to influence business activities. Future trends of 'over 180 major economic indicators' are presented.

Contact details: Economist Intelligence Unit, 15 Regent Street, London SW1Y 4LR, UK. Tel. +44 (0)20 7830 1000. Fax +44 (0)20 7499 9767 Email: london@eiu.com URL:http://www.eiu.com
In the US: Economist Intelligence Unit, The Economist Building, 111 West 57th Street, NY, NY 10019, USA . Tel. +1 212 554 060/1 800 938 4685 (USA and Canada only). Fax +1 212 586 0248. Email: newyork@eiu.com URL: http://www.eiu.com

Cost: £395/$625 pa

Country RiskLines: Hungary

This **monthly,** brief, report (usually 4 pages) rates the risk of trading with the country in terms of earnings and international payment obligations, political and economic stability, investment climate, etc.

Contact details: Dun & Bradstreet, Holmers Farm Way, High Wycombe, Bucks HP12 3BR, UK. Tel. +44 (0)1494 422 000. Fax +44 (0)1494 422 929.

Cost: £35 pa

ECONEWS

This service, one providing economic and financial news, is available in fax and email formats. It is available also directly on the Internet. The notable feature of the service is its five times a day updating routine. The reported news items are brief in the alerting, newsletter, style.

Contact details: MTI-ECO, Naphegy tér. 8, 1016 Budapest, Hungary. Tel. +36 1 201 2972. Fax +36 1 318 8204. Email: info@mtieco.hu URL: http://www.econews.hu

Cost: $100 a month (Internet direct); $85 a month (Email); $70 a month (fax).

Financing Operations: Hungary
This service offers a **quarterly** review of financial conditions reporting on, for example, national monetary policy, banks and other financial institutions, investment incentives, trade financing, various financing techniques. *Financing Operations* is also 'available through on line databases, direct network feeds and the Internet'.

Contact details: Economist Intelligence Unit, 15 Regent Street, London SW1Y 4LR, UK. Tel. +44 (0)20 7830 1000. Fax +44 (0)20 7499 9767 Email: london@eiu.com URL: http://www.eiu.com

Cost: £245 pa

Grant Guide to Hungary
This **monthly** newsletter monitors the complex official world of grants, incentives, preferential tendering, subsidies, credit facilities and the like on offer to business interests.

Contact details: Gazella Publishing House, Victor Hugo u. 2-4, 1132 Budapest, Hungary. Tel/Fax +3 61 340 3924.

Cost: $299 pa

Hungarian Quarterly
The economy features as a strong concern of this stimulating **quarterly** which also provides general coverage of cultural and social issues.

Contact details: Hungarian Quarterly, PO Box 3, H-1426, Budapest, Hungary. Tel. +36 1 175 6722. Fax +36 1 118 8297. URL: http://www.hungary.com/hungq/

Cost: $30 pa

Hungary A.M.
This **daily** news digest service reports on the business scene in two pages of fax or email. The news items include, for example, stock market activities, business events, political and economic developments.

Contact details: Warsaw Business Journal, Ul. Słoneczna 29, 00 789 Warsaw, Poland. Tel. +48 22 646 0575. Fax +48 22 646 0576. URL: http://www.ceebiz.com

Cost: £495 pa

Hungary Around the Clock

Three levels of news coverage are on offer: *HAC Comprehensive*, *HAC Business Daily*, *HAC Business Weekly*, covering in various depths corporate, economic and financial news. An excellent monitoring source.

Contact details: Hungary Around the Clock. Tel. +36 1 351 7142. Fax +36 1 351 7141. Email: info@kingfish.hu   URL: http://www.access-hungary.hu/h_hac.html

Cost: On application

Investing, Licensing and Trading: Hungary

This service consists of 'one main report and an updater six months later'. It is a guide to operating conditions covering such topics as foreign trade regulations, the legal requirements when setting up a company, the licensing of trading activities, private and personal taxation, labour laws and practices. The report is 'available through on line databases, direct network feeds and the Internet'.

Contact details: Economist Intelligence Unit, 15 Regent Street, London SW1Y 4LR, UK. Tel. +44 (0)20 7830 1000. Fax +44 (0)20 7499 9767
Email: london@eiu.com   URL:http://www.eiu.com
Economist Intelligence Unit, The Economist Building, 111 West 57th Street, NY, NY 10019, USA . Tel. +1 212 554 060/1 800 938 4685 (USA and Canada only). Fax +1 212 586 0248. Email: newyork@eiu.com URL: http://www.eiu.com

Cost: £225/$310 pa

Monthly Information for Managers

This two-page report combines an analysis of the past month's economic developments with a forward look at possible future trends. Intended as a planning aid for the highest levels of large organisations which might explain the price.

Contact details: GKI Economic Research, Semmelweis u. 9, H-1052 Budapest, Hungary. Tel. +36 1 118 1868. Fax +36 1 118 4023. Email: gerl@gki.hu URL: http://www.gki.hu/english.html

Cost: HUF 396,000 pa

Monthly Macroeconomic Review

Macroeconomic data compiled by national agencies are re-presented and analysed for trends in a number of economic sectors. A working tool for planners.

Contact details: GKI Economic Research, Semmelweis u. 9,H-1052 Budapest, Hungary. Tel. +36 1 118 1868. Fax +36 1 118 4023. Email: gerl@gki.hu URL: http://www.gki.hu/english.html

Cost: HUF 720,000 pa

Companies and Contacts

A respectable repertoire of sources, with major contributions from Hungarian providers.

Budapest Business Journal Book of Lists
This **annual** lists 1000 companies in 66 industry sectors. The company detail includes contact data, name of CEO, revenue, number of employees.

Contact details: VP International, Red Hill House, Hope Street, Chester CH4 8BU, UK. Tel. +44 (0)1244 681619. Fax +44 (0)1244 681617. Email: helen@vpinternational.com URL: http://www.vpinternational.com/

Cost: £25/$38 (Europe); $48 (elsewhere).

Foreign Companies in Emerging Markets Yearbook: Hungary
This **annual** lists the numerous foreign companies operating in the Republic highlighting their potential as buyers and suppliers. The company details are standard including, for example, contact data, business activity descriptions, sales volumes. Available in hard copy and CD-ROM formats.

Contact details: Business Monitor International, 179 Queen Victoria Street, London EC4V 4DU, UK. Tel. +44 (0)20 7248 0468. Fax +44 (0)20 7248 0467. URL: http://www.businessmonitor.com

Cost: £240/$390 (print); £390/$650 (CD-ROM)

Kompass Hungary
One of the standard directories (1998) listing over 20,000 companies. The usual contact and descriptive data, and supporting indexes are provided.

Contact details: Kompass UK, Reed Information Services, Windsor Couort, East Grinstead House, East Grinstead, West Sussex RH19 1XA, UK. Tel. +44 (0)1342 326972. Fax +44 (0)1342 335612.

Cost: £300

Major Companies in Hungary
This CD-ROM **annual** profiles over 17,000 firms. The data provided include the usual locational and contact details, plus number of employees, annual sales, subsidiaries, imports/exports, products. There are two ver-

sions – the more limited is searchable, and can print out full company profiles; the fuller version 'is also capable of printing address labels'.

Contact details: VP International, Red Hill House, Hope Street, Chester CH4 8BU, UK. Tel. +44 (0)1244 681619. Fax +44 (0)1244 681617. Email: helen@vpinternational.com URL: http://www.vpinternational.com/

Cost: £175/$263 (standard – Europe), $272 (standard – elsewhere). £625/$940 (full – Europe), $950 (full – elsewhere)

Yelloweb Hungary
Telephone directories are useful tools for tracing companies. Their utility is increased when their data are to be found on the Internet and searchable by company name and by activity sector – and in English, as well as Hungarian.

Contact details: URL: http://www.yelloweb.hu/index.asp?lang=1

Industries and Services

The range of sectoral sources is not extensive. The following examples indicate that western and local interests are producing helpful material, but less than might be expected in the country's developing economy.

Agriculture

Agricultural Situation and Perspectives in the Central and East European Countries: Hungary
This report, from the European Union, 'aims to provide an analysis of the current situation and the medium-term outlook for the agricultural and agri-food industries' in the CEE countries aiming for EU membership – Bulgaria, Czech Republic, Hungary, Poland, Romania, Slovakia, Slovenia. The report is freely available on the Internet.

Contact details: URL: http://www.europa.eu.int/comm/dg06/publi/peco.index-en.htm

Automotive

Hungarian Automotive Industry
This report (1997) reviews and analyses the current state and performance of the sector, and sets out possible future scenarios. The aim, with the assistance of numerous statistical tables, is to provide current and potential investors with data and news for decision-taking. The major companies in the sector are profiled and appraised. There is a list of useful contacts.

Contact details: FT Automotive, Maple House, 149 Tottenham Court Road, London W1P 9LL, UK. Tel. +44 (0)20 7896 2241. Fax +44 (0)20 7896 2275. URL: http://www.ftauto.com

Cost: £395/$624

Electronics

Hungarian Federation for Electronics and Informatics
This sectoral directory profiles 38 major companies. In addition to the usual contact details there are descriptions of technologies employed, revenue, products, quality assurance.

Contact details: Hungarian Federation for Electronics and Informatics, Szemere u. 17, 1054, Hungary. Tel. +36 1 311 6271. Fax +36 1 331 6320. Email: meisz@dbassoc.hu

Cost: On application.

Finance and Banking

Budapest Stock Exchange
Reopened in 1990 – among the first in CEE countries. A source of information about companies.

Contact details: Budapest Stock Exchange, Déak Ferenc u.5,Budapest 1052, Hungary. Tel. +36 1 117 5226. Fax +36 1 118 1737.

Citibank Magyarorzag
Naturally, the web site of this bank has a lot to say about the bank itself; but it also provides data on a wide range of financial matters.

Contact details: URL: http://www.citibank.com/hungary/

Hungarian Financial and Stock Exchange Almanac
This **annual** provides information about companies and institutions operating in the financial, banking, insurance and capital markets, as well as being a guide to the stock exchange. The company profiles include balance sheets and future plans.

Contact details: TAS 11 Ltd, PO Box 477, 4 Bank Street, Budapest H-1242, Hungary.

Cost: $50

Information House Company Register Online
This subscription database contains 'all the public information' about 350,000 companies registered by the Company Court. The database is updated **twice a month**. There is an 'easy to use' searching facility. The

service also provides Bankruptcy Watch Online to keep an eye on 'judicial proceedings concerning the companies you are interested in'. A complete service, it might be claimed.

Contact details: URL: http://infohaz.euroweb.hu/ceg/ceglefta.htm

Cost: On application

Monetary Forecasts
This **twice-a-year** report presents future monetary scenarios based on the canvassed opinion of major institutions and economists.

Contact details: GKI Economic Research, Semmelweis u. 9, H-1052 Budapest, Hungary. Tel. +36 1 118 1868. Fax +36 1 118 4023. Email: gerl@gki.hu URL: http://www.gki.hu/english.html

Cost: HUF 600,000 per issue

National Bank of Hungary
The National Bank monitors developments in banking and financial institutions, as well government activities in these and other financial sectors. Information and statistics are made public through the *Monthly Report*. More considered analyses appear in such reports as *Hungarian Banking Sector: Developments in the First Half of 1998*. The financial standing of the banking system is closely reviewed. Both publications are free.

Contact details: National Bank of Hungary, Szabadság ter. 8-9. H-1850 Budapest V, Hungary. Tel. +36 1 153 2326. Fax +36 1 153 0286. URL: http://www.mnb.hu/main.htm

Legislation

English language sources are numerous. Examples are:

Business Law Handbook: Hungary
This *Handbook* is updated **annually** to take account of changes in the laws and regulations governing business activities generally, and those of foreigners in particular. A readable introduction for the layman.

Contact details: Russian Information and Business Center, PO Box 15343, Washington DC 20003, USA. Tel. +1 202 546 2103. Fax +1 202 546 3275. Email: rusline@erols.com URL: http://www.rusline.com/

Cost: $89

Legal Guide: Hungary
A layman's guide, from the Department of Trade and Industry, to the more important aspects of business law concentrating especially on the processes of establishing a business. A good introduction.

Contact details: DTI, Admail 528, London SW1w 8YT, UK. Tel. +44 (0)20 7510 0171. Fax +44 (0)20 7510 0197. URL: http://www.dti.gov.uk/ots/publications

Cost: £12

Hungarian Businesses and the EU Law Focus
A booklet (1997) for the layman produced by Cameron McKenna, a law firm with interests in CEE countries. Attention is concentrated upon important legal issues arising from the enlargement of the European Union. A brief introduction, no more; but helpful and informative.

Contact details: Cameron McKenna, Mitre House, 160 Aldersgate Street, London EC1A 4DD, UK. Tel. +44 (0)20 7367 3000. Fax +44 (0)20 7367 2000.

Cost: Free on application.

Hungarian Newsletter
The coverage of this English-language **bimonthly** is broad – trade policy, foreign trade statistics, privatisation developments, foreign capital and banking news, for example, are regular features. It also publishes 'laws and other regulations concerning trading relations ... Special editions include full texts of the most important foreign economic legislation'. It is edited 'by the Ministry of International Economic Relations', so whatever is published has full official sanction – an important point.

Contact details: VP International, Red Hill House, Hope Street, Chester CH4 8BU, UK. Tel. +44 (0)1244 681619. Fax +44 (0)1244 681617. Email: helen@vpinternational.com URL: http://www.vpinternational.com/

Cost: On application.

Hungarian Rules of Law in Force
This **fortnightly** bulletin, in Hungarian, English and German, records changes in laws.

Contact details: VP International, Red Hill House, Hope Street, Chester CH4 8BU, UK. Tel. +44 (0)1244 681619. Fax +44 (0)1244 681617. Email: helen@vpinternational.com URL: http://www.vpinternational.com/

Cost: £215/$323 pa (Europe); $333 (elsewhere)

Organisations
The expected array of helpful organisations is available. For example:

American Embassy
The Embassy's web site has informative sections on commercial services, public affairs, news and hot issues.

Contact details: U.S. Embassy, Szabságtér. 12, H-1054 Budapest, Hungary. Tel. +36 1 267 4400. Fax + 36 1 269 9337. URL: http://www.usis.hu/emb.htm

British Chamber of Commerce in Hungary
Established to maintain and foster British business interests. The experience of its members makes it an obviously useful point of contact.

Contact details: British Chamber of Commerce in Hungary, Iskola u. 37, 1011 Budapest, Hungary. Tel./Fax +36 1 201 9142.

British Embassy
Available for advice and support. Office hours: Summer 07.00-15.00. Winter 08.00-16.00.

Contact details: British Embassy, Harminca utca 6, Budapest 1051, Hungary. Tel. +36 1 266 2888. Fax +36 1 266 0907. Email: info@britemb.hu

Embassy of the Republic of Hungary: UK
Willing to provide guidance and advice.

Contact details: Hungarian Embassy, Commercial Section, 35 Easton Place, London SW1X 8QB, UK. Tel. +44 (0)20 7235 8767. Fax +44 (0)20 7235 4319.

Embassy of the Republic of Hungary: USA
The Embassy's web site has an informative section on country facts and figures, economy, trade and investment. Good on links, too.

Contact details: Embassy of the Republic of Hungary, 3910 Shoemaker Street, NW, Washington DC 20008, USA. Tel. +1 202 362 6730. Fax +1 202 686 6412. URL: http://www.hungaryemb.org/

Hungarian Central Statistical Office
The web site lists publications, periodicals and major surveys. It also provides access to *Hungary in Figures, Major Annual Figures,* and samples of *Most Recent Data*. The chief paper-based sources are *Statistical Yearbook of Hungary*, *Statistical Report* (**monthly**), and *Living Standard* (**annual**). The latter is especially useful for the market research material it contains. A handy portable collection of more generally required national statistics is to be found in the **annual** *The Statistical Pocket Book of Hungary*. Fuller details are available on the web site but, when searching for detail, you will come up against the warning 'the figures above are accessible only against payment' – the clear indication that the most interesting, and up-to-date, data cost money to access.

Contact details: Hungarian Central Statistical Office, Keleti Károly u. 5-7, H-1024 Budapest, Hungary. Tel. +36 1 345 6000. Fax +36 1 345 6378. URL: http://www.ksh.hu/eng/homeng.html

Hungarian Chamber of Commerce and Industry

The Hungarian Chamber of Commerce and Industry has a keen promotional eye – publishes a number of English-language information sources, arranges exhibitions and fairs, advises on contacts. It has a large membership, over 400,000, but then, membership is compulsory on all business enterprises.

Contact details: Hungarian Chamber of Commerce and Industry, POB 452, 1372 Budapest V, Hungary. Tel. +36 1 153 0835.Fax +36 1 153 4125. Email: mkik@mail.mkik.hu URL: http://www.mkik.cos.hu/aindex.html

Hungarian Investment and Trade Development Agency

The Agency's role includes the fullest possible assistance to intending business investors. It has developed an extensive publications programme extolling the merits of Hungary as an investment prospect. With information seen as one of its main resources the Agency has capitalised upon this belief with the establishment of a European Information and Business Centre (Euro Info Centre), linked to numerous databanks, which can be put at the disposal of its clients. The expected forms of business and economic information are on offer.

Contact details: Hungarian Investment and Trade Development Agency, Dorottya u. 4, 1051 Budapest, Hungary. Tel. +361 318 3986. Fax +361 318 3732. Email: info@itd.hu URL: http://www.itd.hu/english/index.htm

Hungarian Ministry of Economic Affairs

The Ministry maintains a web site providing general information and data about the country and its economy. There are pages devoted to the *Investors' Handbook*, a guide to doing business in Hungary. It forms a useful introduction to major business laws, investor incentives on offer, taxation, setting up a business, etc.

Contact details: Ministry of Economic Affairs, Honvéd utca 13-15, H-1880 Budapest, Hungary. Tel. +36 1 302 2355. Fax +36 1 302 2394. URL: http://www.ikm.iif.hu/investor/index.htm

Chapter 8

FYR Macedonia

Population 2m. Impoverished and with only slight prospects of improvement. Unemployment is close to 30%, economic reform is laggardly, inward investment is inadequate. The consequences of the movement of huge numbers of Kosovar refugees into Macedonia have worsened the country's already chronic economic imbalance.

There are English language business information sources but, overall, provision is of the sparsest.

Overview

Media attention has focused on the country during the period of the Kosovo conflict. Some of the more normal sources of information for overview purposes, which include the Internet even for this impoverished country, are:

Business Investment Opportunity Yearbook: Macedonia
This **annual** covers 'business, investment, export-import, economic and other opportunities in respected countries. Foreign economic assistance projects, sources of financing , strategic government and business contacts, and more...'. The annual publication cycle precludes 'hot' investment news. The series titles, of which this is one, cover numerous countries throughout the world. It is difficult to know what weight to attach to the description 'respected'.

Contact details: Russian Information and Business Center, PO Box 15343, Washington DC 20003, USA. Tel. +1 202 546 2103. Fax +1 202 546 3275. Email: rusline@erols.com URL: http://www.rusline.com/

Cost: $89

Country Profile: Macedonia
This **annual** publication is a standard reference source. Comment, analysis and statistics cover the main industrial sectors, economic policies, political background, population, finance, prices and wages – with remarkable succinctness.

Contact details: Economist Intelligence Unit, 15 Regent Street, London SW1Y 4LR, UK. Tel. +44 (0)20 7830 1000. Fax +44 (0)1708 371 850.

Email: london@eiu.com URL: http://www.eiu.com
In the US: Economist Intelligence Unit, The Economist Building, 111
West 57th Street, NY, NY 10019, USA . Tel. +1 212 554 060/1 800
938 4685 (USA and Canada only). Fax +1 212 586 0248. Email:
newyork@eiu.com URL: http://www.eiu.com

Cost: £120/$205

EBRD Country Profiles: Macedonia
The main headings for this **annually** produced report are – economic
survey, investment climate, financial sector, multilateral funding, EBRD
activities, contact list. The report is prepared for the Annual Meeting of
the European Bank for Reconstruction and Development.

Contact details: Effective Technology Marketing, PO Box 171, Grimsby
DN35 0TP, UK. Tel/Fax +44 (0)1472 816660. Email:
sales@etmltd.demon.co.uk URL: http://www.etmltd.demon.co.uk

Cost: £10/$17

Facts on the Republic of Macedonia
An Internet site providing basic data and information about the economy.
A useful first source to consult.

Contact details: URL: http://www.macedonian.se.org/facts/
economy.htm

IMF Staff Country Reports: Macedonia
The International Monetary Fund monitors the economic and financial
affairs of its member countries. A series of reports, updated at irregular
intervals, are produced for the consultations and assessments that take
place. These appear as reviews of recent economic developments, selected
issues and statistical annexes. The result, for each country surveyed, is a
useful source of general and specialised knowledge of the economy, with
an emphasis upon financial issues. The reports can be downloaded from
the Internet.

Contact details: IMF Publication Services, 700 19th Street, NM, Washington DC 20431, USA. Tel. +1 202 623 7430. Fax +1 202 623 7201.
Email: pubweb@imf.org URL: http://www.imf.org/external/pubs/
pubs/dist.htm In the UK – The Stationery Office, PO Box 276, London
SW8 5DT, UK. Tel. +44 (0)870 600 5522. Fax +44 (0)20 7873 8247. URL:
http://www.tso-online.co.uk

Cost: $15

Investment and Business Guide: Macedonia
This introductory **annual** source provides 'basic information on economy, business and investment climate and opportunities, export-import, industrial development, banking and finance, government and business, contacts'. All from the point of view of those contemplating doing business in the country. Readable and informative.

Contact details: Russian Information and Business Center, PO Box 15343, Washington DC 20003, USA. Tel. +1 202 546 2103. Fax +1 202 546 3275. Email: rusline@erols.com   URL: http://www.rusline.com/

Cost: $89

Macedonia
This is a general Internet site providing geographic, climatic, demographic, historical, cultural information and data. In addition it profiles the larger cities, and has a privatisation page.

Contact details: URL: http://www.soros.org.mk/mk/

The Macedonian Directory
An excellent subject directory with links to other relevant sites. Sections on business and the economy, news and media, government and politics, etc.

Contact details: URL: http://www.sit.wisc.edu/~laskoski/mk.html

Republic of Macedonia: The First Macedonian WWWPage
An Internet site providing a wide range of information about the country, including all major towns. For example – facts and figures (from *CIA World Factbook*), geography, pictures of Macedonia, descriptions of the cities of Skopje, Ohrid, Bitola, Prilep, Kumanova, Veles and other places of interest., culture and links with related electronic sources.

Contact details: URL: http://b-info.com/places/Macedonia/republic/

Current Developments

Again sparser than most countries in the region. Examples are:

Country Reports: Macedonia
The *Reports* are produced **quarterly.** Each issue describes the political and economic structures, reviews political and economic prospects for the next 12 - 18 months, critically reviews major economic and political issues. Economic trends are illustrated with graphs and tables, and there are a number of statistical appendices.

Contact details: Economist Intelligence Unit, 15 Regent Street, London SW1Y 4LR, UK. Tel. +44 (0)20 7830 1000. Fax +44 (0)20 7499 9767 URL:http://www.eiu.com
In the US: Economist Intelligence Unit, The Economist Building, 111 West 57th Street, NY, NY 10019, USA . Tel. +1 212 554 060/1 800 938 4685 (USA and Canada only). Fax +1 212 586 0248. Email: newyork@eiu.com URL: http://www.eiu.com

Cost: £235/$425 pa. The *Country Profile* **annual** is included in the sub-scription.

Country Risk Service: Macedonia
The *Risk Service* takes a two-year 'forecasting horizon' on a **quarterly** basis when presenting assessments of political, economic and financial risks likely to influence business activities. Future trends of 'over 180 major economic indicators' are presented.

Contact details: Economist Intelligence Unit, 15 Regent Street, London SW1Y 4LR, UK. Tel. +44 (0)20 7830 1000. Fax +44 (0)20 7499 9767 URL: Email: london@eiu.com http://www.eiu.com
In the US: Economist Intelligence Unit, The Economist Building, 111 West 57th Street, NY, NY 10019, USA . Tel. +1 212 554 060/1 800 938 4685 (USA and Canada only). Fax +1 212 586 0248. Email: newyork@eiu.com URL: http://www.eiu.com

Cost: £395/$625 pa

Country RiskLines: Macedonia
This **monthly**, brief, report (usually 4 pages) rates the risk of trading with the country in terms of earnings and international payment obligations, political and economic stability, investment climate, etc.

Contact details: Dun & Bradstreet, Holmers Farm Way, High Wycombe, Bucks HP12 3BR, UK. Tel. +44 (0)1494 422 000. Fax +44 (0)1494 422 929.

Cost: £35 pa

MILS – News
This service, described as 'non-profit, non-governmental', provides a **daily** email, fax and mailed digest of the latest events and developments in the country. The web site has a small number of links to other related sites.

Contact details: Macedonian Information and Liaison Service, Skopje, Macedonia. Tel/Fax +389 91 223319. Email: mils@lotus.mk URL: http://enws121.eas.asu.edu/places/Macedonia/republic/MILS.html

Cost: Subscription details on application.

Companies and Contacts

At present it is possible only to recommend approaches to the agencies listed under Organisations below. However, a *Kompass Macedonia* is in the pipeline awaiting a firm publication date.

Industries and Services

Apart from the financial sector there are no sectoral sources of note. Sectoral queries are best directed at the organisations listed below.

Finance and banking

National Bank of the Republic of Macedonia

The Bank's *Quarterly Bulletin* provides monetary, banking and financial statistics The web site maintained by the Bank provides access to business laws and regulations and official publications. The latter include the statistical *Quarterly Bulletin.*

Contact details: National Bank of the Republic of Macedonia, Box 401, Kompleks banki, 91000 Skopje, Republic of Macedonia. Tel +389 91 108 108. Fax +389 91 111 161. URL http://www.nbrm.gov.mk/main.htm

Macedonian Stock Exchange

Provides listing requirements, information on regulation and taxation, law on issuance and trading securities, trading, etc.

Contact details: Macedonian Stock Exchange, Mito Hadživasilev Jasmin 20, 91000 Skopje, Macedonia. Tel. +389 91 122055. Fax +389 91 122069. URL: http://www.mne.org.mk/frrtop.htm

Legislation

The lack of competing English language sources reflects western uninterest in the economy and its potential.

Business Law Handbook: Macedonia

This *Handbook* is updated **annually** to take account of changes in the laws and regulations governing business activities generally, and those of foreigners in particular. A readable introduction for the layman.

Contact details: Russian Information and Business Center, PO Box 15343, Washington DC 20003, USA. Tel. +1 202 546 2103. Fax +1 202 546 3275. Email: rusline@erols.com URL: http://www.rusline.com/

Cost: $89

Macedonian Laws
Unofficial translations of Republic of Macedonia laws into English are available from the Macedonian Privatisation Agency. A list of these can be found on their Internet site.

Contact details: Macedonian Privatisation Agency, Nikola Vapcarov 7, POB 410, 91000 Skopje, Macedonia. Tel. +389 91 117564. Fax +389 91 126022. Email: agency@mpa.org.mk URL: http://www.mpa.org.mk/laws.htm

Macedonian Legal Resource Center
Information on courts, lawyers, notaries, legal databases, legal library, constitutional court, etc.

Contact details: URL: http://www.ius.org.mk/

Organisations

There are organisations willing to help business people:

American Embassy
Can assist with business enquiries.

Contact details: U.S. Embassy, Ilindenska BB, 91000 Skopje, Macedonia. Tel. +389 91 116-180. Fax +389 91 117-103.

British Embassy
Available for advice and support. Office hours: Summer 06.00-14.30. Winter 07.00-15.30.

Contact details: British Embassy, Veljko Vlahović 26, 4th Floor, Skopje 9100, Macedonia. Tel. +389 91 116 772, +389 91 237 637. Fax +389 91 117 005, +389 91 119 555.

Economic Chamber of Macedonia
Eager to help potential foreign investors and business people. The Chamber's most useful information contributions are the *Commercial Directory of Macedonia* (1999), and the promotional CD-ROM *Macedonia, Your Business Partner*. The *Directory* provides contact data and brief activity descriptions for the relatively few commercial firms. The CD-ROM is presented as a 'variety of information about Macedonian State, its political and economic structure, history, culture'. The objective of this latter source 'is to motivate and inform businessmen about the possibilities available in Macedonia, the incentives provided by the Macedonian state, in order

to increase their presence both in terms of quality and quantity'. A clear enough message. The Chamber's web site gives access to a *Database of Business Opportunities* and to a register of companies.

Contact details: Economic Chamber of Macedonia, Dimitrie Čupovski 13, PO Box 324, 91000 Skopje, Macedonia. Tel. +389 91 118 088. Fax +389 91 116 210. Email: ic@ic.mchamber.org.mk URL: http://www.mchamber.org.mk

Embassy of the Republic of Macedonia: UK
Can assist with business issues.

Contact details: Macedonian Embassy, Suite 10, Harcourt House, 19a Cavendish Square, London W1M 9AD, UK. +44 (0)20 7499 5152. Fax +44 (0)20 7499 2864.

Embassy of the Republic of Macedonia: USA
Can assist with business issues.

Contact details: Embassy of the Republic of Macedonia, 3050 K Street, NW, Suite 210, Washington DC 20007, USA. Tel. +1 202 337 3063. Fax +1 202 337 3093. Email: macedonia@aol.com

Macedonian Information Centre
The Centre provides country and economic information. It provides a *Daily News Service* – a **daily** fax service monitoring current events including those of the business and economic worlds. The news items are brief.

Contact details: Macedonian Information Centre, Dame Gruev 5, Block 3, 81000 Skopje, Macedonia. Tel. +389 91 117 876. Fax +389 91 221 842. Email: mic@itl.com.mk URL: http://www.makedonija.com/

Macedonian Privatization Agency
The Agency, formally known as the Agency of the Republic of Macedonia for the Transformation of Enterprises with Social Capital is 'self-funded by the proceeds from the sales of enterprises'. It offers assistance and advice to potential foreign investors. Among its 'official' informative documents are – *Current Privatisation and Investment Topics Newsletter, Guidelines for Evaluation of Bids, Privatisation Facts, Perspectives*. There is also a guide for investors *Doing Business in Romania* which can be downloaded from the Internet site.

Contact details: Macedonian Privatisation Agency, Nikola Vapcarov 7, POB 410, 91000 Skopje, Macedonia. Tel. +389 91 117564. Fax +389 91 126022. Email: agency@mpa.org.mk URL: http://www.mpa.org.mk/front/htm

Statistical Office of the Republic of Macedonia
The main publications of the Statistical Office are the *Statistical Yearbook* and the *Monthly Statistical Bulletin*. Both are in Macedonian and English.

Contact details: Statistical Office of the Republic of Macedonia, Dame Gruev 4, Skopje, Macedonia. Tel. +389 91 115 022. Fax +389 91 111 336.

Chapter 9

Poland

Population 38.7m. The largest CEE country, with the second highest GDP and the closest to achieving a state of sustainable growth. It has enjoyed consistently high growth rates. It is not surprising that Poland is an attractive country for foreign investors. A verdict seconded by the EU when praising Poland's economic progress. There are still blemishes – a single company monopoly of telecommunications, a disregard for the environment, slowness of legal reforms required to bring Poland into line with EU expectations – but the country is still favoured as one of the earliest entrants into the EU.

The English language business information sector is extensive, reflecting western and Polish inputs. Poland has developed a range of Internet sites and, in this respect, is ahead of most other CEE countries.

Overview

Curiously, in such an information aware economy, most of the English language overview sources are produced outside Poland. But, as in most CEE countries, the emergence of home-based Internet sites must be viewed as the preferred method for presenting general country data and information to outsiders, especially business persons. Examples in this category are:

Business Investment Opportunity Yearbook: Poland
This **annual** covers 'business, investment, export-import, economic and other opportunities in respected countries. Foreign economic assistance projects, sources of financing , strategic government and business contacts, and more...'. The annual publication cycle precludes 'hot' investment news. The series titles, of which this is one, cover numerous countries throughout the world. It is difficult to understand what weight to attach to the description 'respected'.

Contact details: Russian Information and Business Center, PO Box 15343, Washington DC 20003, USA. Tel. +1 202 546 2103. Fax +1 202 546 3275. Email: rusline@erols.com
URL: http://www.rusline.com/

Cost: $89

Country Commercial Guide: Poland

Titles in the *Guides* series are published **annually**. They review the country's commercial environment 'using economic, political and market analysis', and 'consolidate various reporting documents prepared for the U.S.Embassies community'. There are informative sections on the investment climate, trade regulations and standards, economic trends and outlook, and useful summary statistics in appendices. A good country introduction. Available on the Internet, in hard copy and as a diskette.

Contact details: URL: http://www.stat-usa.gov/Newstand

Cost: $20 (hard copy)

Country Guide: Poland

A well presented **annual** package of information, data and advice about business conditions and operations. A convenient reference source to keep close to hand.

Contact details: Euromoney Publications, Nestor House, Playhouse Yard, London, EC4V 5EX, UK. Tel. +44 (0)20 7779 8999. Fax +44 (0)20 7779 8617.

Cost: £95/$170

Country Profile: Poland

This **annual** publication is a standard reference source. Comment, analysis and statistics cover the main industrial sectors, economic policies, political background, population, finance, prices and wages – with remarkable succinctness.

Contact details: Economist Intelligence Unit, 15 Regent Street, London SW1Y 4LR, UK. Tel. +44 (0)20 7830 1000. Fax +44 (0)1708 371 850. Email:london@eiu.com URL:http://www.eiu.com
In the US: Economist Intelligence Unit, The Economist Building, 111 West 57th Street, NY, NY 10019, USA . Tel. +1 212 554 060/1 800 938 4685 (USA and Canada only). Fax +1 212 586 0248. Email: newyork@eiu.com URL: http://www.eiu.com

Cost: £120/$205

Dun & Bradstreet Country Report: Poland

This **annual** report profiles the country in terms of the economy, political situation, financial information, its debts and payment potential, the business climate. There are **monthly** monitoring updates. The report is available on diskette also.

Contact details: Dun & Bradstreet, Holmers Farm Way, High Wycombe, Bucks HP12 3BR, UK. Tel. +44 (0)1494 422 000. Fax +44 (0)1494 422 929.

Cost: £245 (hard copy; diskette); £335 (report + monthly updates).

EBRD Country Profiles: Poland
The main headings for this **annually** produced report are – economic survey, investment climate, financial sector, multilateral funding, EBRD activities, contact list. The report is prepared for the Annual Meeting of the European Bank for Reconstruction and Development.

Contact details: Effective Technology Marketing, PO Box 171, Grimsby DN35 0TP, UK. Tel/Fax +44 (0)1472 816660.
Email: sales@etmltd.demon.co.uk
URL: http://www.etmltd.demon.co.uk

Cost: £10/$17

The First Polish Economic Guide
An excellent **annual** introduction to the Polish economy. Major companies are listed, business laws explained, investment opportunities reviewed, the banking system described, etc. Useful desk tool.

Contact details: Warsaw Voice Marketing, 64 Księcia Janusza Street, 01-452 Warsaw, Poland. Fax +48 22 37 1995.

Cost: $75

Government Information Centre
A general Internet site including pages of news, promotional material, institutional information, progress of reforms.

Contact details: Government Information Centre, Al. Ujazdowskie 1/3, 00-583 Warsaw, Poland. Email: cirinfo@kprm.gov.pl URL: http://www.kprm.gov.pl/welcomee.html

IMF Staff Country Reports: Poland
The International Monetary Fund Monitors the economic and financial affairs of its member countries. A series of reports, updated at irregular intervals, are produced for the consultations and assessments that take place. These appear as reviews of recent economic developments, selected issues and statistical annexes. The result, for each country surveyed, is a useful source of general and specialised knowledge of the economy, with an emphasis upon financial issues. The reports can be downloaded from the Internet.

Contact details: IMF Publication Services, 700 19th Street, NM, Washington DC 20431, USA. Tel. +1 202 623 7430. Fax +1 202 623 7201. Email: pubweb@imf.org URL: http://www.imf.org/external/pubs/pubs/dist.htm In the UK – The Stationery Office, PO Box 276, London SW8 5DT, UK. Tel. +44 (0)870 600 5522. Fax +44 (0)207 873 8247. URL: http://www.tso-online.co.uk

Cost: $15

Investing, Licensing and Trading: Poland
This **annual** service consists of 'one main report and an updater six months later'. It is a guide to operating conditions covering such topics as foreign trade regulations, the legal requirements when setting up a company, the licensing of trading activities, private and personal taxation, labour laws and practices. The report is 'available through on line databases, direct network feeds and the Internet'.

Contact details: Economist Intelligence Unit, 15 Regent Street, London SW1Y 4LR, UK. Tel. +44 (0)20 7830 1000. Fax +44 (0)20 7499 9767 Email: london@eiu.com URL:http://www.eiu.com
In the US: Economist Intelligence Unit, The Economist Building, 111 West 57th Street, NY, NY 10019, USA . Tel. +1 212 554 060/1 800 938 4685 (USA and Canada only). Fax +1 212 586 0248. Email: newyork@eiu.com URL: http://www.eiu.com

Cost: £225/$310 pa

Investment and Business Guide: Poland
This introductory **annual** source provides 'basic information on economy, business and investment climate and opportunities, export-import, industrial development, banking and finance, government and business, contacts'. All from the point of view of those contemplating doing business in the country. Readable and informative.

Contact details: Russian Information and Business Center, PO Box 15343, Washington DC 20003, USA. Tel. +1 202 546 2103. Fax +1 202 546 3275. Email: rusline@erols.com URL: http://www.rusline.com/

Cost: $89

OECD Economic Surveys 1997-1998: Poland
An authoritative analysis (1998) of what has been, and has not been, achieved in terms of economic reform. Problems and solutions are viewed from the perspective of liberalising economists.

Contact details: OECD Publications, 2 rue André-Pascal, 75775 Paris, Cedex 16, France. Tel. +33 (0)145 24 8200. Fax +33 (0)149 10 4276. Email: compte.PUBSINQ@oecd.org

Cost: FF130

Poland 1999
This **annual** provides succinct summaries of the current economic and political state of the country, with a rolling three-year look into the future. Also provides market intelligence, selected economic statistics.

Contact details: Business Monitor International, 179 Queen Victoria Street, London EC4V 4DD, UK. Tel. +44 (0)20 7248 0468. Fax +44 (0)20 7248 0467. URL: http://www.businessmonitor.com

Cost: £295/$485

Poland to 2005
A review and analysis (1997) of the problems and issues confronting Poland, with an assessment of future possibilities and prospects. An interesting overview.

Contact details: Economist Intelligence Unit, PO Box 200, Harold Hill, Romford RM3 8UX, UK. Tel. +44 (0)207 830 1007. Fax +44 (0)1708 371850 URL: http://www.eiu.com/

Cost: £325

Polish Home Page
This Internet site provides pages of descriptive data and information; especially strong on setting the historical scene. The strength of homepages of this type, however, is in the links provided to numerous other, related, web sources. A good place to search for background country information.

Contact details: URL: http://www.info.fuw.edu.pl/pl/PolandHome.html

PolishWorld
Polish net directory which includes sections on business and the economy, politics and government, news and media.

Contact details: URL: http://www.polishworld.com/

Political Risk Services: Country Reports: Poland
Reports in this series are produced **annually.** They include 'fact sheets' of basic national data, background information, 'eighteen month and five year forecasts' indicating the risks that lie ahead, profiles of individuals likely to influence the business climate. The attendant hype suggests that 'this may be the only site you will ever need for country research'. Arguable, but not too far off the mark. The publishers maintain an especially informative web site.

Contact details: The PRS Group, 6320 Fly Road, Suite 102, East Syracuse, NY 13057-0248, USA. Tel. +1 315 431 0511. Fax +1 315 431 0200. URL: http://www.prsgroup.com/

Cost: $395

The Warsaw Voice Business and Economy Yearbook
An **annual** providing 'the main facts about Poland's economy, commentaries from independent experts and analysts, ranking of companies from

recognised sources, investment opportunities, useful contacts and addresses'.

Contact details: The Warsaw Voice, 64 Księcia Janusza St., 5th Floor, 01-452 Warsaw, Poland. Tel. +48 22 36 6377. Fax +48 22 37 1995.

World of Information Country Report: Poland
A concise **annual** report reviewing the economic and political scene, with selected supporting statistics. Ideal for quick familiarisation.

Contact details: Walden Publishing, 2 Market Street, Saffron Walden, Essex CB10 1HZ, UK. Tel. +44 (0)1799 521150. Fax +44 (0)1799 524805.

Cost: £30/$65

Current Developments

Poland is well supplied with an extensive array of English language sources aimed at describing the business environment, providing guidance for business operations, analysing current events – generally catering to the information needs of business interests. Many of these are the products of Polish enterprise although, given the relatively promising economic prospects of the country, western providers of information services are also strongly represented. Internet services, with general and specialised coverage, are a feature of the Polish information scene. Examples of conventional print and electronic forms are:

Business News Poland: A Weekly Bulletin of Boss Economic Information
This **weekly** business newspaper has wide coverage – 'reports on the Polish economy and investment opportunities, sector analyses, legal and tax regulations, business forecasts and assessments, statistics, current company news and a review of business developments'. The publishers maintain an informative Internet site.

Further information: Boss Information and Publishing Agency, ul. Usypiskowa 12, 02-386 Warsaw, Poland. Tel. +48 22 668 8602. Fax +48 22 668 9196. Email: boss@boss.com.pl URL: http://www.boss.com.pl

Cost: $490 pa.

Business Operations Report: Poland
This is a **quarterly** analysis of the wide range of local and other factors bearing upon business decisions. Examples of such factors are: labour relations, the expected impact of political changes, assessments of future developments. Lessons are drawn from informative case studies. There are supporting statistics. The Report is 'also available through on line databases, direct network feeds and the Internet'.

Contact details: Economist Intelligence Unit, 15 Regent Street, London SW1Y 4LR, UK. Tel. +44 (0)20 7830 1000. Fax +44 (0)20 7499 9767 Email:london@eiu.com URL: http://www.eiu.com

Cost: £315 pa

Business Polska
This Internet site reports a broad range of business information. For example, the *News* section monitors current business developments, the *Market Reports* section lists the various sectoral reports published, while the *Organisations* section provides an excellent list of agencies and other bodies relevant to business activities. Other sections are: *Investor's Guide, Companies, Warsaw Stock Exchange, Partner's Forum, Contacts.*

Contact details: URL: http://www.polska.net/newpage/main2.html

Country Forecasts: Poland
This **quarterly** source presents 'five-year forecasts of political, economic and business trends'. Issues examined include, for example, prospects for political stability, business operating climate, government economic policies, labour market developments, sectoral matters.

Contact details: Economist Intelligence Unit, 15 Regent Street, London SW1Y 4LR, UK. Tel. +44 (0)20 7830 1000. Fax +44 (0)20 7499 9767 Email:london@eiu.com URL:http://www.eiu.com
In the US: Economist Intelligence Unit, The Economist Building, 111 West 57th Street, NY, NY 10019, USA . Tel. +1 212 554 060/1 800 938 4685 (USA and Canada only). Fax +1 212 586 0248. Email: newyork@eiu.com URL: http://www.eiu.com

Cost: £450/$645 pa

Country Reports: Poland
The Reports are produced **quarterly**. Each issue describes the political and economic structures, reviews political and economic prospects for the next 12 - 18 months, critically reviews major economic and political issues. Economic trends are illustrated with graphs and tables, and there are a number of statistical appendices.

Contact details: Economist Intelligence Unit, 15 Regent Street, London SW1Y 4LR, UK. Tel. +44 (0)20 7830 1000. Fax +44 (0)20 7499 9767 URL: Email:london@eiu.com http://www.eiu.com
In the US: Economist Intelligence Unit, The Economist Building, 111 West 57th Street, NY, NY 10019, USA . Tel. +1 212 554 060/1 800 938 4685 (USA and Canada only). Fax +1 212 586 0248. Email: newyork@eiu.com URL: http://www.eiu.com

Cost: £235/$425 pa. The *Country Profile* **annual** is included in the sub-scription.

Country Risk Service: Poland

The Risk Service takes a two-year 'forecasting horizon' on a **quarterly** basis when presenting assessments of political, economic and financial risks likely to influence business activities. Future trends of 'over 180 major economic indicators' are presented.

Contact details: Economist Intelligence Unit, 15 Regent Street, London SW1Y 4LR, UK. Tel. +44 (0)20 7830 1000. Fax +44 (0)20 7499 9767 Email:london@eiu.com URL:http://www.eiu.com
In the US: Economist Intelligence Unit, The Economist Building, 111 West 57th Street, NY, NY 10019, USA . Tel. +1 212 554 060/1 800 938 4685 (USA and Canada only). Fax +1 212 586 0248. Email: newyork@eiu.com URL: http://www.eiu.com

Cost: £395/$625 pa

Country RiskLines: Poland

This **monthly,** brief, report (usually 4 pages) rates the risk of trading with the country in terms of earnings and international payment obligations, political and economic stability, investment climate, etc.

Contact details: Dun & Bradstreet, Holmers Farm Way, High Wycombe, Bucks HP12 3BR, UK. Tel. +44 (0)1494 422 000. Fax +44 (0)1494 422 929.

Cost: £35 pa

Financing Operations: Poland

This service offers a **quarterly** review of financial conditions reporting on, for example, national monetary policy, banks and other financial in-stitutions, investment incentives, trade financing, various financing techniques. *Financing Operations* is also 'available through on line databases, direct network feeds and the Internet'.

Contact details: Economist Intelligence Unit, 15 Regent Street, London SW1Y 4LR, UK. Tel. +44 (0)20 7830 1000. Fax +44 (0)20 7499 9767 URL: http://www.eiu.com

Cost: £245 pa.

Master Page

Business, tourist and cultural information. Free *Poland Today* news serv-ice available. There is also *Economic Outlook* which is described as 'a professional journal dedicated to professionals and business people who have an interest in Poland and Polish business matters'. It is available

daily on an Internet site, and can be obtained in email format. Both services are free as a 'public service'. The site 'provides coverage of banking, law, corporate finance, market analysis, economic analysis, real estate, employment, income tax, accounting, marketing and more'. 'A major library of all articles published is maintained in an electronic library'. A great deal of business and country information is on offer, obviously; but it should be noted that 'articles are accepted from any responsible source [but] are unedited'. The site carries a very lively, not say acrimonious, 'letters' section.

Contact details: Poland Business Association, Pl. Defilad 1, PKiN#1809, 00-901 Warsaw, Poland. Tel. +48 22 826 4980. Fax +48 22 5149. Email: sales@masterpage.com.pl URL: http://www.masterpage.com.pl/aibg/

Poland A.M.

This is **daily** news digest with prominent business coverage, including the Warsaw Stock Exchange. Entries are of the briefest. It is available by fax and email.

Contact details: Warsaw Business Journal, Ul. Słoneczna 29, Warsaw 00-789, Poland. Tel: +48 22 646 0575. Fax +48 22 646 0576. Email: wbj@wbj.pl URL: http://www.ceebiz.com

Cost: On application

Polish Business

A **monthly** magazine reporting on business events and developments in readable fashion. There is an Internet version called *Polish Business Online*.

Contact details: Polish Business, 238-246 King Street, London W6 0RF, UK. Tel. +44 (0)20 8748 6537. Fax +44 (0)20 8748 2779. Email: staff@polishbusiness.com URL: http://www.polishbusiness.com/

Cost: £29.50 pa

Polish Economy: Analyses and Forecasts

This **bimonthly** bank publication provides a continuing survey of the economic scene, with statistical data, as well as attempting to forecast trends. There are few better freebies.

Contact details: Bank Handlowy w Warszawie, 16 Eastcheap, London EC3M 1BD, UK. Tel. +44 (0)20 7369 1150. Fax +44 (0)20 7369 1155.

Cost: Free on application.

Polish Market Review

This is a **bimonthly** newsletter covering investing, investment management, product research and marketing in Poland. The associated Internet site provides a wide coverage of business news, with links to other relevant business sources.

Contact details: PMR, ul Sarego 12/1A, 31-047 Krakow, Poland. Tel/Fax +48 12 637 5438. Email: pmr.polishmarket.com URL: http://www.polishmarket.com/main.html

Cost: On application

Warsaw Business Journal
This **weekly** source monitors economic and financial developments, provides sectoral and stock exchange news, as well as general news with a bearing upon business operations and foreign investments.

Contact details: VP International, Red Hill House, Hope Street, Hope House, Chester CH4 8BU, UK. Tel. +44 (0)1244 681619. Email: helen@vpinternational.com URL: http://www.vpinternational.com/

Cost: £130/$195 pa.

Warsaw Voice
A **weekly** newspaper with a strong Internet presence. General news coverage, but with pronounced emphasis upon economic and business issues.

Contact information: The Warsaw Voice, 64 Księcia Janusza St., 5th Floor, 01-452 Warsaw, Poland. Email: voice@warsawvoice.com.pl URL: http://www.warsawvoice.com.pl

Companies and Contacts

In comparative terms well supplied with competing company information sources providing the standard, basic, locational, contact and activity data. Examples are:

Business Foundation Book
This directory (1998) provides basic details of major companies, but also 'provides information on doing business in Poland, ranging from the economic potential to investment law'. Available in hard copy and CD-ROM formats.

Contact details: VP International, Red Hill House, Hope Street, Chester CH4 8BU, UK. Tel. +44 (0)1244 681619. Fax +44 (0)1244 681617. Email: helen@vpinternational.com URL: hrrp://www.vpinternational.com/

Cost: £175/$273 (outside Europe)

Foreign Companies in Emerging Markets Yearbook: Poland
This **annual** lists the numerous foreign companies operating in the Republic highlighting their potential as buyers and suppliers. The company details are standard including, for example, contact data, business activ-

ity descriptions, sales volumes. Available in hard copy and CD-ROM formats.

Contact details: Business Monitor International, 179 Queen Victoria Street, London EC4V 4DU, UK. Tel. +44 (0)20 7248 0468. Fax +44 (0)20 7248 0467. URL: http://www.businessmonitor.com

Cost: £240/$390 (print); £390/$650 (CD-ROM)

Kompass Poland
This standard directory (8th edition, 1999) lists 43,000 enterprises. In addition to the usual locational details and activity descriptions, trade marks, bank details, annual turnover, number of employees are included. This is the largest of the *Kompass* range of directories.

Contact details: Kompass UK, Reed Information Services, Windsor Court, East Grinstead House, East Grinstead, West Sussex RH19 1WA, UK. Tel. +44 (0)1342 326972. Fax +44 (0)1342 335612.

Cost: £330

Major Companies in Poland
This CD-ROM provides, **annually,** basic company details which may be accessed using company name, city, branch or region. Over 22,000 companies are listed. The CD-ROMs are searchable, but the simpler version has only the facility to print labels.

Contact details: VP International, Red Hill House, Hope Street, Chester CH4 8BU, UK. Tel. +44 (0)1244 681619. Fax +44 (0)1244 681617. Email: helen@vpinternational.com URL: http://www.vpinternational.com/vpi2b.htm

Cost: £175/$263 (in Europe – viewing only), $273 (outside Europe); £725/$1090 (in Europe – full profile printing), $1100 (outside Europe).

Polish Company Directory – TeleAdreson Online
This is a huge Internet company directory with over 70,000 enterprises of all types listed. Company profiles include activity descriptors. The file is searchable by names, sector and geographical area.

Contact details: URL: http://www.teleadreson.com.pl

Warsaw Business Journal Book of Lists
This **annual** lists over 1500 major companies in 76 sectors. Company data include contact details, names of CEOs, revenues.

Contact details: VP International, Red Hill House, Hope Street, Hope House, Chester CH4 8BU, UK. Tel. +44 (0)1244 681619. Email: helen@vpinternational.com URL: http://www.vpinternational.com/

Cost: £25/$38 (Europe); $48 (elsewhere)

Industries and Services

Poland's industrial and service sectors are well provided with varied and competing English language sources – the result of contributions by western information suppliers and an increasing number of indigenous producers. The impact of Internet services is significant.

Agriculture

Agricultural Situation and Perspectives in the Central and East European Countries: Poland

This report, from the European Union, 'aims to provide an analysis of the current situation and the medium-term outlook for the agricultural and agri-food industries' in the CEE countries aiming for EU membership – Bulgaria, Czech Republic, Hungary, Poland, Romania, Slovakia, Slovenia. The report is freely available on the Internet.

Contact details: URL: http://www.europa.eu.int/comm/dg06/publi/peco.index-en.htm

Automotive

Directory of Polish Automotive Component Manufacturers

This directory (1997) reviews developments in the sector; analyses trends, productive capacity and sub-group activities. There is a directory of component suppliers, with contact data and product descriptions.

Contact details: FT Automotive, Maple House, 149 Tottenham Court Road, London W1P 9LL, UK. Tel. +44 (0)20 7896 2241. Fax +44 (0)20 7896 2275. URL: http://www.ftauto.com

Cost: £195/$305

Polish Automotive Industry

A description (1997) and analysis of sectoral developments set in the political, social, economic and demographic situation. Developments in the various sub-sectors are reviewed, and the industry's future assessed. Major companies are profiled and assessed.

Contact details: FT Automotive, Maple House, 149 Tottenham Court Road, London W1P 9LL, UK. Tel. +44 (0)20 7896 2241. Fax +44 (0)20 7896 2275. URL: http://www.ftauto.com

Cost: £395/$624

Chemicals

Poland's Chemical Sector
This **annual** is compiled by Red Square Trade Information, with a record of providing more interesting financial and strategic detail than most other directory makers. Apart from contact data there are details of the privatisation process, sales figures, product information, and sectoral statistics.

Contact details: VP International, Red Hill House, Hope Street, Chester CH4 8BU, UK. Tel +44 (0)1244 681619. Fax +44 (0)1244 681617. Email: helen@vpinternational.com URL: http://www.vpinternational.com

Cost: £295/$445

Poland's Paint and Varnish Sector: A Directory of Companies
A listing (1998) of 200 producers and suppliers in the sector. The company data provided include contact details, names of chief personnel, brief activity outlines. There are print and diskette versions. A Red Square Trade Information product.

Contact details: VP International, Red Hill House, Hope Street, Chester CH4 8BU, UK. Tel +44 (0)1244 681619. Fax +44 (0)1244 681617. Email: helen@vpinternational.com URL: http://www.vpinternational.com

Cost: £175 (print version); £250 (Diskette version, with mailing list facility).

Poland's Plastics and Rubber Sector
A list (1998) of some 4000 firms, with contact and descriptive data and sectoral statistics. Another Red Square Trade Information product.

Contact details: VP International, Red Hill House, Hope Street, Chester CH4 8BU, UK. Tel +44 (0)1244 681619. Fax +44 (0)1244 681617. Email: helen@vpinternational.com URL: http://www.vpinternational.com

Cost: £195

Construction

Construction in Poland 1998 - 2010.
This research report (1998) analyses future sectoral possibilities with strong statistical support. Major companies are profiled.

Contact details: European Construction Research, Bredgade 35B, DK-1260 Copenhagen, Denmark. Tel. +45 33 162100. Fax +45 33 162900. Email: ecr@CYBERNET.DK URL: http://www.epi.no/ecr/index/htm

Cost: On application.

EuroBuild Poland

A **monthly** newsletter reporting on developments in the construction industry. Includes reviews of building regulations, forecasts, major projects, tenders, contacts.

Contact details: European Construction Research, Bredgade 35B, DK-1260 Copenhagen, Denmark. Tel. +45 33 162100. Fax +45 33 162900. Email: ecr@CYBERNET.DK URL: http://www.epi.no/ecr/index/htm

Cost: £39 a month.

Energy

Poland's Oil and Gas Sector

All the major companies are profiled in this directory (1998) from Red Square Trade Information. Private petrol retailers are listed, together with foreign oil and gas companies. Import and export statistics for oil and gas are provided.

Contact details: VP International, Red Hill House, Hope Street, Chester CH4 8BU, UK. Tel +44 (0)1244 681619. Fax +44 (0)1244 681617. Email: helen@vpinternational.com URL: http://www.vpinternational.com

Cost: £295/$445

Finance and Banking

Capital Market in Poland

Covers stock market, trust funds, treasury bonds, statistics, currency, etc.

Contact details: URL: http://yogi.ippt.gov.pl/gielda/gielda_e.html

Gazeta Giełdy Parkiet

Events on the Warsaw Stock Exchange are monitored on this web site. Traded companies are profiled.

Contact details: Gazeta Giełdy Parkiet, 12 Saska Street, 03-968 Warsaw, Poland. Tel. +48 22 672 8239. Fax +48 22 672 8039. Email: parkiet1@medianet.com.pl URL: http://www.parkiet.com.pl

National Bank of Poland

Information on legislation, statistics, banks in Poland, etc. is presented in a number of publications.

Contact details: ul. Świętokrzyska 11/21, 00-919 Warsaw, Poland. Tel. +48 22 653 10 00. Fax +48 22 620 85 18. Email: nbp@nbp.pl URL: http://www.nbp.pl/home_en.html

Polish Capital Markets Guide

A reference compilation that gathers scattered information and data about the Warsaw Stock Exchange, traded companies, leading personalities in the financial markets, brokerage houses, investment funds, insurance companies.

Contact details: Aspekt kilcullen, Marszałkowska 60/7, 00-545 Warsaw, Poland. Tel. +48 22 628 7283. Fax +48 22 622 0359. Email: aspekt@aspekt.com.pl URL: http://www.aspekt.com.pl

Warsaw Stock Exchange

Details of regulatory framework, trading systems, listed securities, listed companies, exchange members, derivatives, indices and statistics as well as daily quotations. Includes links to Polish capital market institutions. Publications include *CEDULA – Daily Bulletin, WSE Monthly Bulletin* and *WSE Quarterly Bulletin.*

Contact details: Warsaw Stock Exchange, ul. Nowy Świat 6/12, 00-400 Warsaw, Poland. Tel. +48 22 661 7453. Fax +48 22 661 7484. Email: gielda@wsc.com.pl and gielda@gpw.com.pl URL: http:// www.wse.com.pl/ and http://www.atm.com.pl

Cost: *CEDULA – Daily Bulletin* $250pa; *WSE Monthly Bulletin* $25pa; *WSE Quarterly Bulletin* $12pa.

Who's Who in Polish Banking and Finance

Provides brief biographical and business details of the major figures in the sector classified by areas of operation – investment banks, commercial banks, investment funds, etc.

Contact details: Warsaw Business Journal, Ul. Słoneczna 29, 00-789 Warsaw, Poland. Tel. +48 22 646 0575. Fax +48 22 646 0576. Email: wbj@wbj.pl URL: http://www.ceebiz.com

Cost: $10

Food and Drink

Food Retailing in Poland

A market research report (1998) providing a 'very detailed analysis of food wholesaling and retailing ... The market is analysed by channel in terms of market size, number of retailers, size of outlets, employment, market concentration, modernisation'.

Contact details: Seymour-Cooke Ltd., Food Research International, 42 Colebrooke Row, London N1 8AF, UK. Tel. +44 (0)20 7704 9951. Fax +44 (0)20 7226 5298. URL: http://www.seymour-cooke.com/

Cost: £950/$1660

Food Service Opportunities in Poland
A management report (1999) covering commercial, institutional and catering sectors. It includes data on foodservice sales, consumer trends, major operators, consumer attitudes towards eating out, changing eating habits, and the impact of tourism on the market.

Contact details: Seymour-Cooke Ltd., Food Research International, 42 Colebrooke Row, London N1 8AF, UK. Tel. +44 (0)20 7704 9951. Fax +44 (0)20 7226 5298. URL: http://www.seymour-cooke.com/

Cost: £650/$1140

Metallurgy

Poland's Iron and Steel Industry
This directory (1999) profiles all the major enterprises. In doing so it provides more financial data than is usual – for example, net profit, balance sheets, profit and loss accounts, assessments of future planning decisions, sectoral statistics. From the prolific Red Square Trade Information publishing group.

Contact details: VP International, Red Hill House, Hope Street, Chester CH4 8BU, UK. Tel +44 (0)1244 681619. Fax +44 (0)1244 681617. Email: helen@vpinternational.com URL: http://www.vpinternational.com

Cost: £295/$445

Pharmaceuticals

Poland's Pharmaceutical Sector
A directory (1997) of 200 firms with their balance sheets, profit and loss accounts. Import/export statistics, and domestic production statistics are provided.

Contact details: VP International, Red Hill House, Hope Street, Chester CH4 8BU, UK. Tel +44 (0)1244 681619. Fax +44 (0)1244 681617. Email: helen@vpinternational.com URL: http://www.vpinternational.com

Cost: £175/$263

Telecommunications

Poland: Telecom Opportunities and Risks 1998.
This is a market research report identifying investment opportunities with potential, and those better left alone. Among the topics discussed are authorities and regulations, regulatory structure and policies, developments, independent local operators, local access markets, value added service.

Contact details: ITC Publications, 4340 East West Highway, Suite 1020, Bethesda, MD 20814, USA. Tel. +1 301 907 0060. Fax +1 301 907 6555. Email: itcorp@itcresearch.com URL: http://www.itcresearch.com

Cost: $2500

Legislation

Business law is well catered for at the layman and specialist levels. Examples are:

Business Law Handbook: Poland
This *Handook* is updated **annually** to take account of changes in the laws and regulations governing business activities generally, and those of foreigners in particular. A readable introduction for the layman.

Contact details: Russian Information and Business Center, PO Box 15343, Washington DC 20003, USA. Tel. +1 202 546 2103. Fax +1 202 546 3275. Email: rusline@erols.com URL: http://www.rusline.com/

Cost: $89

Legal Guide: Poland
A layman's guide, from the Department of Trade and Industry, to the more important aspects of business law, concentrating especially on the processes of establishing a business. A good introduction.

Contact details: DTI, Admail 528, London SW1w 8YT, UK. Tel. +44 (0)20 7510 0171. Fax +44 (0)20 7510 0197. URL: http://www.dti.gov.uk/ots/publications

Cost: £12

Poland's Commercial Code
Translations of a number of laws governing business and business transactions, including the *Bankruptcy Act*.

Contact details: VP International, Red Hill House, Hope Street, Chester CH4 8BU, UK. Tel +44 (0)1244 681619. Fax +44 (0)1244 681617. Email: helen@vpinternational.com URL: http://www.vpinternational.com

Cost: £40 (Europe); $70 (elsewhere)

Polish Businesses and the EU Law Focus
A booklet (1997) for the layman produced by Cameron McKenna, a law firm with interests in CEE countries. Attention is concentrated upon important legal issues arising from the enlargement of the European Union.

Contact details: Cameron McKenna, Mitre House, 160 Aldersgate Street, London EC1A 4DD, UK. Tel. +44 (0)20 7367 3000. Fax +44 (0)20 7367 2000. Email: info@cmck.com URL: http://www.cmck.com/pub23.htm

Cost: Free on application.

Polish Law Translation
The Publishing House of the Polish Society of Economics, Legal and Court Translations (Tepis) supplies authoritative versions of commercial laws. These are available as separate issues, for example – *The Polish Commercial Code, The Polish Labour Code, Polish Copyright*. The most comprehensive English language version is the *Polish Law Collection*, a loose-leaf edition which has monthly updating sections. This version includes, for example, the *Companies with Foreign Share-Holding Act, Real Estate Acquisition Act, Foreign Exchange Law* – to name only three of the 36 acts provided.

Contact details: VP International, Red Hill House, Hope Street, Chester CH4 8BU, UK. Tel. +44 (0)1244 681619. Fax +44 (0)1244 681617. Email: helen@vpinternational.com URL: http://www.vpinternational.com/

Cost: On application.

Organisations
Poland's campaign to attract foreign investment has very active informational, advice and assistance strands. Some of the organisations willing and able to help in some, or all, these ways are:

American Embassy
At the Embassy Commercial Officers assist U.S. business – providing counsel on Polish trade regulations, laws and customs; identifying importers, buyers, agents, distributors and joint venture partners for U.S. firms; and arranging appointments with business and government officials'. The Embassy's web site is informative on a wide range of topics.

British Embassy
Available to provide advice, guidance and support. Office hours: Summer 06.30-14.30. Winter 07.30-15.30.

Contact details: British Embassy, Aleje Róż 1, 00 556 Warsaw, Poland. Commercial/Visa/Consular Section: Emilii Plater 28, 00-888 Warsaw, Poland. Tel. +48 22 628 1001/5, +48 22 625 6262, +48 22 625 3030

(Commercial/Visa/Consular). Fax +48 22 621 7161, +48 22 625 3472 (Commercial/Visa/Consular). Email: britemb@com.pl URL: http://www.britemb.it.pl/

British-Polish Chamber of Commerce (BPCC)
'As of 1st January 1999, the British Chamber of Commerce in Poland (BCCP) merged with the British-Polish Chamber of Commerce (UK) (BPCC). The two web sites are currently being redesigned ...'. The result of the merger is to strengthen the claim of the new Chamber as a source of business information and advice.

Contact details: BPCC, 55 Exhibition Road, London SW7 2PG, UK. Tel. +44 (0)20 7591 0057. Fax +44 (0)20 7591 0067. Email: bpcc@mcmail.com BPCC, ul. Zimna 2 m 1, 00-138, Warsaw, Poland. Tel. +48 22 654 5971/5974. Fax +48 22 654 1675. Email: bpcc@bpcc.org.pl URL: http://www.bpcc.org.pl/

Central Statistical Office
Poland got its statistical act together earlier than most CEE countries, both in terms of data collection and presentation. The web site maintained by CSO is informative, describing, for example, the statistical system in technical detail, the sources produced and the services available. Among the many sources published are – *Statistical Yearbook of the Republic of Poland* (available in hard copy and as a CD-ROM), *Concise Statistical Yearbook, Statistical Bulletin, Poland: Quarterly Statistics, Demographic Yearbook.*

Contact details: Statistical Publishing Department, al. Niepodległości 208, 00-925 Warsaw, Poland. Tel. +48 608 3145. Fax +48 608 3867. URL: http://www.stat.gov.pl/english/stale/przewodnik/index.htm

Embassy of Poland: UK
Offers advice, guidance and contact information to interested business parties. The Embassy maintains an Internet site providing information about the economy and country, aspects of business law and travel advice.

Contact details: Commercial Department, 47 Portland Place, London W1N 3AG, UK. Tel. +44 (0)20 7580 5481. Fax +44 (0)20 7323 0195. Polish Commercial Counsellors Office, 15 Devonshire Street, London W1N, UK. Tel. +44 (0)20 7580 5481.URL: http://www.poland-embassy.org.uk

Embassy of Poland: USA
The Embassy's web site is strong on business and economy, travel, news and a wide range of country information.

Contact details: Embassy of Poland, 2640 16ᵗʰ Street, NW, Washington DC 20009, USA. Tel. +1 202 234 3800. Fax +1 202 328 6271. Email: embpol@dgsys.com URL: http://www.polishworld.com/polemb/

Polish Agency for Foreign Investment (PAIZ)

'PAIZ was established to actively promote Poland's investment opportunities and encourage foreign companies to choose Poland as their investment location'. In furtherance of its aims the Agency provides assistance on entering Polish markets, highlights opportunities, identifies potential business partners, explains legal conditions – everything, in short, to promote inward investment. Its information role includes the publication of, for example, the *List of Major Foreign Investors in Poland*, and the CD-ROM (1998), produced with EU assistance, *Thinking Investment – Think Poland*. The latter is obviously heavily promotional, but it contains good background material, with informative descriptions of various sectoral opportunities.

Contact details: Polish Agency for Foreign Investment, Aleje Róż 2, Warsaw, 00-559 Warsaw, Poland. Tel. +48 22 621 6261. Fax +48 22 621 8427. URL: http://www.paiz.gov.pl/

Polish Chamber of Commerce

Promoted as one of the main points of contact for those wishing to enter Polish markets. Provides the usual array of information about companies, opportunities, partners, business law, etc. Need for specific types of information may be satisfied by recourse to the specialist Chambers. There are, for example, Chambers of Commerce for Construction, Electrical Engineering, Exporters and Importers, Electronics, the Chemical Industry.

Contact details: Polish Chamber of Commerce, ul. Trębacka 4, PO Box 361, 00-916 Warsaw, Poland. Tel. +48 22 27-9478. Fax. +48 22 27-4673.

Chapter 10

Romania

Population 22.5m. Internal political differences have crippled the process of economic reform. The result is declining industrial production, a weak currency, continuing inflation and high unemployment. However, 'the Romanian government has decided to fast-track the privatization process for 64 large and medium-sized companies. Investment banks will be chosen by the end of June to prepare these companies for sell-off in 3Q99. While the announcement is related to Romania's attempt to please the IMF and private international lenders, the privatization program would at least keep international investment banks involved in Romania' (*Central Europe Portfolio* May 18, 1999, p3). For many countries economic survival requires policies that have the approval of those with command of international purse-strings.

The business information sector is reasonably developed with numerous sources available for overview and current development purposes. There is good coverage of business law, and the beginnings of sectoral coverage.

Overview

Many of the general, or overview, English language sources are produced in the USA and the UK. The ability of Internet sites to serve this general country information role has been recognised with the emergence of locally based sites.

Business Investment Opportunity Yearbook: Romania
This **annual** covers 'business, investment, export-import, economic and other opportunities in respected countries. Foreign economic assistance projects, sources of financing , strategic government and business contacts, and more...'. The annual publication cycle precludes 'hot' investment news. The series titles, of which this is one, cover numerous countries throughout the world. It is difficult to know what weight to attach to the description 'respected'.

Contact details: Russian Information and Business Center, PO Box 15343, Washington DC 20003, USA. Tel. +1 202 546 2103. Fax +1 202 546 3275. Email: rusline@erols.com URL: http://www.rusline.com/

Cost: $89

Country Commercial Guide: Romania
Titles in the *Guides* series are published **annually**. They review the country's commercial environment 'using economic, political and market analysis', and 'consolidate various reporting documents prepared for the U.S.Embassies community'. There are informative sections on the investment climate, trade regulations and standards, economic trends and outlook, and useful summary statistics in appendices. A good country introduction. Available on the Internet, in hard copy and as a diskette.

Contact details: URL: http://www.stat-usa.gov/Newstand

Cost: $20 (hard copy)

Country Profile: Romania
This **annual** publication is a standard reference source. Comment, analysis and statistics cover the main industrial sectors, economic policies, political background, population, finance, prices and wages – with remarkable succinctness.

Contact details: Economist Intelligence Unit, 15 Regent Street, London SW1Y 4LR, UK. Tel. +44 (0)20 7830 1000. Fax +44 (0)1708 371 850. Email: london@eiu.com URL: http://www.eiu.com
In the US: Economist Intelligence Unit, The Economist Building, 111 West 57th Street, NY, NY 10019, USA . Tel. +1 212 554 060/1 800 938 4685 (USA and Canada only). Fax +1 212 586 0248. Email: newyork@eiu.com URL: http://www.eiu.com

Cost: £120/$205

Doing Business In Romania
One of a series (1998) produced by the CBI as introductions to business practices and environments in CEE countries. Titles are produced to a standard format covering the business context, market potential, business development and building an organisation. Appendices include useful contacts. The advice offered is middle of the road – sensible and with risk avoidance as a priority.

Contact details: VP International, Red Hill House, Hope Street, Chester CH4 8BU, UK. Tel. +44 (0)1244 681619. Fax +44 (0)1244 681617. Email: helen@vpinternational.com URL: http://www.vpinternational.com/

Cost: £30

Doing Business with Romania
A locally produced promotional introduction to investing in Romania. The free pocket-book is informative on topics like banking, contacts, privatisation, tax, businesss law, custom tariffs.

Contact details: Banca Turco-Românã, Str. Ion Câmpineanu 16, Bucharest 1, Romania. Tel. +40 1 312 3143. Fax +40 1 311 1732.

Dun & Bradstreet Country Report: Romania

This **annual** report profiles the country in terms of the economy, political situation, financial information, its debts and payment potential, the business climate. There are **monthly** monitoring updates. The report is available on diskette also.

Contact details: Dun & Bradstreet, Holmers Farm Way, High Wycombe, Bucks HP12 3BR, UK. Tel. +44 (0)1494 422 000. Fax +44 (0)1494 422 929.

Cost: £245 (hard copy; diskette); £335 (report + monthly updates).

EBRD Country Profiles: Romania

The main headings for this **annually** produced report are: economic survey, investment climate, financial sector, multilateral funding, EBRD activities, contact list. The report is prepared for the Annual Meeting of the European Bank for Reconstruction and Development.

Contact details: Effective Technology Marketing, PO Box 171, Grimsby DN35 0TP, UK. Tel/Fax +44 (0)1472 816660. Email: sales@etmltd.demon.co.uk URL: http://www.etmltd.demon.co.uk

Cost: £10/$17

IMF Staff Country Reports: Romania

The International Monetary Fund monitors the economic and financial affairs of its member countries. A series of reports, updated at irregular intervals, are produced for the consultations and assessments that take place. These appear as reviews of recent economic developments, selected issues and statistical annexes. The result, for each country surveyed, is a useful source of general and specialised knowledge of the economy, with an emphasis upon financial issues. The reports can be downloaded from the Internet.

Contact details: IMF Publication Services, 700 19th Street, NM, Washington DC 20431, USA. Tel. +1 202 623 7430. Fax +1 202 623 7201. Email: pubweb@imf.org URL: http://www.imf.org/external/pubs/pubs/dist.htm In the UK – The Stationery Office, PO Box 276, London SW8 5DT, UK. Tel. +44 (0)870 600 5522. Fax +44 (0)20 7873 8247. URL: http://www.tso-online.co.uk

Cost: $15

Investment and Business Guide: Romania
This introductory **annual** source provides 'basic information on economy, business and investment climate and opportunities, export-import, industrial development, banking and finance, government and business, contacts'. All from the point of view of those contemplating doing business in the country. Readable and informative.

Contact details: Russian Information and Business Center, PO Box 15343, Washington DC 20003, USA. Tel. +1 202 546 2103. Fax +1 202 546 3275. Email: rusline@erols.com   URL: http://www.rusline.com/

Cost: $89

OECD Economic Surveys 1997-1998: Romania
A general analysis and assessment (1999) of the country's economic and social development based upon conventional western economic beliefs. Useful source of statistics

Contact details: OECD Publications, 2 rue André-Pascal, 75775 Paris, Cedex 16, France. Tel. +33 (0)1 45 24 8200. Fax +33 (0)1 49 10 4276. Email: compte.pubsinq@oecd.org. URL: http://www.oecd.org

Cost: FF130

Political Risk Services: Country Reports: Romania
Reports in this series are produced **annually.** They include 'fact sheets' of basic national data, background information, 'eighteen month and five year forecasts' indicating the risks that lie ahead, profiles of individuals likely to influence the business climate. The attendant hype suggests that 'this may be the only site you will ever need for country research'. Arguable, but not too far off the mark. The publishers maintain an especially informative web site.

Contact details: The PRS Group, 6320 Fly Road, Suite 102, East Syracuse, NY 13057-0248, USA. Tel. +1 315 431 0511. Fax +1 315 431 0200. URL: http://www.prsgroup.com/

Cost: $395

Romania: Encyclopaedic Survey
This web site provides a wide range of information and data about the country. Topics on the economy include, for example, foreign trade, foreign investment, economic indicators, privatisation. Other sections include business opportunities information, law digest for foreign investors, as well as company and institutional data. For general background information there are pages devoted to history, political life, social aspects, geography and culture.

Contact details: URL: http://www.indis.ici.ro/romania/romania.html

World of Information Country Report: Romania
A concise **annual** report reviewing the economic and political scene, with selected supporting statistics. Ideal for quick familiarisation.

Contact details: Walden Publishing, 2 Market Street, Saffron Walden, Essex CB10 1HZ, UK. Tel. +44 (0)1799 521150. Fax +44 (0)1799 524805.

Cost: £30/$65

Current Developments

Unlike the Overview section current developments is a category in which locally produced English language sources are prominent.

Bucharest Business Week
A well-presented and readable source that allows of close monitoring of business and financial events.

Contact details: VP International, Red Hill House, Hope Street, Chester CH4 8BU, UK. Tel. +44 (0)1244 681619. Fax +44 (0)1244 681617. Email: helen@vpinternational.com URL: http://www.vpinternational.com

Cost: £90 pa

Business Operations Report: Romania
This is a **quarterly** analysis of the wide range of local and other factors bearing upon business decisions. Examples of such factors are: labour relations, the expected impact of political changes, assessments of future developments. Lessons are drawn from informative case studies. There are supporting statistics. The Report is 'also available through on line databases, direct network feeds and the Internet'.

Contact details: Economist Intelligence Unit, 15 Regent Street, London SW1Y 4LR, UK. Tel. +44 (0)20 7830 1000. Fax +44 (0)20 7499 9767 URL: http://www.eiu.com

Cost: £315 pa

Country Forecasts: Romania
This **quarterly** source presents 'five-year forecasts of political, economic and business trends'. Issues examined include, for example, prospects for political stability, business operating climate, government economic policies, labour market developments, sectoral matters.

Contact details: Economist Intelligence Unit, 15 Regent Street, London SW1Y 4LR, UK. Tel. +44 (0)20 7830 1000. Fax +44 (0)20 7499 9767 Email: london@eiu.com URL: http://www.eiu.com
In the US: Economist Intelligence Unit, The Economist Building, 111 West 57th Street, NY, NY 10019, USA . Tel. +1 212 554 060/1 800 938

4685 (USA and Canada only). Fax +1 212 586 0248. Email: newyork@eiu.com URL: http://www.eiu.com

Cost: £450/$645 pa

Country Risk Service: Romania

The Risk Service takes a two-year 'forecasting horizon' on a **quarterly** basis when presenting assessments of political, economic and financial risks likely to influence business activities. Future trends of 'over 180 major economic indicators' are presented.

Contact details: Economist Intelligence Unit, 15 Regent Street, London SW1Y 4LR, UK. Tel. +44 (0)20 7830 1000. Fax +44 (0)20 7499 9767 Email: london@eiu.com URL: http://www.eiu.com
In the US: Economist Intelligence Unit, The Economist Building, 111 West 57th Street, NY, NY 10019, USA . Tel. +1 212 554 060/1 800 938 4685 (USA and Canada only). Fax +1 212 586 0248. Email: newyork@eiu.com URL: http://www.eiu.com

Cost: £395/$625 pa

Country RiskLines: Romania

This **monthly** brief report (usually 4 pages) rates the risk of trading with the country in terms of earnings and international payment obligations, political and economic stability, investment climate, etc.

Contact details: Dun & Bradstreet, Holmers Farm Way, High Wycombe, Bucks HP12 3BR, UK. Tel. +44 (0)1494 422 000. Fax +44 (0)1494 422 929.

Cost: £35 pa

Economics

This electronic service sends out items of economic and business news throughout the day. The reports are brief and factual, in the alerting, newsletter, style.

Contact details: Mediafax, Bd. Marceşal Averescu 8-10, Bucharest, Romania. Tel. +40 1 223 3132. Fax +40 1 222 3503. URL: http://www.mediafax.ro/

Cost: $150 monthly.

InReview Romania

Business magazines the world over tend to adopt a similar style – glossy, features short enough not to tax the management attention span, numerous adverts, with serious news sandwiched between the glamorous. This **monthly** is no exception. A useful window on Romanian business though.

Contact details: IRR, Bd. Unirii, 13, Bl. 2c, sc.2, Ap.32, Bucharest, Romania. Tel/Fax +401 336 2139. Email: RoPR1@aol.com

Cost: On application

Invest Romania

This **quarterly** provides wide coverage of business news, including the promotion of investment opportunities. The style is lively and readable. The Internet site is updated **daily.**

Contact details: MediaGlobe Invest, Calea Călărașilor nr. 167, bl.39, sc.1, ap. 5, Bucharest, Romania. Tel/Fax +40 1 322 8641. Email: investro@bx.logicnet.ro URL: http://www.investromania.ro

Cost: $32 pa

Monitorul Online

This Internet site is maintained by Nord Est Media Group. *Monitorul* is the largest daily Romanian newspaper. The site provides items of general news, but it has 'business pages' that are worth a look.

Contact details: URL: http://www.monitorul.ro/home_e.htm

News Brief

This is a **twice-daily** fax service providing a general range of news items, including alerting reports on business topics.

Contact details: Mediafax, Bd. Marceşal Averescu 8-10, Bucharest, Romania. Tel. +40 1 223 3132. Fax +40 1 222 3503. URL: http://www.mediafax.ro/

Cost: $90 monthly.

Robix

The *Romanian Business Information Express* is intended as a general source of company and business information, including business laws and stock exchange dealings and prices.

Contact details: ROBIX, Tel. +40 1 223 0428. Fax +40 1 222 8807. Email: cia@ccir.ro URL: http://www.robix.ccir.ro

Romania Economic Newsletter

This **quarterly** newsletter reports and analyses economic and financial developments, with selected statistical indicators. Special in-depth analytical reports of specific issues are included as supplements to the newsletter.

Contact details: Cosmos Inc., PO Box 30437, Bethesda MD 20824, USA. Tel. +1 301 718 4305. Fax +1 301 718 4306.

Cost: Free on application.

Romanian Business Journal
A **weekly** with wide coverage of economic, financial, business and sectoral issues.

Contact details: Romanian Business Journal, piaţa Valter Mărăcineanu, etj.2, Sector 1, Bucharest, Romania. Tel. +40 1 312 4997. Fax +40 1 312 4958. Email: rbj@starnets.ro URL: http://www.starnets.ro/rbj

Cost: $15 monthly.

Romanian Economic Daily
Covers the business world in comprehensive fashion. The newspaper has an Internet presence.

Contact details: Nine O'Clock, Spaliul Independeţei 202A, Ground Floor, Bucharest, Romania. Tel. +40 1 222 8280. Fax +40 1 222 3241. Email: nine@nineoclock.ro URL: http://www.romanian-daily.ro/

Cost: $180 pa

Romanian Survey
A **weekly fax** news service covering political and economic affairs in an alerting, factual, fashion. Not for those wanting interpretation and analysis.

Contact details: Mediafax, Bd. Marceşal Averescu 8-10, Bucharest, Romania. Tel. +40 1 223 3132. Fax +40 1 222 3503. URL: http://www.mediafax.ro/

Cost: $30 monthly.

Companies and Contacts

This is a section in transformation. *Kompass Romania,*a standard company directory, was available for consultation until 1997. Contact with Reed Information Services brought the news that the local compilers of the directory had been declared bankrupt. A reminder that the early days of directory mania are over. However, the situation is balanced by the appearance of an upgraded, subscription based, company register on the Internet.

Romania Yellow Pages
An Internet telephone directory of business enterprises. A useful tool searchable by name.

Contact details: URL: http://www.romaniayellowpages.com/~mozaic

Romanian Trade Register
The current web site of the National Trade Register Office provides statistical data, aspects of business law, information on setting up companies, as well as a basic company checking service, free of charge. Change is in the offing, however. A new database – ROLEG Ver. 2.0 – is soon to be posted 'which will contain information, to be available by subscription, on details of a company, company profiles, information on the balance sheet and profit losss statement, etc.'.

Contact details: National Trade Register Office, Expoxitiei Blvd. 4, sector 1, 78334 Bucharest, Romania. Tel. +40 1 223 0893. Fax +40 1 224 4603. Email: onrc@ccir.ro URL: http://www.onrc.ccir.ro

TOP 3000
The 3000 companies profiled on this CD-ROM are listed on the Bucharest Stock Exchange according to the compilers. Other evidence indicates that the Exchange trades on a much smaller number of stocks. Anyhow, 3000 companies are profiled. The descriptions include financial data such as, for example, profit and loss accounts for the last three years, returns on capital, balance sheets, debt ratios, etc.

Contact details: Mediafax, Bd. Marceşal Averescu 8-10, Bucharest, Romania. Tel. +40 1 223 3132. Fax +40 1 222 3503. URL: http://www.mediafax.ro/

Cost: $900

Industries and Services

Our illustrative examples indicate that sectoral sources are appearing. The best description of the situation is of slowly widening coverage, but with little of the active competition that provides any depth of sources under each sectoral heading.

Agriculture

Agricultural Situation and Perspectives in the Central and East European Countries: Romania
This report, from the European Union, 'aims to provide an analysis of the current situation and the medium-term outlook for the agricultural and agri-food industries' in the CEE countries aiming for EU membership – Bulgaria, Czech Republic, Hungary, Poland, Romania, Slovakia, Slovenia. The report is freely available on the Internet.

Contact details: URL: http://www.europa.eu.int/comm/dg06/publi/peco.index-en.htm

Automotive

Romania: Automotive Industry
This is a sector report (1998) produced by the Department of Trade and Industry. A concise package of statistics, company descriptions, and sectoral review. The perspective is that of potential investors, suppliers or buyers in the UK.

Contact details: DTI Publications Orderline, Admail 528, London SW1W 8YT, UK. Tel. +44 (0)870 1502 5000. Fax +44 (0)870 1502 333.

Cost: £50

Construction

Facts About Construction Growth in Romania
This report (1999) 'contains information about construction activity and forecasts of future trends [focusing on] the civil engineering sector, office and housing, retail and industrial construction trends and includes information about price levels, vacancy rates and yields'. The socio-economic structure is described, and numerous statistical indicators provided.

Contact details: European Construction Research, Bredgade 35B, DK-1260 Copenhagen K, Denmark. Tel. +45 33 162 100. Fax +45 33 162 900. Email: ecr@cybernet.dk URL: http://www.sn.no/ne/ecr/construction-reports-europe.htm

Cost: £98/$145

Finance and Banking

Bucharest Stock Exchange
Not in the first line of Stock Exchanges. One reference source records only 12 actively traded companies. As a possible source of company information, however, it holds promise.

Contact details: Bucharest Stock Exchange, Str. Doamnei 8, Bucharest 70421, Romania. Tel. +40 0 3158 209. Fax +40 0 3158 149. Email:bvbrel@ceir.ro

Capital Market
This **daily** electronic service monitors developments on the Bucharest Stock Exchange, providing the expected data about share movements and quotations, with commentaries about the events of the day.

Contact details: Mediafax, Bd. Marceşal Averescu 8-10, Bucharest, Romania. Tel. +40 1 222 3132. Fax +40 1 222 3503. URL: http://www.mediafax.ro/

Cost: $150 monthly.

Forex and the Money Market
A **daily** fax service reporting on money market developments including interest and currency rates.

Contact details: Mediafax, Bd. Marceşal Averescu 8-10, Bucharest, Roamania. Tel. +40 1 222 3132. Fax +40 1 222 3503. URL: http://www.mediafax.ro/

Cost: $50 monthly.

NationalBank of Romania: Monthly Bulletin
The *Bulletin* provides a statistical summary of developments in the economic, financial, capital and money sectors.

Contact details: National Bank of Romania, Str., Lipscani 25, 70421 Bucharest, Romania. Tel. +40 1 312 4375. Fax +40 1 312 6261.

Cost: Free on application.

Legislation

Coverage of business law is adequate, with US information providers making a significant contribution.

Business Law Handbook: Romania
This *Handbook* is updated **annually** to take account of changes in the laws and regulations governing business activities generally, and those of foreigners in particular. A readable introduction for the layman.

Contact details: Russian Information and Business Center, PO Box 15343, Washington DC 20003, USA. Tel. +1 202 546 2103. Fax +1 202 546 3275. Email: rusline@erols.com URL: http://www.rusline.com/

Cost: $89

Commercial and Investment Law: Romania
A survey of laws affecting business operations including, for example, the regulation and protection of foreign investment, securities law, company law. It is updated **annually**.

Contact details: Juris Publishing, Executive Park, 1 Odell Plaza, Yonkers, NY 10701, USA. Tel. +1 914 375 3400. Fax +1 914 375 6047. Email: orders@jurispub.com URL: http://www.jurispub.com

Cost: $95

Law Digest for Foreign Investors
A straightforward translation of laws relevant to the business activities of foreigners. A basic, but essential, service.

Contact details: Romanian Development Agency, Bd. Magheru 7, 70161 Bucharest. Tel. +40 1 315 9229. Fax +40 1 312 0371.

Cost: $40

Lex Structure
Lex Structure, together with its **weekly** updating service, *Juridicial Abridgement*, constitute a general legal database. Business laws can be drawn out from the CD-ROM by the use of flexible searching facilities.

Contact details: Mediafax, Bd. Marceşal Averescu 8-10, Bucharest, Romania. Tel. +40 1 223 3132. Fax +40 1 222 3503. URL: http://www.mediafax.ro/

Cost: $340 per month (single-users); $540 per month (multi-users).

Romanian Digest
The *Digest* is an Internet service which reviews legislative changes on a **monthly** basis. It is a promotional service, but not one to be neglected on that account.

Contact details: Herzfeld & Rubin, Str. Dionisie Lupu 62, Sector 1, Bucharest, Romania. Tel. +40 1 223 3358. Fax +40 1 223 3377. Email: office@hr.ro URL: http://www.hr.ro/more.htm

Organisations
The usual range of promotional agencies is available. For example:

American Embassy
The Embassy's web site features an excellent Commercial Section. Included in the services offered are – a country commercial overview, contact information, trade related events, listing of major foreign firms operating in Romania, business information.

Contact details: U.S. Embassy, Commercial Section, Str. Tudor Arghezi 7-9, Bucharest, Romania. Tel. +40 1 210 4042 Ext. 351. Fax +40 1 210 0690. Email: Bucharest.Office.Box@mail.doc.gov URL: http://www.usembassy.ro/

British Embassy
Staff at the Embassy help to promote British business interests. Enquiries are answered and assistance given in establishing contacts. Office hours: April to October, Monday to Thursday 05.30-14.00, Friday 05.30-10.30. November-March, Monday to Thursday 06.30-15.00, Friday 06.30-11.30.

Contact details: British Embassy, Str. Jules Michelet 24, 70154 Bucharest, Romania. Tel. +40 1 312 0303. Fax +40 1 312 0229, +40 1 312 9652 (Consular), +40 1 312 9742 (Commercial).

Chamber of Commerce and Industry of Romania
The Chamber engages in the usual range of promotional activities, and is willing to extend assistance to any and all potential investors. Its information programme includes *PRO Business Romania* – a diskette, listing and describing its major member companies. The diskette also provides useful contacts, legal, travel and accommodation information. The 1999 2nd edition covering 7000 companies is now available and costs $49. The Chamber maintains an Internet site giving access to services on offer, with general business information.

Contact details: Chamber of Commerce and Industry of Romania, Bd. Nicolae Bălcescu 22, Bucharest 70122, Romania. Tel. +40 0 3121 312 Fax +40 0 3123 830. Email: cia@ccir.ro   URL: http://www.ccir.ro

Embassy of Romania: UK
Can asist with business issues.

Contact details: Embassy of Romania, 4 Palace Green, London W8 4QD, UK. Tel. +44 (0)20 7937 9666. Fax +44 (0)20 7937 8069

Embassy of Romania: USA
The Trade and Economic Section of the Embassy maintains an Internet site providing a wide range of information relating to Romania. Its main function, however, is to encourage investment in Romania. The service highlights opportunities for foreign investors, outlines legal requirements, notes changes in business laws, provides advice on how best to initiate business enquiries, etc. The site was revamped in October 1999.

Contact details: Embassy of Romania, 1607 23rd Street, NW, Washington DC 20008, USA. Tel. +1 202 332 4846; 4848; 4851; 4852. Fax +1 202 332 4748. Email: info@roembus.org URL: http://www.roembus.org

National Commission for Statistics
The National Commission for Statistics publishes over 50 statistical publications. Noteworthy for general business use are the *Romanian Statistical Yearbook* and the *Monthly Statistical Bulletin*. *Romania in Figures* provides a useful **annual** summary of the main statistical indicators. An informative overview, or background, source is provided by the **annual** *Social Situation* and *Economy of Romania*. These compilations review developments that have occurred in the economy and in society.

Contact details: NCS, Bd. Libertatii 16, Code 70542, Bucharest, Romania. Tel. +401 312 4875. Fax +401 312 4873. Email: romstat@cns.kappa.ro URL: http://www.cns.kappa.ro/address.html

Romanian Development Agency
The Agency has developed an extensive information programme to further its promotional aims. For example, there is a web site to inform and encourage foreign investors which provides a selection of national statistics, a helpful digest of business laws, and a directory of investment opportunities. In addition there is *Romanian Investment Review*, which appears **twice yearly** with reports of economic surveys, news of interest to foreign investors, news of regional developments, etc.

Contact details: Romanian Development Agency, Bd. Magheru 7, 70161 Bucharest, Romania. Tel. +40 1 312 3311, 315 6686, 312 2886. Fax +40 1 312 0371, 313 2415. URL: http://www.rda.ro

Chapter 11

Serbia and Montenegro

Population 10.4 m. Like other Balkan countries, Serbia suffered problems of unemployment, lack of investment, inflation, slow adaptation to more liberal market requirements and low productive performance. All this before the troubles arising from the Kosovo conflict. The economic and business consequences of the conflict have yet to be revealed, but a worsening of the country's economic situation seems inevitable.

The pre-conflict English language business information sector was developing slowly. The consequence here, too, are uncertain at present. The established sources are listed in the hope that effective use of business information will contribute to the reconstruction phase.

Overview

Only a small number of sources, but there should be no difficulty in obtaining general background information and data from multi-country and Internet sources.

Country Profile: Yugoslavia
This **annual** publication is a standard reference source. Comment, analysis and statistics cover the main industrial sectors, economic policies, political background, population, finance, prices and wages – with remarkable succinctness.

Contact details: Economist Intelligence Unit, 15 Regent Street, London SW1Y 4LR, UK. Tel. +44 (0)20 7830 1000. Fax +44 (0)1708 371 850.
Email: london@eiu.com URL: http://www.eiu.com
In the US: Economist Intelligence Unit, The Economist Building, 111 West 57th Street, NY, NY 10019, USA . Tel. +1 212 554 060/1 800 938 4685 (USA and Canada only). Fax +1 212 586 0248.
Email: newyork@eiu.com URL: http://www.eiu.com

Cost: £120/$205

Doing Business in Yugoslavia
This is 'the first Yugoslav Business Electronic Magazine for Foreign Investors'. It is published on the Internet on a **monthly** basis. The magazine features legal changes as these affect foreign investments and investors,

articles about the economy, company and product advertisements, projects in need of financing, real estate opportunities, leisure advice.

Contact details: URL: http://www.YUbusiness.co.yu

Federal Republic of Yugoslavia Official Web Site
The national home page provides general data and information about the country.

Contact details: URL: http://www.gov.yu/index/index.html

Political Risk Services: Country Reports: Yugoslavia
These reports are produced **annually.** They include 'fact sheets' of basic national data, background information, 'eighteen month and five year forecasts' indicating the risks that lie ahead, profiles of individuals likely to influence the business climate. The attendant hype suggests that 'this may be the only site you will ever need for country research'. Arguable, but not too far off the mark. The publishers maintain an especially informative web site.

Contact details: The PRS Group, 6320 Fly Road, Suite 102, East Syracuse, NY 13057-0248, USA. Tel. +1 315 431 0511. Fax +1 315 431 0200. URL: http://www.prsgroup.com/.

Cost: $395

Serbia.net
The service includes the *Serbian Business and Professional Directory.* At the time of writing this site was being updated. In the past it provided general information about the country, with company descriptions.

Contact details: URL: http://serbia.net/directory/directory_frame.html

Yugoslav Chamber of Commerce and Industry of the United States of America
The Chamber maintains an Internet site with basic data about the economy of FR Yugoslavia, a list of projects and background country information. The site produced the *Yugoslav Daily Survey,* but the Kosovo conflict appears to have disrupted its publication.

Contact details: URL: http://www.artanet.com/ycciinus/index.html

Yugoslavia Infomap
Provides a subject directory with links to relevant sites. Includes news and business categories.

Contact details: URL: http://www.yu/

Current Developments

A small selection of sources but, again, there should be no difficulty in monitoring political and economic developments.

Beta News Agency
Daily news in English from Yugoslavia and the former Yugoslav republics.

Contact details: URL: http://beta-press.com/bnewsone.htm

Country Reports: Yugoslavia
The *Reports* are produced **quarterly.** Each issue describes the political and economic structures, reviews political and economic prospects for the next 12 - 18 months, critically reviews major economic and political issues. Economic trends are illustrated with graphs and tables, and there are a number of statistical appendices.

Contact details: Economist Intelligence Unit, 15 Regent Street, London SW1Y 4LR, UK. Tel. +44 (0)20 7830 1000. Fax +44 (0)20 7499 9767
Email: london@eiu.com URL: http://www.eiu.com
In the US: Economist Intelligence Unit, The Economist Building, 111 West 57th Street, NY, NY 10019, USA . Tel. +1 212 554 060/1 800 938 4685 (USA and Canada only). Fax +1 212 586 0248.
Email: newyork@eiu.com URL: http://www.eiu.com.

Cost: £235/$425 pa. The *Country Profile* **annual** is included in the subscription.

Country Risk Service: Yugoslavia
The *Risk Service* takes a two-year 'forecasting horizon' on a **quarterly** basis when presenting assessments of political, economic and financial risks likely to influence business activities. Future trends of 'over 180 major economic indicators' are presented.

Contact details: Economist Intelligence Unit, 15 Regent Street, London SW1Y 4LR, UK. Tel. +44 (0)20 7830 1000. Fax +44 (0)20 7499 9767
Email: london@eiu.com URL: http://www.eiu.com.

Cost: £395

Economic Barometer
The *Barometer,* on a **quarterly** basis, offers 'an overview of the current trends and short-term prognosis for leading economic indicators in the following three months'. An issue consists of gathered views of 300 managers as to the state of the economy, the current situation as portrayed by official statistics, the use of economoetric models to estimate the future

trends of leading economic indicators, and analyses of selected topics of interest.

Contact details: Economics Institute (for Economic Barometer), Srpskih Vladara 16, 11000 Belgrade, Yugoslavia. Tel. +381 11 644 581. Fax +381 11 687 627. Email: gpitic@eunet.yu

Yugoslavia Weekly Survey
This Internet site provides a selective digest of political and business news. The selection is in the hands of the Federal Ministry of Foreign Affairs. There is also a *Daily Survey* on the same site, subject to the same control. There are links to other relevant sites.

Contact details: URL: http://www.yugoslavia.com/news/default.htm

Companies and Contacts

Not much choice, although there is one of standard directories devoted to the area.

Kompass Yugoslavia
A standard company directory. The 6th edition is promised for August, 1999, listing 16,000 companies. Profile details include locational data, names of top executives, annual turnover, product and activity descriptions.

Contact details: Kompass UK, Reed Information Services, Windsor Court, East Grinstead House, East Grinstead, West Sussex RH19 1XA, UK. Tel. +44 (0)1342 326972. Fax +44 (0)1342 335612.

Cost: £225

Industries and Services

For sectoral information the various agencies listed in the Organisations section below should be contacted.

Finance and Banking

Belgrade Stock Exchange
Can be used as a source of company information. Publishes bulletin, reports, analyses.

Contact details: Belgrade Stock Exchange, Omladinskih brigada 1, POB 214, 11070 Belgrade, Serbia. Tel. +381 11 311 74 10, 311 75 69. Fax +381 11 311 45 70. URL: http://www.belex.co.yu

National Bank of Yugoslavia: Quarterly Bulletin
A source for financial and monetary data. For comparative purposes the monthly data sets cover the past two years.

Contact details:National Bank of Yugoslavia, POB 1010 Bulevar Revolucije 15, Belgrade, Yugoslavia. Tel. +381 11 324 8841.

Cost: Free on application.

Legislation

There is little choice in this area.

Regulations
This Internet site is devoted to describing and explaining the laws applicable to foreign investors and investments.

Contact details: URL: http://www.yugoslavia.com/economy/regula.htm

Organisations

In a still heavily controlled economy government agencies are the likeliest sources for company, investment and business law enquiries.

American Embassy
The Economic/Commercial Section at the American Embassy 'provides information and services to help U.S. businesses succeed in Serbia and Montenegro, and to assist businesses to locate American business partners'. Among the items of business information provided are a country commercial guide, a quarterly report on the economy, key economic indicators. The Embassy's Internet site lists all the services available.

Contact details: U.S. Embassy, Kneza Milosa 50, Belgrade, Serbia. Tel. +381 11 645 655 Ext. 247. Email: tkuzminac@statebg.co.yu URL: http://www.amembbg.co.yu

British Embassy
Business activities have been disrupted by the Kosovo conflict. In the hope that relations will improve the last known details of the Embassy are provided. Office hours Monday to Thursday 07.00-15.30. Friday 07.00-112.00.

Contact details: British Embassy, Generia Ždanova 46, 11000 Belgrade, Serbia. Tel. +38 11 645055/645034/645053/646644/643742/645087. Fax +38 11 659651/642293 (Information Section). URL: http://www.britemb.org.yu/

Embassy of the Federal Republic of Yugoslavia
Will assisy with business issues.

Contact details: Embassy of the Federal Republic of Yugoslavia, 5 Lexham Gardens, London W8 5JJ, UK. Tel. +44 (0)20 7370 6105. Fax +44 (0)20 7370 3838.

Embassy of the Federal Republic of Yugoslavia: USA
The Embassy's web site provides country and business information.

Contact details: Embassy of the Former S.F. Republic of Yugoslavia, 2410 California Street, NW, Washington DC 20008, USA. Tel. +1 202 462 6566. Email: yuembassy@compuserve.com

Federal Statistical Office of Yugoslavia
The FSO publishes a range of basic statistics, but with less abandon than its neighbours. Among the more useful for business purposes are the *Statistical Yearbook, Monthly Review of Economic Statistics*, and the **annual** *Yugoslavia in Figures*. The latter is a handy brochure format presenting the main descriptive data.

Contact details: Federal Statistical Office, 20 Kneza Miloša Street, 11000 Beograd, Yugoslavia. Tel. +381 11 361 7437. Fax +381 11 361 7297. URL: http://www.szs.sv.gov.yu/homee.htm

Foreign Trade Institute
The concern of this government agency is to monitor and foster foreign trade. Requests for information about trading conditions and regulations are accepted.

Contact details: Foreign Trade Institute, Moše Pijade 8, 11000 Belgrade, Yugoslavia. Tel. +381 11 339041.

Yugoslav Chamber of Commerce and Industry
The Chamber will advise and assist foreign business investors. Its publication programme is on a much smaller scale than its counterparts in the region. Two helpful background and introductions to doing business in the country are – *Doing Business in Yugoslavia* (1998) and *Principles of Economic Development of Yugoslavia* (1998). The former sets out the procedures for establishing a company and the relevant legal requirements. The *Principles* ... describes and explains the industrial set-up and future development plans. All rather irrelevant in the current circumstances, but the Chamber will be required to play its part in the inevitable process of reconstruction as an information source. The Internet site maintained by the Chamber provides a description of the economy. The circumstances of the time are plainly reflected in the pages devoted to 'Nato Aggression on Yugoslavia'.

Contact details: Yugoslav Chamber of Commerce and Industry, POB 1003, Terazije 23, 11000 Belgrade, Yugoslavia. Tel. +381 11 3248 222, 3248 123. Fax +381 11 3248 754. Email: info@pjk.co.yu URL: http://f.pkj.co.yu/eindex.html

Chapter 12

Slovakia

Population 5.4m. Falling industrial production, double-figure inflation and unemployment, banks in an unreconstructed state, unresolved political difficulties, and a still uncompleted privatisation process explain the EU's expressed concern over Slovakia's progress towards a place around the Union table. The country has an indifferent record in attracting foreign direct investment. However, the UK and the USA appear to be taking a sanguine view of prospects. In 1998 the UK was the leading investor, followed by the USA. An unusually high placing for British business investments in CEE countries.

The business information sector is not as well endowed as some of those in neighbouring countries. The weight of government on business activities is reflected in the fact that, internally, the largest publishers of business and sectoral information sources are the Statistical Office of the Slovak Republic and the Slovak National Agency for Foreign Investment and Development (SNAZIR) – both government agencies. Over 60% of English language sources are from official sources.

Overview

The general overview sources are mainly of western origin. Examples are:

Business Investment Opportunity Yearbook: Slovakia
This **annual** covers 'business, investment, export-import, economic and other opportunities in respected countries. Foreign economic assistance projects, sources of financing , strategic government and business contacts, and more...'. The annual publication cycle precludes 'hot' investment news. The series titles, of which this is one, cover numerous countries throughout the world. In the circumstances it is difficult to understand the weight to be attached to the description 'respected'.

Contact details: Russian Information and Business Center, PO Box 15343, Washington DC 20003, USA. Tel. +1 202 546 2103. Fax +1 202 546 3275. Email: rusline@erols.com URL: http://www.rusline.com/

Cost: $89

Country Commercial Guide: Slovakia
Titles in the *Guides* series are published **annually**. They review the country's commercial environment 'using economic, political and market analysis', and 'consolidate various reporting documents prepared for the U.S.Embassies community'. There are informative sections on the investment climate, trade regulations and standards, economic trends and outlook, and useful summary statistics in appendices. A good country introduction. Available on the Internet, in hard copy and as a diskette.

Contact details: URL: http://www.stat-usa.gov/Newstand

Cost: $20 (hard copy)

Country Profile: Slovakia
This **annual** publication is a standard reference source. Comment, analysis and statistics cover the main industrial sectors, economic policies, political background, population, finance, prices and wages – with remarkable succinctness.

Contact details: Economist Intelligence Unit, 15 Regent Street, London SW1Y 4LR, UK. Tel. +44 (0)20 7830 1000. Fax +44 (0)1708 371 850. Email: london@eiu.com URL: http://www.eiu.com
In the US: Economist Intelligence Unit, The Economist Building, 111 West 57th Street, NY, NY 10019, USA . Tel. +1 212 554 060/1 800 938 4685 (USA and Canada only). Fax +1 212 586 0248.
Email: newyork@eiu.com URL: http://www.eiu.com

Cost: £120/$205

EBRD Country Profiles: Slovakia
The main headings for this **annually** produced report are – economic survey, investment climate, financial sector, multilateral funding, EBRD activities, contact list. The report is prepared for the Annual Meeting of the European Bank for Reconstruction and Development.

Contact details: Effective Technology Marketing, PO Box 171, Grimsby DN35 0TP, UK. Tel/Fax +44 (0)1472 816660. Email:
sales@etmltd.demon.co.uk URL: http://www.etmltd.demon.co.uk

Cost: £10/$17

IMF Staff Country Reports: Slovakia
The International Monetary Fund monitors the economic and financial affairs of its member countries. A series of reports, updated at irregular intervals, are produced for the consultations and assessments that take place. These appear as reviews of recent economic developments, selected issues and statistical annexes. The result, for each country surveyed, is a useful source of general and specialised knowledge of the economy, with an emphasis upon financial issues. The reports can be downloaded from the Internet.

Contact details: IMF Publication Services, 700 19th Street, NM, Washington DC 20431, USA. Tel. +1 202 623 7430. Fax +1 202 623 7201. Email: pubweb@imf.org URL: http://www.imf.org/external/pubs/pubs/dist.htm In the UK – The Stationery Office, PO Box 276, London SW8 5DT, UK. Tel. +44 (0)870 600 5522. Fax +44 (0)20 7873 8247. URL: http://www.tso-online.co.uk

Cost: $15

Investment and Business Guide: Slovak Republic
This introductory **annual** source provides 'basic information on economy, business and investment climate and opportunities, export-import, industrial development, banking and finance, government and business, contacts'. All from the point of view of those contemplating doing business in the country. Readable and informative.

Contact details: Russian Information and Business Center, PO Box 15343, Washington DC 20003, USA. Tel. +1 202 546 2103. Fax +1 202 546 3275. Email: rusline@erols.com URL: http://www.rusline.com/

Cost: $89

OECD Economic Surveys: Slovak Republic 1999
An informative description (1999) of the state of the country and its economy seen from a conservative perspective. The main sections review main economic developments, macroeconomic policies, the banking sector and enterprise restructuring and development. There are statistical appendices. A lengthy summary of the report is available on the Internet.

Contact details: OECD Paris Centre, 2 rue André-Pascal, 75775 Cedex 16, France. Tel. +33 (0)1 49 104235. Fax +33 (0)1 49 104276. Email: sales@oecd.org. Also – The Stationery Office, PO Box 276, London SW8 5DT, UK. Tel. +44 (0)870 600 5522. Fax +44 (0)20 7873 8247. URL: http://www.tso-online.co.uk

Cost: 150FF

Political Risk Service Country Report: Slovakia
This report assesses future political stability and, within this context, examines the implications for the economy.

Contact details: PRS Group, 6320 Fly Road, Suite 102, PO Box 248, East Syracuse, NY 13057-0248, USA. Tel. +1 315 431 0511. Fax +1 315 431 0200. Email: custserve@prsgroup.com URL: http://www.prsgroup.com/

Cost: $375

Slovakia
An Internet source for general background country information, and for an introduction to the economy and business.

Contact details: URL: http://www.slovak.sk

Slovakia: A Business and Investment Guide
A general, introductory, concise account of some of the main issues and conditions associated with doing business in Slovakia. An informative starter.

Contact details: PricewaterhouseCoopers, Plum Tree Court, London EC4A 4HI, UK. Tel. +44 (0)20 7212 4100. Fax +44 (0)20 7212 4995.

Cost: Free on application

Slovakia Since Independence
This book (1998) reviews the problems encountered following the break with what is now the Czech Republic. Provides a sound basis for understanding the present through an analysis of such issues as economic organisation, external relations, political structure, government structure and policies.

Contact details: Praeger Publishers, 3 Henrietta Street, Covent Garden, London WC2E 8LU, UK. Tel. +44 (0)20 7240 0856. Fax +44 (0)20 7379 0609. Email: orders@eurospan.co.uk

Cost: £43.95

Slovakia.org
This is an Internet site 'dedicated to presenting objective and non-partisan information about Slovak politics, society, history, culture, and the Slovak economy'.

Contact details: URL: http://www.slovakia.org

World of Information Country Report: Slovakia
A concise **annual** report reviewing the economic and political scene, with selected supporting statistics. Ideal for quick familiarisation.

Contact details: Walden Publishing, 2 Market Street, Saffron Walden, Essex CB10 1HZ, UK. Tel. +44 (0)1799 521150. Fax +44 (0)1799 524805.

Cost: £30/$65

Current Developments

The day-to-day current news is produced locally and appears in newspapers and on the Internet, but the more considered approach to current events, in English, are produced mainly outside the country.

Business Operations Report: Slovakia
This is a **quarterly** analysis of the wide range of local and other factors bearing upon business decisions. Examples of such factors are – labour relations, the expected impact of political changes, assessments of future developments. Lessons are drawn from informative case studies. There are supporting statistics. The *Report* is 'also available through on line databases, direct network feeds and the Internet'.

Contact details: Economist Intelligence Unit, 15 Regent Street, London SW1Y 4LR, UK. Tel. +44 (0)20 7830 1000. Fax +44 (0)20 7499 9767 Email: london@eiu.com URL: http://www.eiu.com

Cost: £315 pa

Country Forecasts: Slovakia
This **quarterly** source presents 'five-year forecasts of political, economic and business trends'. Issues examined include, for example, prospects for political stability, business operating climate, government economic policies, labour market developments, sectoral matters.

Contact details: Economist Intelligence Unit, 15 Regent Street, London SW1Y 4LR, UK. Tel. +44 (0)20 7830 1000. Fax +44 (0)20 7499 9767 Email: london@eiu.com URL: http://www.eiu.com
In the US: Economist Intelligence Unit, The Economist Building, 111 West 57th Street, NY, NY 10019, USA . Tel. +1 212 554 060/1 800 938 4685 (USA and Canada only). Fax +1 212 586 0248.
Email: newyork@eiu.com URL: http://www.eiu.com

Cost: £450/$645 pa

Country Reports: Slovakia
The *Reports* are produced **quarterly.** Each issue describes the political and economic structures, reviews political and economic prospects for the next 12 - 18 months, critically reviews major economic and political issues. Economic trends are illustrated with graphs and tables, and there are a number of statistical appendices.

Contact details: Economist Intelligence Unit, 15 Regent Street, London SW1Y 4LR, UK. Tel. +44 (0)20 7830 1000. Fax +44 (0)20 7499 9767 URL: Email: london@eiu.com http://www.eiu.com
In the US: Economist Intelligence Unit, The Economist Building, 111 West 57th Street, NY, NY 10019, USA . Tel. +1 212 554 060/1 800 938

4685 (USA and Canada only). Fax +1 212 586 0248.
Email: newyork@eiu.com URL: http://www.eiu.com

Cost: £235/$425 pa. The *Country Profile* annual is included in the sub-
scription.

Country Risk Service: Slovakia

The *Risk Service* takes a two-year 'forecasting horizon' on a **quarterly**
basis when presenting assessments of political, economic and financial
risks likely to influence business activities. Future trends of 'over 180
major economic indicators' are presented.

Contact details: Economist Intelligence Unit, 15 Regent Street, London
SW1Y 4LR, UK. Tel. +44 (0)20 7830 1000. Fax +44 (0)20 7499 9767
Email: london@eiu.com URL: http://www.eiu.com
In the US: Economist Intelligence Unit, The Economist Building, 111
West 57th Street, NY, NY 10019, USA . Tel. +1 212 554 060/1 800 938
4685 (USA and Canada only). Fax +1 212 586 0248.
Email: newyork@eiu.com URL: http://www.eiu.com

Cost: £395/$625 pa

Country RiskLines: Slovakia

This **monthly,** brief, report (usually 4 pages) rates the risk of trading with
the country in terms of earnings and international payment obligations,
political and economic stability, investment climate, etc.

Contact details: Dun & Bradstreet, Holmers Farm Way, High Wycombe,
Bucks HP12 3BR, UK. Tel. +44 (0)1494 422 000. Fax +44 (0)1494 422
929.

Cost: £35 pa

Slovakia Today

This is a **fortnightly** email service reporting on economic, financial, political and cultural developments and events.

Contact details: Bonus Real, Štefánikova 2, 81000 Bratislava, Slovak
Republic. Tel. +421 7 533 4467. Fax +421 7 533 4467. URL: http://
www.sia.gov.sk/sltoday.html

Cost: On application

Trend

Trend provides English language news summaries on the Internet site
maintained by EUnet Slovakia.

Contact details: URL: http://www.trend.sk

Companies and Contacts

Probably benefitting from its association with what is now the Czech Republic, Slovakia is relatively well supplied with sources of company information of the basic type. Czech publishers produce company sources which cover the 'old' Czecho-Slovakia (see the Czech Republic), as well as producing sources limited to Slovakia.

Inform Katalog: Slovakia

This **annual** directory provides over 5000 basic locational and contact company details. Companies are listed alphabetically and by industrial classification. Not the largest number of listings, but it is a useful source for locating details of major companies. Available in hard copy and CD-ROM formats. The latter, in the more expensive versions, has the 'capacity to modify and print labels'.

Contact details: VP International, Red Hill House, Hope Street, Chester CH4 8BU, UK. Tel. +44 (0)1244 681619. Fax +44 (0)1244 681617. Email: helen@vpinternational.com URL: http://www.vpinternational.com/

Cost: £50/$75 (Europe);$85 (elsewhere)

Kompass Slovakia

Over 16,000 companies are listed in this directory. The company profiles include locational and contact data, annual turnover, number of employees, product and activity descriptions. A new edition is promised for October, 1999.

Contact details: Kompass UK, Reed Information Services, Windsor Court, East Grinstead House, East Grinstead, West Sussex RH19 1XA, UK. Tel. +44 (0)1342 326972. Fax +44 (0)1342 335612.

Cost: £285

Resources Slovakia

This is a loose-leaf reference directory (1998) to assist business people navigate the complexities of business life in Slovakia. The directory provides an introduction to doing business the Slovakian way, and provides a number of contact sections – in government, banks, major companies, etc. Half the directory is updated every **three months**. There is a CD-ROM version.

Contact details: Resources s.r.o., Ječná 39, 120 00 Prague, Czech Republic. Tel. +420 2 2494 1800. Fax +420 2 2494 3082. Email: resources@inbox.vol.cz URL: http://www.resources.cz

Cost: $270 pa (print); $425 (CD-ROM)

Industries and Services

External agencies have produced a number of helpful sectoral sources. In addition, there are numerous sectoral reports produced by the government agency SNAZIR covering, for example – chemicals, pharmaceuticals, machine tools, food processing, wood processing, electro-technics. For details of SNAZIR see under Organisations. Other examples of sectoral sources are:

Agriculture

Agricultural Situation and Perspectives in the Central and East European Countries: Slovakia
This report, from the European Union, 'aims to provide an analysis of the current situation and the medium-term outlook for the agricultural and agri-food industries' in the CEE countries aiming for EU membership – Bulgaria, Czech Republic, Hungary, Poland, Romania, Slovakia, Slovenia. The report is freely available on the Internet.

Contact details: URL: http://www.europa.eu.int/comm/dg06/publi/peco.index-en.htm

Chemicals

Slovak Chemical Guide
This **annual** provides 'more than 1000 Slovak firms and more than 300 firms active in the Slovak Republic'. The strength of the Guide is in its 'classification index of 123 chemical product groups including chemical machinery'. The company data are basic.

Contact details: EXIN, Šeřikova 32, 63700 Brno, Czech Republic. Tel. +420 5 432 360040 1. Fax +420 5 432 36040. URL: http://www.exin.cz/

Cost: 40 EUR (hard copy); 120 EUR (diskette/CD-ROM)

Slovak Plastics and Rubber Guide
This **annual** profiles 'more than 800 Slovak firms and institutions ... and more than 100 foreign companies acting in the Slovak Republic'.

Contact details: EXIN, Šeřikova 32, 63700 Brno, Czech Republic. Tel. +420 5 432 360040 1. Fax +420 5 432 36040. URL: http://www.exin.cz/

Cost: 40 EUR (hard copy); 120 EUR (diskette/CD-ROM)

Construction

Facts About Construction Growth in Slovakia
This report (1999) 'contains information about construction activity and forecasts of future trends [focusing on] the civil engineering sector, office and housing, retail and industrial construction trends and includes information about price levels, vacancy rates and yields'. The socio-economic structure is described, and numerous statistical indicators provided.

Contact details: European Construction Research, Bredgade 35B, DK-1260 Copenhagen K, Denmark. Tel. +45 33 162 100. Fax +45 33 162 900. Email: ecr@cybernet.dk URL: http://www.epi.no/ecr/index.htm

Cost: £98/$145

Energy

Energy Policies of the Slovak Republic
An International Energy Agency report (1997) describing and analysing the efficiency and performance of the various energy sectors. National energy policies are reviewed, and recommendations made regarding future developments.

Contact details: OECD, 2 rue André-Pascal, 75775 Paris Cedex 16, France. Tel. +33 1 45 248200. Fax +33 1 49 104276. Email: Compte.PUBSINQ@oecd.org URL: http://www.oecd.org/

Finance and Banking

Bratislava Stock Exchange
The future as an effective western style stock exchange has yet to arrive, but the Exchange can be used as a source of information.

Contact details: Bratislava Stock Exchange, Vysoká 17, POB 151, Bratislava, Slovkia. Tel. +412 7 503 6111. Fax +412 7 503 6103.

Fact Book
A reference **annual** (CD-ROM) providing information and data about the capital market, and about selected companies.

Contact details: RM-System Slovakia, Zámocké schody 2/A, PO Box 301, 810 00 Bratislava, Slovakia. Tel. +421 7 532 9313. Fax +421 7 532 9121. URL: http://www.rms.sk/

Cost: $340

Narodna Banka Slovenska: Monetary Survey
This **monthly** records, in statistical terms, developments in the capital and foreign exchange markets, and the results of the government's monetary policies.

Contact details: Narodna Banka Slovenska, Štúrova 2, 81854 Bratislava, Slovakia. Tel. +421 7 5953 1111. Fax +421 7 5413 1167. URL: http://www.nbs.sk/indexa.htm

Cost: Free on application.

Legislation

As far as can be ascertained, most of the English language versions of business law are produced outside the country.

Business Law Handbook: Slovakia
This *Handbook* is updated **annually** to take account of changes in the laws and regulations governing business activities generally, and those of foreigners in particular. A readable introduction for the layman.

Contact details: Russian Information and Business Center, PO Box 15343, Washington DC 20003, USA. Tel. +1 202 546 2103. Fax +1 202 546 3275. Email: rusline@erols.com URL: http://www.rusline.com/

Cost: $89

Commercial and Investment Law: Slovakia
A survey, with **annual** updates, of the laws and regulations governing business affairs including, for example, regulation and protection of foreign investment, banking and insurance, labour regulations.

Contact details: Juris Publishing, Executive Park, 1 Odell Plaza, Yonkers, NY 10701, USA. Tel. +1 914 375 3400. Fax +1 914 375 6047. Email: orders@jurispub.com URL: http://www.jurispub.com

Cost: $165

Legal Guide: Slovak Republic
A layman's guide (1998), from the Department of Trade and Industry, to the more important aspects of business law concentrating especially on the processes of establishing a business. A good introduction.

Contact details: DTI, Admail 528, London SW1W 8YT, UK. Tel. +44 (0)20 7510 0171. Fax +44 (0)20 7510 0197. URL: http://www.dti.gov.uk/ots/publications

Cost: £12

Trade-Related Legislation

English-language versions of the *Consumer Protection Act, Bankruptcy and Composition Act, Economic Competition Act*, for example. From Trade Links.

Contact details: VP International, Red Hill House, Hope Street, Chester CH4 8BU, UK. Tel. +44 (0)1244 681619. Fax +44 (0)1244 681617. Email: helen@vpinternational.com URL: http://www.vpinternational.com/

Cost: £35

Organisations

Official agencies with responsibility for promotional work are quite active.

American Embassy

The Embassy's web site describes commercial services available to businessmen, and provides general information.

Contact details: U.S. Embassy, Hviezdoslavovo nám. 4, 811 02 Bratislava, Slovak Republic. Tel. +421 7 5443 3338. Fax +421 7 5443 0096. URL: http://www.usis.sk/

British Embassy

Available for guidance, advice and support.

Contact details: British Embassy, Panská 16, 811 01 Bratislava, Slovak Republic. Tel. +421 7 531 9632/9633/0005/0007 (out of hours). Fax +421 7 531 0002/0003 (Commercial)/0004 (Defence). Email: bebra@internet.sk

Embassy of the Slovak Republic: UK

Can be approached with business issues.

Contact details: Embassy of the Slovak Republic, 25 Kensington Palace Gardens, London W8 4QY, UK. Tel. +44 (0)20 7243 0803. Fax +44 (0)20 7727 3667.

Embassy of the Slovak Republic: USA

The Embassy's web site includes business information, business opportunities and general country information.

Contact details: Embassy of the Slovak Republic, 2201 Wisconsin Avenue, NW, Suite 250, Washington DC 20007, USA. Tel. +1 202 965 5160. Fax +1 202 965 5166. Email: sykemb@concentric.net URL: http://www.slovakemb.com/

National Agency for Development of Small and Medium Enterprises
The Agency was established in 1993 with European assistance. Its over-all responsibility is to encourage and coordinate the establishment and activities of small and medium sized firms. Under the Agency's umbrella are carried out such activities as the identification of suitable partners for cooperation, the presentation of industrial information and financial data about Slovak companies, provision of consulting services. The web site maintained by the Agency presents brief country details and addresses of likely useful contacts.

Contact details: National Agency for Development of Small and Medium Enterprises, Nevädzová 5, 821 01 Bratislava, Slovakia. Tel. +42 07 237 563. Fax +42 07 5222 434. Email: agency@nadsme.sanet.sk URL: http://www.savba.savba.sk/logos/trade/nadsme/index.htm

Slovak Business Links
A commercial enterprise 'able to identify trade contacts for specific product areas'. In effect the company acts as research agents providing a 'shortlist of recommended companies', obtaining quotations, establishing personal contacts.

Contact details: Slovak Business Links, 48 Courthope Road, London NW3 2LD, UK. Tel/Fax +44 (0)20 7428 0608. Email: gt20@dial.pipex.com

Slovak Chamber of Commerce and Industry
Among the promotional publications of the Chamber is *Slovak Foreign Trade*, a free magazine which describes the economy and its various sectors in an attractive manner. The English version of the web site, although promised, was still not operational on our last visit to the site (June, 1999).

Contact details: Slovak Chamber of Commerce and Industry, Gorkého str. 9, SK - 81603 Bratislava, Slovak Republic. Tel: +421 7 5443 3846. Fax: +421 7 5443 0754.

Email: sopkurad@scci.sk URL: http://www.scci.sk/

Slovak National Agency for Foreign Investment and Development (SNAZIR)
SNAZIR has a most active promotional programme. Its main tasks include identifying potential partners, leading negotiations between local and foreign partners, arranging visit programmmes, offering guidance and advice. SNAZIR's information role has a wider remit than usual, allowing it to publish a number of well-produced sectoral reports for the machine-tool, chemical, electro-technics, engineering and automotive components industries, among others. Of more general use is the guide to doing business in Slovakia – *Business Guide: The Slovak Republic*, an **an-**

nual available as a diskette and in print form. It is helpful as an introduction to needed business information, even though the evident promotional aim links prospects and optimism a little too closely. For investors there is the *Foreign Investor's Guide to the Legal System* which provides a useful first approach to laws and regulations governing business activities. Available as a brochure and diskette. This can be updated by the **monthly** English-language magazine *Slovakia – News for Investors*. Each issue reports on legislative developments, sectoral issues and opportunities, individual companies and their activities. The Agency maintains a number of databases providing company, sectoral and regional information.

Contact details: SNAZIR, Sládkovičova 7, 811 06 Bratislava, Slovak Republic. Tel. +421 7 5443 5175. Fax +421 7 5443 5022.. Email: snazir@ba.pubnet.sk URL: http://www.pubnet.sk/~snazir/

Statistical Office of the Slovak Republic
The Statistical Office produces an array of English language statistical sources. For example – *Statistical Yearbook of the Slovak Republic* (print and CD-ROM), *Yearbook of Industry, Yearbook of Transport, Yearbook of Construction, Environment in Slovak Republic*. Updating statistical data is possible with the **quarterly** *Economic Monitor of the Economy*. The Statistical Office's web site makes freely available *Slovak Republic in Figures* and *Basic Economy Indicators of the Slovak Republic*, as well as listing published sources.

Contact details: SOSR, Miletičova 3, 824 67 Bratislava, Slovak Republic. Email: heidinger@statistics.sk URL: http://www.statistics.sk/ webdata.english/index2.htm

Chapter 13

Slovenia

Population 2.0m. This small country has claims to being the richest in eastern Europe. It has a substantial private sector, producing around 60% of GDP. Its application for EU membership has been regarded favourably, although there have been failures to adopt EU legislation, and little has been done to strengthen very weak position of shareholders in companies privatised in favour of managers and workers. The continuing state control of financial institutions, and the monopoly of the national telecoms company are other problems needing attention.

English language business information sources for overview and current purposes are in reasonable supply – largely due to the activities of western information suppliers. There are signs of indigenous business publishing in English; a trend likely to be reinforced by the increasing resort to the Internet for business activities. Official promotional agencies, and statistical agencies, publish in English.

Overview

Business Investment Opportunity Yearbook: Slovenia
This **annual** covers 'business, investment, export-import, economic and other opportunities in respected countries. Foreign economic assistance projects, sources of financing , strategic government and business contacts, and more ...'. The annual publication cycle precludes 'hot' investment news. The series titles, of which this is one, cover numerous countries throughout the world. In the circumstances 'respected' is an empty word.

Contact details: Russian Information and Business Center, PO Box 15343, Washington DC 20003, USA. Tel. +1 202 546 2103. Fax +1 202 546 3275. Email: rusline@erols.com URL: http://www.rusline.com/

Cost: $89

Country Commercial Guide: Slovenia
Titles in the *Guides* series are published **annually**. They review the country's commercial environment 'using economic, political and market analysis', and 'consolidate various reporting documents prepared for the U.S. Embassies community'. There are informative sections on the investment climate, trade regulations and standards, economic trends

and outlook, and useful summary statistics in appendices. A good country introduction. Available on the Internet, in hard copy and as a diskette.

Contact details: URL: http://www.stat-usa.gov/Newstand

Cost: $20 (hard copy)

Country Profile: Slovenia

This **annual** publication is a standard reference source. Comment, analysis and statistics cover the main industrial sectors, economic policies, political background, population, finance, prices and wages – with remarkable succinctness.

Contact details: Economist Intelligence Unit, 15 Regent Street, London SW1Y 4LR, UK. Tel. +44 (0)20 7830 1000. Fax +44 (0)1708 371 850. Email: london@eiu.com URL: http://www.eiu.com
In the US: Economist Intelligence Unit, The Economist Building, 111 West 57th Street, NY, NY 10019, USA . Tel. +1 212 554 060/1 800 938 4685 (USA and Canada only). Fax +1 212 586 0248. Email: newyork@eiu.com URL: http://www.eiu.com

Cost: £120/$205

Doing Business In Slovenia

General advice (1999) on how to do business within the legal parameters and according to national custom.

Contact details: Centre for International Cooperation and Development, Kardeljeva ploščad 1, 1109 Ljubljana, Slovenia. Tel. +386 61 168 3597. Fax +386 61 168 1585.

Cost: DEM 90

Dun & Bradstreet Country Report: Slovenia

This **annual** report profiles the country in terms of the economy, political situation, financial information, its debts and payment potential, the business climate. There are **monthly** monitoring updates. The report is available on diskette also.

Contact details: Dun & Bradstreet, Holmers Farm Way, High Wycombe, Bucks HP12 3BR, UK. Tel. +44 (0)1494 422 000. Fax +44 (0)1494 422 929.

Cost: £245 (hard copy; diskette); £335 (report + monthly updates).

EBRD Country Profiles: Slovenia

The main headings for this **annually** produced report are: economic survey, investment climate, financial sector, multilateral funding, EBRD activities, contact list. The report is prepared for the Annual Meeting of the European Bank for Reconstruction and Development.

Contact details: Effective Technology Marketing, PO Box 171, Grimsby DN35 0TP, UK. Tel/Fax +44 (0)1472 816660. Email: sales@etmltd.demon.co.uk URL: http://www.etmltd.demon.co.uk

Cost: £10/$17

Guide to Virtual Slovenia

An Internet site with information and data about the country, including the *CIA World Factbook*. Like most web sites, a useful starting point for background material. In-depth satisfaction requires recourse to additional sources however.

Contact details: URL: http://www.ijs.si/slo/country/

IMF Staff Country Reports: Slovenia

The International Monetary Fund monitors the economic and financial affairs of its member countries. A series of reports, updated at irregular intervals, are produced for the consultations and assessments that take place. These appear as reviews of recent economic developments, selected issues and statistical annexes. The result, for each country surveyed, is a useful source of general and specialised knowledge of the economy, with an emphasis upon financial issues. The reports can be downloaded from the Internet.

Contact details: IMF Publication Services, 700 19th Street, NM, Washington DC 20431, USA. Tel. +1 202 623 7430. Fax +1 202 623 7201. Email: pubweb@imf.org URL: http://www.imf.org/external/pubs/pubs/dist.htm In the UK – The Stationery Office, PO Box 276, London SW8 5DT, UK. Tel. +44 (0)870 600 5522. Fax +44 (0)20 7873 8247. URL: http://www.tso-online.co.uk

Cost: $15

Investment and Business Guide: Slovenia

This introductory **annual** source provides 'basic information on economy, business and investment climate and opportunities, export-import, industrial development, banking and finance, government and business, contacts'. All from the point of view of those contemplating doing business in the country. Readable and informative.

Contact details: Russian Information and Business Center, PO Box 15343, Washington DC 20003, USA. Tel. +1 202 546 2103. Fax +1 202 546 3275. Email: rusline@erols.com URL: http://www.rusline.com/

Cost: $89

Political Risk Services: Country Reports: Slovenia
Reports in this series are produced **annually.** They include 'fact sheets' of basic national data, background information, 'eighteen month and five year forecasts' indicating the risks that lie ahead, profiles of individuals likely to influence the business climate. The attendant hype suggests that 'this may be the only site you will ever need for country research'. Arguable, but not too far off the mark. The publishers maintain an especially informative web site.

Contact details: The PRS Group, 6320 Fly Road, Suite 102, East Syracuse, NY 13057-0248, USA. Tel. +1 315 431 0511. Fax +1 315 431 0200. URL: http://www.prsgroup.com/

Cost: $395

Slovenia '98
This **annual** reference source, now in CD-ROM format, provides background country information – geography, climate, history, political system, demography, main economic indicators, infrastructure.

Contact details: Vitrum Publishing, Hradeckega 38, 1000 Ljubljana, Slovenia. Tel. +386 61 140 2027. Email: marketing@vitrum.si URL: http://www.vitrum.si/

Cost: $65 (Europe); $69.50 (elsewhere)

Slovenian Business Catalogue
The 5th edition of the *Catalogue* (1998) is described as 'an exclusive but information-rich publication detailing the most important export products, services and investment opportunities'. Seventeen activity sectors and their companies are listed. The economy of the country is described, with an emphasis upon the 'stable Slovenian environment'. The introduction devotes 'special attention to the preconditions and necessary adjustments for successful economic and monetary integration' with the EU. Available on the Internet, and in CD-ROM format.

Contact details: Kabi, Šmartinska 106, 1000 Ljubljana, Slovenia. Tel. +386 (0)61 141 9280. Email: info@kabi.si. URL: http://www.kabi.si/si21/SBC/

Cost: on application

World of Information Country Report: Slovenia
A concise **annual** report reviewing the economic and political scene, with selected supporting statistics. Ideal for quick familiarisation.

Contact details: Walden Publishing, 2 Market Street, Saffron Walden, Essex CB10 1HZ, UK. Tel. +44 (0)1799 521150. Fax +44 (0)1799 524805.

Cost: £30/$65

Current Developments

A variety of Internet sites are catching and reporting current events. This is a development only at its beginnings here. Among the conventional sources monitoring and assessing developments in Slovenia are:

Business Operations Report: Slovenia
This is a **quarterly** analysis of the wide range of local and other factors bearing upon business decisions. Examples of such factors are: labour relations, the expected impact of political changes, assessments of future developments. Lessons are drawn from informative case studies. There are supporting statistics. The *Report* is 'also available through on line databases, direct network feeds and the Internet'.

Contact details: Economist Intelligence Unit, 15 Regent Street, London SW1Y 4LR, UK. Tel. +44 (0)20 7830 1000. Fax +44 (0)20 7499 9767 Email: london@eiu.com URL: http://www.eiu.com
In the US: Economist Intelligence Unit, The Economist Building, 111 West 57th Street, NY, NY 10019, USA . Tel. +1 212 554 060/1 800 938 4685 (USA and Canada only). Fax +1 212 586 0248. Email: newyork@eiu.com URL: http://www.eiu.com

Cost: £315 pa

Country Reports: Slovenia
The *Reports* are produced **quarterly.** Each issue describes the political and economic structures, reviews political and economic prospects for the next 12 - 18 months, critically reviews major economic and political issues. Economic trends are illustrated with graphs and tables, and there a number of statistical appendices.

Contact details: Economist Intelligence Unit, 15 Regent Street, London SW1Y 4LR, UK. Tel. +44 (0)20 7830 1000. Fax +44 (0)20 7499 9767 Email: london@eiu.com URL: http://www.eiu.com
In the US: Economist Intelligence Unit, The Economist Building, 111 West 57th Street, NY, NY 10019, USA . Tel. +1 212 554 060/1 800 938 4685 (USA and Canada only). Fax +1 212 586 0248. Email: newyork@eiu.com URL: http://www.eiu.com

Cost: £235/$425 pa. The *Country Profile* **annual** is included in the subscription.

Country Risk Service: Slovenia
The *Risk Service* takes a two-year 'forecasting horizon' on a **quarterly** basis when presenting assessments of political, economic and financial risks likely to influence business activities. Future trends of 'over 180 major economic indicators' are presented.

Contact details: Economist Intelligence Unit, 15 Regent Street, London SW1Y 4LR, UK. Tel. +44 (0)20 7830 1000. Fax +44 (0)20 7499 9767 Email: london@eiu.com URL: http://www.eiu.com

Cost: £395 pa

Country RiskLines: Slovenia
This **monthly** brief report (usually 4 pages) rates the risk of trading with the country in terms of earnings and international payment obligations, political and economic stability, investment climate, etc.

Contact details: Dun & Bradstreet, Holmers Farm Way, High Wycombe, Bucks HP12 3BR, UK. Tel. +44 (0)1494 422 000. Fax +44 (0)1494 422 929.

Cost: £35 pa

Slovenia Weekly
This magazine provides general news coverage, with a pronounced emphasis upon economic and business issues. It is informative, but from an official perspective. It is produced with the cooperation of the Government Public Relations and Media Office and the Ministry of Foreign Affairs. It is available in print and on the Internet.

Contact details: Vitrum, Hradeckega 38, 61000 Ljubljana, Slovenia. Tel. +386 61 140 2027. Fax +386 61 133 2301. Email: marketingj@vitrum.si URL: http://www.vitrum.si

Cost: DEM 120.75 pa (print); DEM 241.50 pa (electronic format)

Slovenian Business Report
This is a **bimonthly** English-language publication aimed at foreign business interests and official agencies. It reports on recent developments in the economy, including business legislation and finance, with statistical indicators and tables.

Contact details: Gospodarski Vestnik, Dunajska 5, Ljubljana 61000, Slovenia. Tel. +386 61 132 1230. Fax +386 61 132 1012.

Companies and Contacts

Not an over-endowed sector, but a start has been made on providing basic company data.

Business Directory of the Republic of Slovenia (PIRS)
PIRS 1999 is a CD-ROM which 'includes up to date information on more than 80,000 businesses ... on the territory of the Republic of Slovenia'. By most directory standards this is a substantial figure. The company pro-

files are basic, providing locational, contact and activity descriptions. The system allows searches 'by title, street, town, phone, director and activity', as well as by more complex search strings. There are maps, and label printing is possible. The Internet site of the publishers gives access to economic statistics, as well as to the searchable company database.

Contact details: URL: http://www.slo-knjiga.si/pdemo_gb.htm

Cost: SIT 6000

Jasico Yellow Pages
An Internet directory of companies searchable by name and sector heading.

Contact details: URL: http://www.yellow.eunet.si/yellowpage/a/index.html

Kompass Slovenia
Over 10,000 companies are listed in this standard directory. Company data include, for example, locational details, names of top executives, descriptions of activities and products, annual turnover, trade marks. The 7th edition is promised for June, 1999.

Contact details: Kompass UK, Reed Information Services, Windsor Court, East Grinstead House, East Grinstead, West Sussex RH19 1XA, UK. Tel. +44 (0)1342 326972. Fax +44 (0)1342 335612.

Cost: £225

Industries and Services

Not many examples of sectoral sources. The best developed, not unexpectedly perhaps, is the banking and finance sector. There all the English language examples are home produced.

Agriculture

Agricultural Situation and Perspectives in the Central and East European Countries: Slovenia
This report, from the European Union, 'aims to provide an analysis of the current situation and the medium-term outlook for the agricultural and agri-food industries' in the CEE countries aiming for EU membership – Bulgaria, Czech Republic, Hungary, Poland, Romania, Slovakia, Slovenia. The report is freely available on the Internet.

Contact details: URL: http://www.europa.eu.int/comm/dg06/publi/peco.index-en.htm

Finance and Banking

Bank of Slovenia

Publishes a *Monthly Bulletin* and an *Annual Report*. The activities of the Bank, the banking and financial sectors, are described in statistical terms, without comment or interpretation. The main national economic indicators are included.

Contact details: Bank of Slovenia, Slovenska 35, 1505 Ljubljana, Slovenia. Tel. +386 61 1719000. Fax +386 61 215516, 215541. Email: bsi@bsi.si URL: http://www.bsi.si/html/eng/publications/bulletins/index.html

Cost: Free on application

Finance

This **fortnightly** newspaper is well defined by its title. The main issues reported are finance and the stock exchange. Regional news on these sectors are also reported and commented upon.

Contact details: Gospodarski Vestnik, Dunajaska 5, 1509 Ljubljana, Slovenia. Tel. +386 6 132 1230. Fax +386 61 132 1012.

Cost: SIT 23,520

Ljubljana Stock Exchange

The Exchange publishes the *Ljubljana Stock Exchange Newsletter*. This is an irregular, official, publication providing information about new members, company news, trading data and Stock Exchange events. The Exchange accepts requests for information from foreigners.

Contact details: Ljubljana Stock Exchange, Slovenska cesta 56, 1000 Ljubljana, Slovenia. Tel. +386 61 171 0211. Fax +386 61 171 0231. Email: info@ljse.si URL: http://www.ljse.si/index.html

Cost: Free on application

SKB Banka D. D.

The Bank maintains a web site providing financial sector data. It also has information and data about the country in general and about the economy under the heading *Slovenia and Economic Outlook*.

Contact details: URL: http://ww.skh.si/html98/eng/menu.html

Statistical Insurance Bulletin

The Bulletin sets out, for this new business sector, the role and aims of commercial insurance companies. Developments in the insurance industry, as well as the main companies, are described.

Contact details: Slovenian Insurance Association, Zelezna cesta 14, 1000 Ljubljana, Slovenia. Tel. +386 61 173 5699. Fax +386 61 173 5692. Email: info@zav-zdruzenje.si URL: http://www.zav-zdruzenje.si

Cost: Free on application.

Legislation

English language introductory and monitoring guides to business law exist. For those seeking to understand the law on particular business issues the advice, as always, is to employ the services of a competent lawyer. The official promotional agencies (see below) are sources of assistance in such cases.

Business Law Handbook: Slovenia
This *Handbook* is updated **annually** to take account of changes in the laws and regulations governing business activities generally, and those of foreigners in particular. A readable introduction for the layman.

Contact details: Russian Information and Business Center, PO Box 15343, Washington DC 20003, USA. Tel. +1 202 546 2103. Fax +1 202 546 3275. Email: rusline@erols.com URL: http://www.rusline.com/

Cost: $89

Legal Guide: Slovenia
A layman's guide (1997), from the Department of Trade and Industry, to the more important aspects of business law concentrating especially on the processes of establishing a business. A good introduction.

Further information: DTI, Admail 528, London SW1W 8YT, UK. Tel. +44 (0)20 7510 0171. Fax +44 (0)20 7510 0197. URL: http://www.dti.gov.uk/ots/publications

Cost: £12

Organisations

A fairly standard array of official agencies to assist and encourage foreign investment. For example,

American Embassy
Provides a range of services for businessmen.

Contact details: U.S. Embassy, Prazakova 4, 1000 Ljubljana, Slovenia. Tel. +386 61 301427. Fax +386 61 301401. URL: http://www.usembassy.si/

British Embassy
Available for advice, guidance and support.

Contact details: British Embassy, trg Republike 3/IV, 1000 Ljubljana, Slovenia. Tel. +386 61 125 7191/3266 (Commercial). Fax +386 61 125 0174/9080 (Commercial). Email: info@british-embassy.si URL: http://www.british-embassy.si/

Chamber of Commerce and Industry
A flagship publication of the Chamber is *SLO-Export*. This is a directory of 2000 firms 'which account for more than 90% of Slovenia's total exports'. It is available in print form and as a CD-ROM with additional country and economic data. A wide range of business news items is reported in *Slovenia Business Week*. Access to this newsletter, as well as to country, economic and business information and data, is available through the Internet site maintained by the Chamber.

Contact details: Chamber of Economy of Slovenia, Slovenska cesta 41, 1504 Ljubljana, Slovenia. Tel. +386 61 223 1571. Fax +386 61 219 536. Email: infolink@hq.gzs.si URL: http://www.gzs.si/eng/

Embassy of the Republic of Slovenia: UK
Can be approached with business issues.

Contact details: Embassy of the Republic of Slovenia, Suite 1, Cavendish Court, 11-15 Wigmore Street, London W1H 9LA, UK. Tel. +44 (0)20 7495 7775. Fax +44 (0)20 7495 7776.

Embassy of the Republic of Slovenia: USA
The Embassy's web site highlights 'attractive business opportunities'. There are news and country information pages.

Contact details: Embassy of the Republic of Slovenia, 1525 New Hampshire Avenue, NW, Washington DC 20036, USA. Tel. +1 202 667 5363. Fax +1 202 667 4563. URL: http://www.embassy.org/slovenia/

Institute of Macroeconomic Analysis and Development
The Institute publishes the **monthly** *Slovenian Economic Mirror* with the aim of 'providing standard macroeconomic analyses, estimates and forecasts'. Reviews the changes in key indicators, and relates these to declared aspects of government economic policies. There is a statistical appendix, and summaries of major developments in the current month and 'in the near past'.

Contact details: Institute of Macroeconomic Analysis and Development, Gregorčičeva 27, 1000 Ljubljana, Slovenia. Tel. +386 61 178 2112. Fax +386 61 178 2070. URL: http://www.sigov.si/zmar

Statistical Office of the Republic of Slovenia

Unusually prompt in the publication of statistical sources. The *Statistical Yearbook* is the standard reference source, with *Slovenia in Figures*, another **annual**, providing sets of the most commonly needed data. Many of the time series, including the *Statistical Yearbook*, are freely available on the web site. The web site is also the best means of discovering the availability of general and specialist sources.

Contact details: SORS, Vožarski pot 12, 1000 Ljubljana, Slovenia. Tel. +386 61 125 5322. Fax +386 61 216 932. URL: http://www.sigov.si/zrs/eng/start.html

Trade and Investment Promotion Office (TIPO)

The Internet site of TIPO provides information and data likely to encourage and inform foreign investors. The range is wide from business contacts to business laws, from investment incentivess to trade exhibitions.

Contact details: TIPO, Kotnikova 5, 1000 Ljubljana, Slovenia. Tel. +386 61 176 3557. Fax +386 61 176 3599. Email: tipo@meor.sigov.mail.si URL: http://www.sigov.si/tipo

Index

About the Republic of Hungary 120

Access Hungary 120

Accounting Legislation 1998 114

Agency for Privatization in the Federation of Bosnia and Herzegovina 73

Agrarian Economies of Central and Eastern Europe and the Commonwealth of Independent States: Situation and Perspectives 28

Agricultural Policies in Emerging and Transition Economies 28

Agricultural Situation and Perspectives in the Central and East European Countries: Bulgaria 84

Agricultural Situation and Perspectives in the Central and East European Countries: Czech Republic 110

Agricultural Situation and Perspectives in the Central and East European Countries: Hungary 130

Agricultural Situation and Perspectives in the Central and East European Countries: Poland 155

Agricultural Situation and Perspectives in the Central and East European Countries: Romania 172

Agricultural Situation and Perspectives in the Central and East European Countries: Slovakia 192

Agricultural Situation and Perspectives in the Central and East European Countries: Slovenia 204

agriculture

    Bulgaria 84

    Central and Eastern Europe 28-9

    Czech Republic 110

    Hungary 130

    Poland 155

    Romania 172

    Slovakia 192

    Slovenia 204

Akcie.cz 112

Albanews 59

Albania
    companies and contacts 64
    current developments 62-4
    industries and services 64
    legislation 64-5
    organisations 65-7
    overview 59-62
Albania – Land of Eagles 60
Albania Law Report 64-5
Albania On-Line 60
Albanian American Trade and Development Association 60
Albanian Centre for Foreign Investment Promotion 66
Albanian Daily News 63
Albanian Economic Development Agency 66
Albanian Home Page 60
Albanian Times 63
Albanian Yellow Pages Business Directory 64
Albertina Company Register 107
Albertina Financial Profiles 107
Alcoholic Drinks in Eastern Europe 43
American Embassy
    Albania 66
    Bosnia-Herzegovina 73
    Bulgaria 87
    Croatia 97-8
    Czech Republic 117
    Hungary 133-4
    Macedonia 141
    Poland 161
    Romania 175
    Serbia and Montenegro 182
    Slovakia 195
    Slovenia 206
automotive
    Central and Eastern Europe 29-30
    Czech Republic 110
    Hungary 130-1

Poland 155-6

Romania 173

Automotive Emerging Markets 29

Automotive Sectors of Central and Eastern Europe, The 29

Baby Food in Central and Eastern Europe 43

Bank of Slovenia 205

Banka Magazine 96

banking see *finance and banking*

Bankruptcy and Composition Act, Trades Licensing Act, Act on Prices 114-15

BBC Summary of World Broadcasts 16

Belgrade Stock Exchange 181

Beta News Agency 180

BIH Press 70

Biscuits Market in Eastern Europe 44

BNA's Eastern Europe Reporter 16

bol.bg 80

Bosnia-Herzegovina

    companies and contacts 71

    current developments 70-1

    industries and services 71-2

    legislation 72-3

    organisations 73-4

    overview 68-70

Bratislava Stock Exchange 193

British Chamber of Commerce in Hungary 134

British Embassy

    Albania 66

    Bosnia-Herzegovina 73

    Bulgaria 87

    Croatia 98

    Czech Republic 117-18

    Hungary 134

    Macedonia 141

    Poland 161-2

    Romania 175-6

    Serbia and Montenegro 182

Slovakia 195
Slovenia 207
British Trade International 56
British-Polish Chamber of Commerce (BPCC) 162
Bucharest Business Week 168
Bucharest Stock Exchange 173
Budapest Business Journal 125
Budapest Business Journal Book of Lists 129
Budapest Stock Exchange 131
Bulgaria 80
Bulgaria: Business and Investment Opportunities 80
Bulgaria
    companies and contacts 82-3
    current developments 80-2
    industries and services 84-5
    legislation 86-7
    organisations 87-9
    overview 75-9
Bulgaria Business 75
Bulgaria Business Catalog 82-3
Bulgarian Business Adviser 75-6
Bulgarian Business News 80
Bulgarian Chamber of Commerce and Industry (BCCI) 87-8
Bulgarian Economic Outlook 80
Bulgarian Economic Review 81
Bulgarian Foreign Investment Agency (BIEA) 88
Bulgarian National Bank: Monthly Bulletin 84
Bulgarian Press Digest 81
Bulgarian Privatisation Agency 88
Bulgarian Small and Medium Sized Enterprises 83
Bulgarian Stock Exchange 85
Business Central Europe 16-17
Business Directory of the Republic of Slovenia (PIRS) 203-4
Business Eastern Europe 17
Business Europa: Central European Business Magazine 17
Business Executive Resources Worldwide 7-8

Business Foundation Book 153

Business in Hungary: The Essential Guide 121

Business International 8

Business Investment Opportunity Yearbook: Albania 61

Business Investment Opportunity Yearbook: Bosnia-Herzegovina 68

Business Investment Opportunity Yearbook: Bulgaria 76

Business Investment Opportunity Yearbook: Croatia 90

Business Investment Opportunity Yearbook: Czech Republic 100-1

Business Investment Opportunity Yearbook: Hungary 121

Business Investment Opportunity Yearbook: Macedonia 136

Business Investment Opportunity Yearbook: Poland 144

Business Investment Opportunity Yearbook: Romania 164

Business Investment Opportunity Yearbook: Slovakia 185

Business Investment Opportunity Yearbook: Slovenia 198

Business Law Guide: Bulgaria 86

Business Law Handbook: Albania 65

Business Law Handbook: Bosnia-Herzegovina 72-3

Business Law Handbook: Bulgaria 86

Business Law Handbook: Croatia 97

Business Law Handbook: Czech Republic 115

Business Law Handbook: Hungary 132

Business Law Handbook: Macedonia 140

Business Law Handbook: Poland 160

Business Law Handbook: Romania 174

Business Law Handbook: Slovakia 194

Business Law Handbook: Slovenia 206

Business News Poland: A Weekly Bulletin of Boss Economic Information 149

Business Operations Report: Bulgaria 76

Business Operations Report: Croatia 93

Business Operations Report: Czech Republic 104

Business Operations Report: Hungary 125

Business Operations Report: Poland 149-50

Business Operations Report: Romania 168

Business Operations Report: Slovakia 189

Business Operations Report: Slovenia 202

Business Polska 150

Business Strategies for Eastern Europe 8

BusinessBiH 71

Capital Market 173
Capital Market in Poland 157
Capital Weekly 85
CEEBICnet 8
CeeSource: Central and East European Legal, Political, Business and Economics WWW Resources 9
Central Bank of Bosnia and Herzegovina 72
Central Bureau of Statistics 98
Central and East European Agriculture and the European Union 28
Central and East European Business Directory (CEEBD) 9
Central and East European Tax Directory 36
Central and Eastern Europe
    companies and contacts 25-7
    current developments 15-25
    industries and services 27-54
    legislation 54-6
    organisations 56-8
    overview 7-15
Central and Eastern European Directory 26
Central and Eastern European Legal Materials 54
Central Europe Automotive Report (CEAR) 29-30
Central Europe Business Journal 18
Central Europe Daily Bulletin 18
Central Europe Online 18
Central Europe Portfolio: The Central European Securities Newsletter 36
Central Europe Review 18
Central European 18-19
Central European Business Daily 19
Central European Business and Finance 19
Central European Business Weekly 19
Central European Construction Journal 32
Central European Downstream Service 33
Central European Economic Review 19-20
Central and North West European Department: Foreign and Commonwealth Office (FCO) 56-7

Central and South-East Europe Monitor 17

Central Statistical Office 162

Chamber of Commerce and Industry 207

Chamber of Commerce and Industry of Romania 176

Chamber of Commerce of the Republic of Albania 66-7

Chamber of Economy of Bosnia and Herzegovina 73

Chemical Producers in Central and Eastern Europe 31

chemicals

    Central and Eastern Europe 31

    Czech Republic 111

    Poland 156

    Slovakia 192

CIA Factbook 9

Cigarettes - Central and Eastern Europe 44

CIS and East European Energy Databook 33

Citibank Magyarorzag 131

Collection of Bulgarian Laws 86

Commercial and Investment Law: Bulgaria 86

Commercial and Investment Law: Czech Republic 115

Commercial and Investment Law: Romania 174

Commercial and Investment Law: Slovakia 194

Communications Markets in Eastern Europe 51

companies and contacts

    Albania 64

    Bosnia-Herzegovina 71

    Bulgaria 82-3

    Central and Eastern Europe 25-7

    Croatia 95

    Czech Republic 107-10

    Hungary 129-30

    Macedonia 140

    Poland 153-5

    Romania 171-2

    Serbia and Montenegro 181

    Slovakia 191

    Slovenia 203-4

Confectionery in Central and Eastern Europe 44

construction
    Bosnia-Herzegovina 71-2
    Bulgaria 84
    Central and Eastern Europe 32
    Czech Republic 111-12
    Poland 156-7
    Romania 173
    Slovakia 193
Construction in Poland 1998-2010 156-7
Consumer Eastern Europe 15
Consumer Lifestyles in Eastern Europe 15
contacts see *companies and contacts*
Corporate Security in Eastern Europe 9
cosmetics, Central and Eastern Europe 32-3
Cosmetics and Toiletries in Eastern Europe 32-3
Countries in Transition 14-15
Country Commercial Guide: Bulgaria 76-7
Country Commercial Guide: Czech Republic 101
Country Commercial Guide: Hungary 121
Country Commercial Guide: Poland 145
Country Commercial Guide: Romania 165
Country Commercial Guide: Slovakia 186
Country Commercial Guide: Slovenia 198-9
Country Forecasts: Bulgaria 81
Country Forecasts: Czech Republic 104
Country Forecasts: Poland 150
Country Forecasts: Romania 168-9
Country Forecasts: Slovakia 189
Country Guide: Poland 145
Country Profile: Albania 61
Country Profile: Bosnia and Herzegovina 69
Country Profile: Bulgaria 77
Country Profile: Croatia 91
Country Profile: Czech Republic 101
Country Profile: Hungary 121
Country Profile: Macedonia 136-7
Country Profile: Poland 145

Country Profile: Romania 165

Country Profile: Slovakia 186

Country Profile: Slovenia 199

Country Profile: Yugoslavia 178

Country Reports: Albania 63

Country Reports: Bosnia and Herzegovina 70-1

Country Reports: Bulgaria 81

Country Reports: Croatia 93-4

Country Reports: Czech Republic 104

Country Reports: Hungary 126

Country Reports: Macedonia 138-9

Country Reports: Poland 150-1

Country Reports: Slovakia 189-90

Country Reports: Slovenia 202

Country Reports: Yugoslavia 180

Country Risk Service: Bulgaria 81-2

Country Risk Service: Croatia 94

Country Risk Service: Czech Republic 105

Country Risk Service: Hungary 126

Country Risk Service: Macedonia 139

Country Risk Service: Poland 151

Country Risk Service: Romania 169

Country Risk Service: Slovakia 190

Country Risk Service: Slovenia 202-3

Country Risk Service: Yugoslavia 180

Country RiskLines: Albania 63-4

Country RiskLines: Bulgaria 82

Country RiskLines: Croatia 94

Country RiskLines: Czech Republic 105

Country RiskLines: Hungary 126

Country RiskLines: Macedonia 139

Country RiskLines: Poland 151

Country RiskLines: Romania 169

Country RiskLines: Slovakia 190

Country RiskLines: Slovenia 203

Croatia

    companies and contacts 95

current developments 93-5
industries and services 96
legislation 97
organisations 97-9
overview 90-3
Croatian Almanac 95
Croatian Business Directory 1997 95
Croatian Business Pages 95
Croatian Chamber of Economy 98
Croatian Income Tax and Profit Tax Acts 97
Croatian Ministry of Finance 99
Croatian News Agency 94
Croatian Privatisation Fund 98-9
Croatian Value Added Tax Act 97
CSOB Newsletter 112
Czech A.M. 105
Czech Business Directory 107
Czech Business Links 118
Czech Business Navigator 101
Czech Businesses and the EU Law Focus 115
Czech Chemical Guide 111
Czech Commercial Code 115
Czech Company Profiles (CFR) 107
Czech Construction: Sector Analysis Report 111
Czech Engineering: Sector Analysis Report 112
Czech Exporters 1999 108
Czech Financial Services Legislation 1998 116
Czech Happenings 101-2
Czech Info Centre 105
Czech Information Centre 108
Czech International Market 102
Czech Ministry of Industry and Trade 118
Czech National Bank 113
Czech Pharmaceuticals, Chemicals and Rubber: Sector Analysis Report 114
Czech Plastics and Rubber Guide 111
Czech Republic
    companies and contacts 107-10

current developments 104-6

industries and services 110-14

legislation 114-17

organisations 117-19

overview 100-3

Czech and Slovak Automotive Industries 110

Czech and Slovak Construction Journal 111

Czech and Slovak Pharmaceutical Guide 113-14

Czech Statistical Office 118

Czech Stock Market Guide and Directory, The 113

Czech Taxation 1999 116

Czech Telecom Weekly 114

Czech Welcome Page 102

CzechInvest 118-19

CzechTrade (UK) 119

Daily News 82

Dairy Industry in Eastern Europe 28-9

Database of Pulp, Paper and Board Mills in Central and Eastern Europe 48

Datafile of Eastern European Communications 51

Directory of Chemical Producers and Products 31

Directory of Companies, Institutions and Their Activities in Bosnia and Herzegovina 71

Directory of Consumer Brands and their Owners 1998: Eastern Europe 26

Directory of Industrial Companies in the Republic of Bulgaria 83

Directory of Polish Automotive Component Manufacturers 155

Distribution and Retailing in Eastern Europe 50

Doing Business in Croatia 91

Doing Business in Hungary 122

Doing Business in Romania 165

Doing Business with Romania 165-6

Doing Business in Slovenia 199

Doing Business in Yugoslavia 178-9

drink see *food, drink and tobacco*

Dun & Bradstreet Country Report: Bulgaria 77

Dun & Bradstreet Country Report: Croatia 91

Dun & Bradstreet Country Report: Czech Republic 102

Dun & Bradstreet Country Report: Hungary 122

Dun & Bradstreet Country Report: Poland 145

Dun & Bradstreet Country Report: Romania 166

Dun & Bradstreet Country Report: Slovenia 199

East Europe Agriculture and Food 29

East Europe and CIS Chemicals Briefing 31

East European Automotive Industry Forecast Report 30

East European Banking Review 36

East European Business Database 26

East European Business Intelligence on Disc 20

East European Business Law 54

East European Clothing and Textile Industry Directory 53

East European Emerging Markets 20

East European Energy Report 34

East European Insurance Report 36

East European Legislative Monitor 54-5

East European Privatisation News 37

East European Report 33

East European Telecoms Newsletter 51

East European Trade Council (EETC) 57

East/West Executive Guide 55

Eastern Bloc Energy 34

Eastern Europe: A Directory and Sourcebook 10

Eastern Europe at a Glance 10

Eastern Europe and the Commonwealth of Independent States 10

Eastern Europe Consensus Forecasts: A Digest of Economic Forecasts 20

Eastern Europe Monitor 21

Eastern Europe Newsletter 51-2

Eastern Europe Snacks 44

Eastern Europe's Emerging Cities: Operating Beyond the Region's Capitals 11

Eastern Europe's Largest Construction Companies 32

EBRD Business Information Centre 57

EBRD Country Profiles 11

EBRD Country Profiles: Albania 61

EBRD Country Profiles: Bosnia and Herzegovina 69

EBRD Country Profiles: Bulgaria 77

EBRD Country Profiles: Croatia 91-2

EBRD Country Profiles: Czech Republic 102

EBRD Country Profiles: Hungary 122

EBRD Country Profiles: Macedonia 137

EBRD Country Profiles: Poland 146

EBRD Country Profiles: Romania 166

EBRD Country Profiles: Slovakia 186

EBRD Country Profiles: Slovenia 199-200

EBRD Transition Report 11

ECONEWS 126-7

Economic Barometer 180-1

Economic Chamber of the Czech Republic 119

Economic Chamber of Macedonia 141-2

Economic Trends in Eastern Europe 21

Economics 169

EIU Country Forecasts 12

EIU Country Reports 21

EIU Country Risk Service 12

EIU ViewsWire Eastern Europe 21-2

electronics

    Central and Eastern Europe 33

    Hungary 131

Embassy of the Czech Republic: UK 119

Embassy of the Czech Republic: USA 119

Embassy of the Federal Republic of Yugoslavia 183

Embassy of the Federal Republic of Yugoslavia: USA 183

Embassy of Poland: UK 162

Embassy of Poland: USA 162-3

Embassy of the Republic of Albania: UK 67

Embassy of the Republic of Albania: USA 67

Embassy of the Republic of Bosnia-Herzegovina: UK 74

Embassy of the Republic of Bosnia-Herzegovina: USA 74

Embassy of the Republic of Bulgaria: UK 88-9

Embassy of the Republic of Bulgaria: USA 89

Embassy of the Republic of Croatia: UK 99

Embassy of the Republic of Croatia: USA 99

Embassy of the Republic of Hungary: UK 134

Embassy of the Republic of Hungary: USA 134

Embassy of the Republic of Macedonia: UK 142

Embassy of the Republic of Macedonia: USA 142

Embassy of the Republic of Slovenia: UK 207

Embassy of the Republic of Slovenia: USA 207

Embassy of Romania: UK 176

Embassy of Romania: USA 176

Embassy of the Slovak Republic: UK 195

Embassy of the Slovak Republic: USA 195

Emerging Markets Database 37

Emerging Markets Monitor 37

Emerging Markets Securities Handbook: Europe and Central Asia 1998/1999 38

Emerging Stock Markets Factbook 38

Emerging Stock Markets Review 38

Emerging Telecoms and Wireless Operators in Eastern Europe 52

EMIC's Guide to Export Sites 22

energy

    Central and Eastern Europe 33-6

    Poland 157

    Slovakia 193

Energy Markets Service: Europe 34

Energy Policies of the Slovak Republic 193

engineering, Czech Republic 112

Environmental Legislation 116

Equity Central Europe 1998-1999 37

Euro-east 22

EuroBuild Poland 157

Euromoney Bank Register 38-9

European Banker 39

European Newspaper Industry Report 46

European Retail Handbook 50

Fact Book 193

Fact Sheet 105-6

Facts About Construction Growth in Bosnia 71-2

Facts About Construction Growth in Bulgaria 84

Facts About Construction Growth in Czech Republic 112

Facts About Construction Growth in Romania 173
Facts About Construction Growth in Slovakia 193
Facts on the Republic of Macedonia 137
Federal Republic of Yugoslavia Official Web Site 179
Federal Statistical Office of Yugoslavia 183
Finance 205
finance and banking
    Bosnia-Herzegovina 72
    Bulgaria 84-5
    Central and Eastern Europe 36-43
    Croatia 96
    Czech Republic 112-13
    Hungary 131-2
    Macedonia 140
    Poland 157-8
    Romania 173-4
    Serbia and Montenegro 181-2
    Slovakia 193-4
    Slovenia 205-6
Finance East Europe 39
Financial Markets of Eastern Europe and the Former Soviet Union 39
Financing Operations: Czech Republic 113
Financing Operations: Hungary 127
Financing Operations: Poland 151
First Polish Economic Guide, The 146
Food and Drink in Central/Eastern Europe 45
food, drink and tobacco
    Central and Eastern Europe 43-5
    Poland 158-9
Food Retailing in Poland 158-9
Food Service Opportunities in Poland 159
Foreign Companies in Emerging Markets Yearbook: Czech Republic 108
Foreign Companies in Emerging Markets Yearbook: Hungary 129
Foreign Companies in Emerging Markets Yearbook: Poland 153-4
Foreign Direct Investment in Central and Eastern Europe 39-40
Foreign Investment in Central and Eastern Europe 55
Foreign Investor's Legal Guide to Bulgaria 86-7

Foreign Investor's Legal Guide to Bulgarian Securities Market 87

Foreign Residents in the Czech Republic 116

Foreign Trade Institute 183

Forex and the Money Market 174

Fundline: Investment Funds and Equity Resources for Eastern Europe and the Former Soviet Union 40

Future of Media in Eastern Europe and Russia 46-7

Gazeta Gieldy Parkiet 157

Global Treasury News 40

Government Information Centre 146

Grant Guide to Hungary 127

Guide to Virtual Slovenia 200

healthcare and medical, Central and Eastern Europe 46

Hints to Exporters Visiting Bulgaria 78

Hints to Exporters Visiting Croatia 92

Hungarian Automotive Industry 130-1

Hungarian Businesses and the EU Law Focus 133

Hungarian Central Statistical Office 134-5

Hungarian Chamber of Commerce and Industry 135

Hungarian Federation for Electronics and Informatics 131

Hungarian Financial and Stock Exchange Almanac 131

Hungarian Investment and Trade Development Agency 135

Hungarian Ministry of Economic Affairs 135

Hungarian Newsletter 133

Hungarian Quarterly 127

Hungarian Rules of Law in Force 133

Hungary 1999 123

Hungary: A Business and Investment Guide 123

Hungary

    companies and contacts 129-30

    current developments 125-9

    industries and services 130-2

    legislation 132-3

    organisations 133-5

    overview 120-5

Hungary A.M. 127
Hungary Around the Clock 128
HVG Online 123

Image on Central + Eastern Europe 22-3
IMF Staff Country Reports: Albania 61-2
IMF Staff Country Reports: Bosnia and Herzegovina 69
IMF Staff Country Reports: Bulgaria 78
IMF Staff Country Reports: Croatia 92
IMF Staff Country Reports: Czech Republic 102-3
IMF Staff Country Reports: Hungary 123
IMF Staff Country Reports: Macedonia 137
IMF Staff Country Reports: Poland 146
IMF Staff Country Reports: Romunia 166
IMF Staff Country Reports: Slovakia 186-7
IMF Staff Country Reports: Slovenia 200
industries and services
    Albania 64
    Bosnia-Herzegovina 71-2
    Bulgarian 84-5
    Central and Eastern Europe 27-54
    Croatia 96
    Czech Republic 110-14
    Hungary 130-2
    Macedonia 140
    Poland 155-60
    Romania 172-4
    Serbia and Montenegro 181-2
    Slovakia 192-4
    Slovenia 204-6
Inform Base: Czech Republic 108
Inform Katalog: Czech Republic 109
Inform Katalog: Slovakia 191
Inform Katalog Export 1998/1999 109
Information House Company Register Online 131-2
InReview Romania 169-70
Institute of Macroeconomic Analysis and Development 207

Insurance in East and Central Europe 40

Insurance Market in Central and Eastern Europe 41

Insurance and Reinsurance Companies in the Republic of Croatia 96

International Construction Week: Eastern Europe 32

International Country Risk Guide (ICRG) 23

Invest Romania 170

Investing, Licensing and Trading: Czech Republic 106

Investing, Licensing and Trading: Hungary 128

Investing, Licensing and Trading: Poland 147

Investment and Business Guide: Albania 62

Investment and Business Guide: Bosnia-Herzegovina 70

Investment and Business Guide: Bulgaria 78

Investment and Business Guide: Croatia 92-3

Investment and Business Guide: Czech Republic 103

Investment and Business Guide: Hungary 124

Investment and Business Guide: Macedonia 138

Investment and Business Guide: Poland 147

Investment and Business Guide: Romania 167

Investment and Business Guide: Slovak Republic 187

Investment and Business Guide: Slovenia 200

Investment Guarantee Trust Fund 72

Investment Guide to Central and Eastern Europe 41

Investor's Guide to Eastern Europe 12-13

ISI Emerging Markets 23

Jasico Yellow Pages 204

Kompass Bosnia and Herzegovina 71

Kompass Bulgaria 83

Kompass Croatia 95

Kompass Czech Republic 109

Kompass Eastern Europe 26

Kompass Hungary 129

Kompass Poland 154

Kompass Slovakia 191

Kompass Slovenia 204

Kompass Yugoslavia 181

Lafferty Cards Databank: Central and Eastern Europe 41

Law Digest for Foreign Investors 174-5

Legal Guide: Czech Republic 117

Legal Guide: Hungary 132-3

Legal Guide: Poland 160

Legal Guide: Slovak Republic 194

Legal Guide: Slovenia 206

legislation

    Albania 64-5

    Bosnia-Herzegovina 72-3

    Bulgaria 86-7

    Central and Eastern Europe 54-6

    Croatia 97

    Czech Republic 114-17

    Hungary 132-3

    Macedonia 140-1

    Poland 160-1

    Romania 174-5

    Serbia and Montenegro 182

    Slovakia 194-5

    Slovenia 206

Lex Structure 175

Litigation and Arbitration in Central and Eastern Europe 55

Ljubljana Stock Exchange 205

LPG in Eastern Europe 34

Macedonia 138

Macedonia (FYR)

    companies and contacts 140

    current developments 138-9

    industries and services 140

    legislation 140-1

    organisations 141-3

    overview 136-8

Macedonian Directory, The 138

Macedonian Information Centre 142

Macedonian Laws 141

Macedonian Legal Resource Center 141

Macedonian Privatization Agency 142

Macedonian Stock Exchange 140

Major Companies of Central and Eastern Europe and the Commonwealth of Independent States 27

Major Companies in Hungary 129-30

Major Companies in Poland 154

Managing Human Resources in Eastern Europe 13

Master Page 151-2

media, Central and Eastern Europe 46-8

Media Map of Eastern Europe 1999 46

medical see *healthcare and medical*

metallurgy, Poland 159

MILS – News 139

Monetary Forecasts 132

Monitor: Croatian Economic Indicators 94-5

Monitorul Online 170

Montenegro see *Serbia and Montenegro*

Monthly Information for Managers 128

Monthly Macroeconomic Review 128-9

Narodna Banka Slovenska: Monetary Survey 194

National Agency for Development of Small and Medium Enterprises 196

National Agency for Privatisation 67

National Bank of Croatia 96

National Bank of Hungary 132

National Bank of Poland 157-8

National Bank of the Republic of Macedonia 140

National Bank of Romania: Monthly Bulletin 174

National Bank of Yugoslavia: Quarterly Bulletin 182

National Commission for Statistics 176-7

National Statistical Institute of Bulgaria (NSI) 89

New Europe 23-4

New Markets Monthly 24

New Vehicle Distribution in Central and Eastern Europe 30

News Brief 170

OECD Economic Surveys 1997-1998: Poland 147
OECD Economic Surveys 1997-1998: Romania 167
OECD Economic Surveys: Bulgaria 1999 79
OECD Economic Surveys: Hungary 1999 124
OECD Economic Surveys: Slovak Republic 1999 187
Opening and Operating Offices in Eastern Europe and the CIS 13
Opportunities in the Energy Markets of Central and Eastern Europe 35
Opportunities in Life, Health and Pensions in Central and Eastern Europe 41-2
organisations
    Albania 65-7
    Bosnia-Herzegovina 73-4
    Bulgaria 87-9
    Central and Eastern Europe 56-8
    Croatia 97-9
    Czech Republic 117-19
    Hungary 133-5
    Macedonia 141-3
    Poland 161-3
    Romania 175-7
    Serbia and Montenegro 182-4
    Slovakia 195-7
    Slovenia 206-8
OTC Healthcare in Eastern Europe 46
Overview of Nuclear Legislation in Central and Eastern Europe and the NIS 35

Packaging in Central/Eastern Europe 48
Packaging in Eastern Europe 48
packaging and paper, Central and Eastern Europe 48-9
PARI Daily 82
PARI Who's Who in Bulgarian Business 83
Pharmaceutical and Cosmetic Producers in Central and Eastern Europe 49
Pharmaceutical Markets in Central Europe 49
pharmaceuticals
    Central and Eastern Europe 49
    Czech Republic 113-14
    Poland 159

Pharmaceuticals in Central and Eastern Europe 49

PlanEcon Energy Outlook 35

PlanEcon Report 24

PlanEcon Review and Outlook 24

PlanEcon Trade and Finance Review 13

Plastic and Rubber Processing Firms in Central and Eastern Europe 31

Poland 1999 147-8

Poland: Telecom Opportunities and Risks 1998 160

Poland

     companies and contacts 153-5

     current developments 149-53

     industries and services 155-60

     legislation 160-1

     organisations 161-3

     overview 144-9

Poland A.M. 152

Poland to 2005 148

Poland's Chemical Sector 156

Poland's Commercial Code 160

Poland's Iron and Steel Industry 159

Poland's Oil and Gas Sector 157

Poland's Paint and Varnish Sector: A Directory of Companies 156

Poland's Pharmaceutical Sector 159

Poland's Plastics and Rubber Sector 156

Polish Agency for Foreign Investment (PAIZ) 163

Polish Automotive Industry 155-6

Polish Business 152

Polish Businesses and the EU Law Focus 161

Polish Capital Markets Guide 158

Polish Chamber of Commerce 163

Polish Company Directory – TeleAdreson Online 154

Polish Economy: Analyses and Forecasts 152

Polish Home Page 148

Polish Law Translation 161

Polish Market Review 152-3

PolishWorld 148

Political Risk Services: Country Reports: Albania 62

Political Risk Services: Country Reports: Bulgaria 79

Political Risk Services: Country Reports: Croatia 92

Political Risk Services: Country Reports: Czech Republic 103

Political Risk Services: Country Reports: Hungary 124

Political Risk Services: Country Reports: Poland 148

Political Risk Services: Country Reports: Romania 167

Political Risk Services: Country Reports: Slovakia 187

Political Risk Services: Country Reports: Slovenia 201

Political Risk Services: Country Reports: Yugoslavia 179

Portrait of the Regions: Volume 5: Hungary 124-5

Power Generation in Central and Eastern Europe 35-6

Prague Business Journal 106

Prague Business Journal Book of Lists 109

Prague Post 106

Prague Post Book of Business Lists 109-10

Prague Stock Exchange 113

Privatisation Agency 89

Privatisation and Emerging Equity Markets 42

Pulp and Paper in Central and Eastern Europe 49

Radio and Television Systems in Central and Eastern Europe 52

Real Estate Legislation and the Building Code 117

Reconnaissance 14

REESWeb 14

Regulations 182

Republic of Macedonia: The First Macedonian WWWPage 138

Resources 1000 110

Resources Slovakia 191

Retail Banking in Central and Eastern Europe 42

retailing, Central and Eastern Europe 50-1

Retailing in Central and Eastern Europe 50-1

Retailing Central Europe 50

Robix 170

Romania: Automotive Industry 173

Romania: Encyclopaedic Survey 167

Romania

    companies and contacts 171-2

current developments 168-71
industries and services 172-4
legislation 174-5
organisations 175-7
overview 164-8
Romania Economic Newsletter 170
Romania Yellow Pages 171
Romanian Business Journal 171
Romanian Development Agency 177
Romanian Digest 175
Romanian Economic Daily 171
Romanian Survey 171
Romanian Trade Register 172

Savoury Snacks in Eastern Europe 45
Secondary Market of Government Securities 85
Serbia and Montenegro
companies and contacts 181
current developments 180-1
industries and services 181-2
legislation 182
organisations 182-4
overview 178-9
Serbia.net 179
services see industries and services
SKB Banka D.D. 205
Slovak Business Links 196
Slovak Chamber of Commerce and Industry 196
Slovak Chemical Guide 192
Slovak National Agency for Foreign Investment and Development
(SNAZIR) 196-7
Slovak Plastics and Rubber Guide 192
Slovakia 188
Slovakia: A Business and Investment Guide 188
Slovakia
companies and contacts 191
current developments 189-90

    industries and services 192-4

    legislation 194-5

    organisations 195-7

    overview 185-8

Slovakia Since Independence 188

Slovakia Today 190

Slovakia.org 188

Slovenia

    companies and contacts 203-4

    current developments 202-3

    industries and services 204-6

    legislation 206

    organisations 206-8

    overview 198-201

Slovenia '98 201

Slovenia Weekly 203

Slovenian Business Catalogue 201

Slovenian Business Report 203

Soft Drinks in Eastern Europe 45

Statistical Insurance Bulletin 205-6

Statistical Office of the Republic of Macedonia 143

Statistical Office of the Republic of Slovenia 208

Statistical Office of the Slovak Republic 197

Survey on East European Law 55

Taking Stock Central Europe: The Investor's Guide to Central Europe's Stock Markets 42

Taxation 65

Taxation in Central Europe: International Tax and Business Guide 42

Taxation and Investment in Central and East European Countries 56

Telecom Market Report: Russia, Central Europe and Central Asia 52

Telecom and Wireless Eastern Europe/CIS 52

telecommunications

    Central and Eastern Europe 51-3

    Czech Republic 114

    Poland 160

Telecommunications in Central and Eastern Europe 53

Television in Central and Eastern Europe 47

Television in Europe to 2007 47

textiles, Central and Eastern Europe 53

Textiles Eastern Europe 53

Thomson Bankwatch 43

tobacco see *food, drink and tobacco*

Tobacco in Eastern Europe 45

TOP 3000 172

Trade and Investment Promotion Office (TIPO) 208

Trade Point 70

Trade-Related Legislation 195

Transition 24-5

Transparency of the Bulgarian Capital Market 85

Trend 190

TV East Europe 47

TV East Europe Handbook 48

Uniting Europe 25

Value Added Taxes in Central and Eastern European Countries: A Corporate Survey and Evaluation 43

Vienna Institute for International Economic Studies (WIIW) 58

Virtual Hungary 125

Warsaw Business Journal 153

Warsaw Business Journal Book of Lists 154-5

Warsaw Stock Exchange 158

Warsaw Voice 153

Warsaw Voice Business and Economy Yearbook, The 148-9

Welcome to Bulgaria 79

What's Happening 65

white goods, Central and Eastern Europe 53-4

White Goods in Eastern Europe 53-4

Who's Who in Bulgarian Banking 85

Who's Who in Polish Banking and Finance 158

World of Information Country Report: Bulgaria 79

World of Information Country Report: Czech Republic 103

World of Information Country Report: Hungary 125
World of Information Country Report: Poland 149
World of Information Country Report: Romania 168
World of Information Country Report: Slovakia 188
World of Information Country Report: Slovenia 201

Yelloweb Hungary 130
Yugoslav Chamber of Commerce and Industry 183-4
Yugoslav Chamber of Commerce and Industry of the United States of
    America 179
Yugoslavia Infomap 179
Yugoslavia Weekly Survey 181

Zagreb Stock Exchange 96